INFORMATION MANAGEMENT FOR THE INTELLIGENT ORGANIZATION

The Art of Scanning the Environment

SECOND EDITION

Chun Wei Choo

ASIS Monograph Series

Published for the
American Society for Information Science by

Information Today, Inc.

Medford, NJ

1998

Library of Congress Cataloging-in-Publication Data

Choo, Chun Wei.
    Information management for the intelligent organization : the art of scanning the environment / by Chun Wei Choo. -- 2nd ed.
       p.   cm. -- (ASIS monograph series)
    Includes bibliographical references and indexes.
    ISBN 1-57387-057-9 (hardcover)
    1. Information resources management. 2. Information technology--Management. I. Title. II. Series.
    HD30.213.C476   1998
    658.4'038--DC21   98-9816
                                          CIP

ISBN: 1-57387-057-9 Hardcover

Published by: Information Today, Inc.
               143 Old Marlton Pike
               Medford, NJ 08055-8750

Distributed in Europe by: Learned Information Ltd.
                           Woodside, Hinksey Hill
                           Oxford OX1 5AU
                           England

Book Editor: Rhonda Forbes
Cover Design: Jacqueline Walters

Printed in the United States of America

To My Parents

Choo Hwee Ming and Lily Low

Table of Contents

Preface . . . . **ix**

Chapter 1   **The Intelligent Organization**. **1**
Organizations and Environments 2
Organizational Information Processing 5
The Intelligent Organization 8
Intelligence Through Organizational Learning. 14
Building the Intelligent Learning Organization 20

Chapter 2   **A Process Model of Information Management**. **23**
Information Needs. 26
Information Acquisition 29
Information Organization and Storage. 33
Information Products and Services 38
Information Distribution 42
Information Use 45
Summary 48

Chapter 3   **Managers as Information Users** **51**
Management as Conversations. 53
Managers as Information Users. 54
Implications for Information Management. 55
Research on Managers as Information Users 56
The Politics of Information Sharing. 67
Managerial Information Processing and Organizational
    Learning 68

Chapter 4   **Environmental Scanning as Strategic**
Organizational Learning. **71**
From Competitor Intelligence to Social Intelligence 74
Competitive Intelligence 76
Business Intelligence. 78

Social Intelligence. 80
Environmental Scanning and Organizational Learning. . . . 82
Research on Environmental Scanning 85
Situational Dimensions: Perceived Environmental
    Uncertainty 87
Organizational Strategies. 88
Managerial Traits 91
Information Needs: Focus of Environmental
    Scanning. 93
Information Seeking (1): Use and Preferences. 94
Information Seeking (2): Scanning Methods 97
Information Use 100
Summary. 103

Chapter 5   **Environmental Scanning in Action** **105**
Perspectives from Neurobiology 105
Environmental Scanning in Action in
    U.S. Corporations 110
Environmental Scanning in U.K. Corporations 115
Environmental Scanning in Swedish Corporations. 117
Environmental Scanning in Japanese Corporations 120
Scanning for Future Learning 124
Close-Up View of Five Canadian CEOs. 125

Chapter 6   **Managing Information Sources** **137**
Managing an Information Ecology for Scanning the
    Environment 138
Selection and Use of Information Sources. 141
Human Sources. 147
Textual Sources. 150

Chapter 7   **Weaving a Web of Online Intelligence** **157**
Managing Online Scanning. 157
The Internet: A Social Information Space 161
Embarrassment of Riches 176
The Value of Online Databases 186

Chapter 8   **Learning to Be Intelligent** **197**
The Intelligent Organization 197
Information Management 198
Understanding Environmental Scanning 201

Designing an Effective Environmental
  Scanning System 203
Looking Ahead 211
Information Partnerships for the Intelligent
  Organization. 211
New Ways of Organizational Learning and
  Understanding the Future 221
The New Dynamics of Competition 227
Coda 231

References **233**
Name Index **255**
Subject Index **263**

Preface

Information is the organization's strategic resource. Yet information is more than just another factor of production. Information is the resource that enables the effective combination and utilization of the other factors of production—it is in effect, the meta-resource that coordinates the mobilization of the other assets in order for the organization to perform. Outside of the organization, the environment is a larger information arena in which people, objects, and organizations jostle and tussle, and create a constant cascade of signals and messages. Competition is the consequence of the unequal distribution of information among organizations and their differential abilities to acquire, absorb and actuate information. Competition has turned into an information race of discovery and learning.

Unfortunately, much of the information that an organization receives is nuance and innuendo, more of a potential than a prescription for action. To become strategic, information must be galvanized into knowledge that can guide action. This transfiguration of information into knowledge is the goal of information management. As rhetoric, information management is often equated with the management of information technology, or the management of information resources, or the management of information policies and standards (Figure 1). While each of these functions is important, we also need a unifying perspective that would bind these functions together. We need to recognize that information, knowledge and insight are forged in the hearts and minds

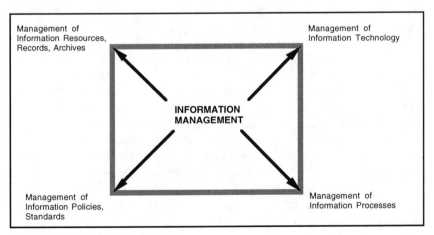

Figure 1. Information Management

of human beings, that the use of information depends on the construction of shared meanings, and that knowledge creation and use are social experiences in which multiple actors participate and exercise their different intellects and interests. This book suggests that the management of information be viewed as the management of a network of processes that acquire, create, organize, distribute, and use information. The intelligent organization is then an organization that is skilled at marshalling its information resources and capabilities, transforming information into knowledge, and using this knowledge to sustain and enhance its performance in a restless environment.

The objective of the book is to develop an understanding of how an organization may manage its information processes more effectively in order to increase its capacity to learn and adapt. Our vista of information management is broad, encompassing information processes, information resources, and information technologies. We will enrich our palette with analogies and metaphors drawn from the fields of anthropology, biology, computer science, economics, hermeneutics, management, information science, library science, neuroscience, organization theory, systems theory, and other disciplines. In the end, the book is about the practice of information management, and the better part of our discussion will dwell on how organizations may act to strengthen its faculty for creating and using knowledge. Our hope is that the deliberations in the book would be of interest to senior managers and administrators, information managers, information specialists and practitioners, information technologists, and indeed anyone whose work in an organization involves acquiring, creating, organizing or using knowledge. Students and instructors in library and information science schools, as well as business administration or management faculties, may also find the book relevant.

The eight chapters of the book fall into three broad thematic sections. The first three chapters are closely related, as they examine the relationship between information management and the intelligent organization. In these chapters, we approach the questions: What makes an organization intelligent? How does information management help an organization to be intelligent? What are the processes that drive the information management cycle? How can we manage these processes better?

Chapter 1, "The Intelligent Organization," develops a profile of the intelligent organization as a learning organization that is adept at creating and gathering knowledge, and at modifying its behavior to reflect the new knowledge. We sketch a cognitive model of the learning organization that describes how the organization senses information about its external and internal environments, develops perceptions and constructs meaning through interpretation, draws upon its memory of past experiences, and takes action based on its interpretation and mental models. To be effective, organizational learning must embrace its own opposites—learning requires the organization to unlearn old norms and assumptions and relearn new frames of reference;

learning about future change in the external environment requires the organization to understand the environment deep enough to be able to envision and shape the future to its own advantage. In this new edition, Chapter 1 has been revised to include a discussion of three types of organizational knowledge: tacit knowledge, rule-based knowledge, and cultural knowledge.

The goal of information management is to harness information resources and information capabilities in order to enable the organization to learn and adapt. Using the organizational learning model outlined in the first chapter, Chapter 2 presents "A Process Model of Information Management" that would underpin the organization's learning capability. The model traces six key information processes that form a continuous, regenerative loop: identifying information needs, acquiring information, organizing and storing information, developing information products and services, distributing information, and using information. We reveal the special problems of managing each process, issues that are often overlooked or overwhelmed by other dominant interests or as a result of historical development. At the same time, we highlight the opportunities for change and revitalization that may be realized by combining our understanding of information use behaviors with a more flexible, user-centered design of information services and systems.

In the learning organization, managers have an important and prominent role. As decision makers, they hold the authority and responsibility to act on the available information. As leaders, they set examples and promote a culture of information sharing and collaboration. As strategists, they ensure that information policies are well aligned with the organization's mission. Unfortunately, providing relevant, actionable information to managers has proved to be a formidable task, and managers are generally less than satisfied with the information they get from existing information systems and services. In Chapter 3, "Managers as Information Users," we review what we know about managers as information seekers and information users, and discuss some important organizational and work-related contingencies that influence managerial information behavior.

One of the greatest challenges facing the intelligent organization is to understand how the external environment is changing, what the changes mean, and how the organization can best respond to the new conditions. The process of learning about the external milieu is environmental scanning, the art of gathering and interpreting information about the environment so that the organization has the knowledge to develop effective courses of action. Chapter 4 and 5 discuss the theory and practice of environmental scanning, provide some insights about scanning as a learning process, and suggest principles for the design and implementation of an effective scanning system.

Chapter 4, "Environmental Scanning as Strategic Organizational Learning," examines the significant corpus of research on scanning that seem to show broad agreement on a number of issues. Research shows that scanning improves organizational performance, especially if the scanning function is well integrated into the organization's strategic planning and learning cycles. Scanning increases with environmental uncertainty, and we may expect the need for scanning to grow as the environment becomes more labile. Scanning is focused on the market sectors of the environment, and longer-term issues tend to be neglected or underemphasized. Managers use a range of sources to scan, but there is a heavy reliance on informal, personal sources. In this new edition, Chapter 4 has been updated to include a selection of studies and papers that were published in 1996 and 1997.

Chapter 5, "Environmental Scanning in Action," presents many case studies of how successful organizations in Canada, Japan, Singapore, Sweden, the United States, the United Kingdom, and other countries have established effective scanning systems and used them to energize organizational learning. From their experiences and those of well-known consultants and practitioners, we distill a number of principles that could enhance the craft of scanning and learning about the environment. Scanning should be planned and managed as a strategic function, much like a research and development program that is given the critical mass of resources to pursue activities with the potential to deliver high payoffs. Scanning should be implemented as a formal, structured, continuous system that maximizes and integrates the information gathering and value-adding capabilities of the organization. Users should participate actively throughout the scanning process, not just as recipients or consumers of information, but also as information partners who contribute their own assessments and commentaries, share and disseminate information, and create fresh insights from the available information. Finally, scanning should be supported by a coherent set of information management strategies that enable the organization to systematically collect, coordinate, store, analyze, and distribute information.

We live in a time of unprecedented access to information—technology, industry and government have lifted the information floodgates, and the waters are still rising. Although organizations may be drowning in information, they often lack the knowledge to illuminate their choices and actions. On the one hand, organizations need to activate a sufficient number and variety of information sources in order to reflect adequately the span and sweep of external phenomena. On the other hand, they need to identify and access specialized sources in order to probe strategic issues in detail. Chapter 6 and 7 discuss the management of information sources, suggest ways of matching sources to information needs, and examine the use and potential of online databases and Internet resources.

Chapter 6, "Managing Information Sources," proposes a holistic approach towards the selection and use of information sources, recognizing that sources effectively "feed" on and off each other in a network of information chains. Sources high on the information chain summarize and interpret data, while sources low on the chain (close to the event) provide details and let users develop their own sense of the situation. Users choose sources by a number of criteria: their accessibility, their ability to offer trustworthy and relevant information, the richness of the information channel, and so on. The chapter examines how human sources and textual sources may be used to scan the environment and initiate organizational learning.

In this new edition, Chapter 7 has been rewritten and reshaped to provide a more up-to-date as well as more in-depth discussion of the role of online information in supporting environmental scanning. Entitled "Weaving a Web of Online Intelligence," the chapter develops a general framework for managing the bewildering array of information resources and services available both on the World Wide Web and through commercial online database vendors. The Web is portrayed as a new kind of social information space that is both a communication and publication medium, where person-to-person communications can take place seamlessly with the looking up of textual and non-textual information. Commercial online databases on the other hand offer the elaborate indexing structures and sophisticated interactive capabilities to finesse focused, pertinent answers to complex, multi-faceted questions. On the whole, the more intensive and creative use of online information resources and information sharing capabilities will enable organizations to scan their environments more intelligently, be more knowledgeable, and respond more effectively to environmental forces.

Chapter 8, the final chapter, "Learning to Be Intelligent," looks at some new tools and methodologies that the smart organization can use to understand the forces and dynamics that are shaping the future. Scenario-based planning helps the organization to expose and, where necessary, unlearn its assumptions in order to be better prepared for external discontinuities. Systems thinking beckons the organization to analyze social and business phenomena as dynamic, holistic networks in which the parts and participants interact through control and communication loops. Complexity theory approaches social systems as complex, adaptive systems that can self-organize, acquire emergent properties, and learn from experience to adapt to the changing environment.

Although it may be impossible to predict the form and function of the future, we may safely assume that the dynamics of competition and organizational growth will become increasingly based on information *and* the knowledge to leverage this information with other physical and intellectual resources. The intelligent organization will foster its own information partnerships that combine user-experts with information technology experts who build the organization's data infrastructure, and information (content) experts who organize knowledge assets to facilitate their productive use. The new charter for information professionals will be to participate as active partners in strategic information alliances that vitalize organizational learning. For the intelligent organization, the first class will be on the delicate art of mobilizing and managing information.

Readers with access to the Internet may wish to visit my home page on the World Wide Web where they will find links to the Web and Gopher resources described in Chapter 7, as well as additional material relevant to the discussions in the book. Please point your Web browser to **http://choo.fis.utoronto.ca/**

Acknowledgements

The author gratefully acknowledges the colleagues, students, and fellow teachers and researchers who have so generously provided feedback, encouragement and moral support. Special thanks are due to Elizabeth Chang, a recent graduate of FIS, who checked the manuscript for this new edition.

I wish to thank Ethel Auster for reading an early version of the manuscript and offering many helpful suggestions; Stevan Dedijer for his papers and insights on business and social intelligence; and Seng Hon Wong, for sharing his know-how on environmental scanning. The book owes an intellectual debt to Robert S. Taylor and Thomas Davenport, whose work on information use environments and information process management respectively have helped to lay the conceptual foundation for the book. I thank my editor, Rhonda Forbes, and publisher, Tom Hogan, who guided and supported this project. Last but not least, I am grateful to my wife Bee Kheng and our two children Ren Min and Ren Ee for their love and encouragement. Although many people have contributed to the creation of the book you hold in your hands, the author admits final responsibility for what you are about to read.

Chun Wei Choo
Faculty of Information Studies
University of Toronto
http://choo.fis.utoronto.ca/

Chapter 1

The Intelligent Organization

*What magical trick makes us intelligent? The trick is that there is
no trick. The power of intelligence stems from our vast diversity,
not from any single, perfect principle. Our species has evolved
many effective although imperfect methods, and each of us individually develops more on our own. Eventually, very few of our
actions and decisions come to depend on any single mechanism.
Instead, they emerge from conflicts and negotiations among societies of processes that constantly challenge one another.*

(Marvin Minsky 1986, The Society of Mind, Section 30.8)

Organizations are societies of minds. Actions and decisions are not the
simple outcome of any single, orderly activity: they emerge from an
ecology of information processes. A diversity of participants and points of
view collaborate together as well as challenge each other. We now recognize
this dynamic, open character of organizations. Yet for a long time we cher-
ished a static view—organizations were places where we went to work every-
day. They could be counted on to produce the goods and services we want,
and some of them were responsible for preserving and protecting structures
and values that underpin our society. Their very stasis and stability was
a source of comfort.

Organizations saw themselves almost as fortresses, with walls and boundaries that etched their domains of activity and influence. From time to time they
would open the gates to send out produce or to receive material, but this was
not their primary concern. Early students of organizations made the simplify-
ing assumption that organizations were closed systems, and the effective organization was one that could buffer its operations from the vicissitudes of the
outside world and thus concentrate on improving its internal form and function.
For most purposes, the external environment was a given in the short run: mar-

kets changed sluggishly, and could sometimes be manipulated; technologies moved in small steps and could be assimilated incrementally; relationships with other organizations were clear-cut and cautious; economic conditions turned in periodic cycles that could occasionally be predicted. On the whole, most organizations, especially the larger ones, felt that they were in control of their own destinies.

Now, this static representation of organizations has become a relic. Today's organizations are no longer circumscribed by walls and boundaries. Their borders are porous, through which materials, energy, and information continuously flow. Instead of trying to do everything, they now parcel out their work to other organizations so that each can maximize its strengths and advantages. A significant proportion of organizations do not live long. Some fail and disappear altogether, while others pursue alliances and linkages to increase their leverage and survivability. They spin networks that include competitors, customers, and suppliers. Rather than fortresses, they are more like species of organisms seeking sustenance and growth in a dynamic environment. Their credo says "evolve or perish." Their eyes are perpetually fixed on the external environment, watching markets shift from day to day, industries jostle to reconfigure themselves, technological innovations intrude at an unremitting pace, and government policies constrain or create options. Today's organizations realize that aiming to insulate themselves from their environments is a lost cause. Instead, they now behave as complex, open systems that share many features with living biological systems. Above all, they recognize that their survival and growth is ultimately conditioned by their capacity to learn and adapt to a changing environment.

This chapter looks closer at the relationship between organizations and environments—why do some organizations survive and grow decade after decade, while something like a third of the companies in the Fortune 500 list have disappeared over the last five years? We suggest that survivability is dependent on the organization's ability to process information about the environment, and to turn this information into knowledge that enables it to adapt effectively to external change. Further, we suggest that such adaptability through learning is the hallmark of the intelligent organization. Learning is the key to intelligent organizational behavior in a fast-changing environment.

Organizations and Environments

Soon after the Second World War, the relationship between organizations and environments became a subject of frequent research. In organization theory, we may differentiate between three ways of analyzing the relationship between organizations and their environments. The external environment may be viewed as a source of information, as a pool of resources, or as an ecological milieu (Aldrich and Mindlin 1978, Aldrich 1979).

Environment as a Source of Information

One of the first researchers to view the environment as a source of information was Dill (1958, 1962). He suggests that the best way to analyze the environment is not to try to understand it as a collection of other systems and organizations but rather to

> treat the environment as information which becomes available to the organization or to which the organization, via search activity, may get access. It is not the supplier or the customer himself that counts, but the information that he makes accessible to the organization being studied about his goals, the conditions under which he will enter into a contract, or other aspects of his behavior (Dill 1962, 96).

Changes, events, and trends in the environment continually create signals and messages. Organizations detect or receive these cues and use the information to adapt to new conditions. Arrow (1964) proposed a theory of control and information in large organizations in which managers receive "signals" from the environment and from other managers. These signals modify their perceptions of the state of the job-related world. When decisions are based on these messages, further information is generated and transmitted, and these in turn lead to new signals and decisions. This informational view of the organizational environment is implicit in the work of several other researchers, with the common thread that because uncertainty is inherent in the environment, a basic management task requires coping with this uncertainty (Burns and Stalker 1961, Cyert and March 1963/1992, Lawrence and Lorsch 1967, Thompson 1967, Galbraith 1973, and Weick 1979).

Early studies examined how organizations adapt to external environments by varying their internal structures. Burns and Stalker (1961) studied twenty firms in the U.K. and found that management structure was related to external environment. Firms in stable environments adopted mechanistic management structures that were characterized by rules, procedures, and clear hierarchy of control. Conversely, firms in rapidly changing environments had organic structures that were freer and more flexible, and decision making was decentralized. They conclude that an essential part of a top manager's job is to interpret correctly the external uncertainties facing the firm, and so decide on the appropriate management structure. Another classic study of organizations in three industries (Lawrence and Lorsch 1967) found that the more varied and uncertain the environment confronted by an organization, the more *differentiated* the organization structure needs to be. At the same time, the more differentiated the structure, the more effort must be given to the *integration* of the various subunits. For an organization to be "co-aligned" with its environment, the differentiation and integration of the organization as a whole should match its environment. According to Thompson (1967), the fundamental problem facing complex organizations is managing the organizational task environment. He proposes that organizations will vary systematically in structure and behavior to reflect the level of uncertainty inherent in their environments. The more heterogeneous and shifting an organization's task environment, the more boundary-spanning differentiation it will show, the more attention it will give to environmental monitoring activities, and the more it will rely on planning to achieve adaptation.

Environment as a Source of Resources

Another perspective views the environment primarily as a source of resources upon which the organization depends. Three structural characteristics of the environment affect resource dependence: munificence, or the abundance of resources; concentration, the extent to which power and authority in the environment is widely dispersed; and interconnectedness, the number and pattern of linkages among organizations in the environment. The degree of dependence would be great when resources are scarce, and when entities in the environment are highly concentrated or interconnected:

> To survive, organizations require resources. Typically, acquiring resources means the organization must interact with others who control those resources. In that sense, organizations depend on their environments. Because the organization does not control the resources it needs, resource acquisition may be problematic and uncertain. Others who control resources may be undependable, particularly when resources are scarce. Organizations transact with others for necessary resources, and control over resources provides others with power over the organization. Survival of the organization is partially explained by the ability to cope with environmental contingencies; negotiating exchanges to ensure the continuation of needed resources is the focus of much organizational action. (Pfeffer and Salancik 1978, 258).

An organization can manage increasing dependence by setting up coordination links and connections among the interdependent organizations in its environment. Pfeffer and Salancik (1978) identify four general strategies. First, it can adapt to or avoid the external demands: for example, when confronted by powerful external organizations, it can use secrecy or restriction of information to avoid influence attempts. Second, it can alter the patterns of interdependence through growth, merger, and diversification—in other words, it can absorb the parts of the environment on which it depends. Third, it can establish collective structures of interorganizational behavior through the use of interlocking directorates, joint ventures, industry associations, and normative restraints—forming a "negotiated environment." Last, it can create the organizational environment through law, political action, and altering the definitions of social legitimacy—forming a "created environment."

Environment as a Source of Variation

In the third perspective, the environment is viewed as an ecological milieu that differentially selects certain types of organizations for survival on the basis of the fit between organizational forms and environmental characteristics. The focus here is on the action of environmental *selection* processes, with the organizations being relatively passive and unable to determine their own fates. This ecological view, developed principally by Hannan and Freeman (1977, 1989) and Aldrich (1979), applies evolutionary biology to explain why certain forms (or species) of organizations survive and thrive, while other types languish and perish (a 1987 *Forbes* magazine survey found that of the top 100 industrial firms in 1917, only 17 survived in 1986).

Organizational change takes place through three stages of variation, selection, and retention. The *variation* stage may be introduced by the creation of new organizations or the transfer of existing organizations to new owners. In the *selection* stage, the purest form of environmental selection is the survival or elimination of entire organizations. Organization forms survive or fail depending on their fitness for a particular environmental niche. In the *retention* stage, several organizational mechanisms preserve structure and knowledge. Bureaucratic administrative structure and procedures, socialization of new members, leadership succession, and so on, help preserve organizational forms, increasing the probability of their retention, if environmental selection criteria are met. Positively selected variations survive and reproduce similar others, which then form a starting point for a new round of selection (Aldrich and Pfeffer 1976).

Summary

The relation between organizations and environments continues to be a major area of study in organization theory. Indeed, the shift towards an "open systems" view of organizations in recent years has concentrated attention on the role of the environment as "the ultimate source of materials, energy, and information, all of which are vital to the continuation of the system." (Scott 1987, 91) In the information view of the environment, decision makers use information from the environment for maintaining or changing organizational structures and processes. The resource view focuses on how dependent the organization is on others (especially other organizations) for the resources it requires. The population ecology model analyzes environmental factors as the forces of change, and studies organizations as populations or species rather than as individual systems.

Organizational Information Processing

Organizations as Information Processing Systems

A number of important theories treat organizations as information processing systems. The information processing approach seeks to understand and predict how organizations perceive stimuli, interpret them, store, retrieve, and transmit information, generate judgments, and solve problems (Larkey and Sproull 1984). Although no unified theory of organizational information processing exists, the field appears to concentrate on organizational participants as information processors, and on organizational systems and structures that contribute to information processing. The accelerating interest in the information processing view is driven by the deficiencies of theoretical views that ignore information processing behaviors, the rapid diffusion of information processing technologies, and the increasing information processing content of organizational tasks.

It is possible to differentiate two research orientations in the literature on organizational information processing (Choo 1991). The first regards organizations as rational, decision making systems. Unfortunately, the individual as decision maker is bounded by cognitive limitations. The task of organization design is thus to control the decision premises that guide decision making behavior. Information is processed in order to reduce or avoid uncertainty. The organization sets its goals first, then searches for alternatives, and selects courses of action which lead to goal attainment. This decision making perspective was first developed by Herbert Simon, James March and Richard Cyert, and became very influential in organization theory.

The second orientation sees organizations as loosely coupled social systems. Individual actors enact or create the environment to which the organization then adapts. The task of organizing is to develop a shared interpretation of the environment and then to act on the basis of this interpretation. Information is processed in order to reduce or resolve equivocality. Actions are often taken first and then interpreted retrospectively: in other words, action can precede goals. This "enactment" perspective was suggested by Karl Weick who, together with Richard Daft, later proposed a model of organizations as interpretation systems.

Organizations as Decision Making Systems

According to Simon (1976), the human mind can only exercise bounded or limited rationality, so that the individual in an organization constructs a simplified model of the real world in order to deal with it and then looks for a course of action that is satisfactory or good enough ("satisfices"). (Simon 1976, xxvii-xxx) A basic problem of organizing is to define the decision premises that form the organizational environment: "The task of administration is so to design this environment that the individual will approach as close as practicable to rationality (judged in terms of the organization's goals) in his decisions" (Simon 1976, 240-241).

The organization influences its members' behaviors by controlling the decision premises upon which decisions are made, rather than controlling the actual decisions themselves (Simon 1976, 223). Because of the limitations of the human mind, decision making in organizations requires "simplifications," particularly in the use of action or performance programs that constrain the decision behaviors of individuals.

A theory of organizational decision making must consist of a theory of *search* and a theory of *choice* (Cyert and March 1963, 10). Decision makers are not automatically presented with problems to solve and alternative solutions to choose from. They must identify problems, search for solutions, and develop methods to generate and evaluate alternatives. In other words, the decision makers must actively search for the required information, since such information is not readily available (Stabell 1978).

According to Cyert and March (1963), information search in organizations is "problem-motivated," "simple-minded," and "biased." The recognition of a problem initiates the search for ways to solve it, and once a way is found then the search stops. Search is "simple-minded"—when a problem occurs, search for a solution is concentrated near the old solution and often relies on available and familiar sources of information. Search is "biased" in that it reflects the training, experience and goals of the participants.

Organizations as Interpretation Systems

In contrast to the perspective of organizations as decision-making systems, Weick (1979) proposes a model of organizations as "loosely coupled" systems in which individual participants have great latitude in interpreting and implementing directions. He stresses the autonomy of individuals and the looseness of the relations linking individuals in an organization. Although he also views organizations as information processing systems, the purpose of processing information is not decision making or problem solving in the first instance. Instead, the focus is on reducing the *equivocality* of information about the organization's external environment. Managers as information processors receive information about the external environment and then create or *enact* the environment to which they will attend. In creating the enacted environment, managers separate out for closer attention selected portions of the environment based on their experience. Weick, together with Daft, later extended this enactment theory into a model of organizations as interpretation systems (Weick and Daft 1983). Organizations receive information about the environment that is ambiguous. Within the organization, various subunits adopt dissimilar frames of reference to view changes in the environment. Weick and Daft conclude that

> organizations must make interpretations. Managers literally must wade into the swarm of events that constitute and surround the organization and actively try to impose some order on them . . . . Interpretation is the process of translating these events, of developing models for understanding, of bringing out meaning, and of assembling conceptual schemes. (Weick and Daft 1983, 74)

What is being interpreted is the organization's external environment, and how the organization goes about its interpretation depends on how analyzable it perceives the environment to be and how actively it intrudes into the environment to understand it. Whether the organization perceives that the environment is objective and that events and developments are analyzable, or that the environment is subjective and essentially unanalyzable, will affect its choice of interpretation mode. Furthermore, some organizations actively search the environment for answers and may also test or manipulate the environment, while others may just accept whatever information the environment gives them (Daft and Weick 1984, 287-88). The organizational learning process then consists of scanning, interpretation, and learning. Scanning is the monitoring of the environment; interpretation takes place when data are given meaning, opinions are exchanged, and "an information coalition of sorts is formed;" and learning occurs when a new action is taken based on the interpretation.

Summary

Both the decision making and interpretation perspectives are complementary ways of understanding information seeking and use in organizations. Rational, systematic decision making is probably better suited to solving problems where issues are clearly identified. On the other hand, collective interpretation may be needed in dealing with problems where issues are unclear and information is ambiguous. Any attempt to study the use of information in organizations would benefit from applying the two points of view. James March, one of the preeminent scholars of organizational decision making, recently observed that

> decision makers often operate in a surveillance mode rather than a problem-solving mode. In contrast to a theory of information that assumes that information is gathered to resolve a choice among alternatives, decision makers scan their environments for surprises and solutions. They monitor what is going on. They characteristically do not "solve" problems; they apply rules and copy solutions from others. (March 1991, 112)

The Intelligent Organization

The picture we have so far is of an organization that behaves as an open system that takes in information, materials, and energy from the environment, and transforms these resources into knowledge, processes, and structures that produce goods or services that, in turn, are consumed by the environment. The relationship between organizations and environment is thus both circular and critical: organizations depend on the environment for resources and for the justification of their continued existence. Because the environment is growing in complexity and volatility, continuing to be viable requires organizations to learn enough about the current and likely future conditions of the environment, *and* to apply this knowledge to change their own behavior and positioning in a timely way.

Students of organizations have wrestled with the concept of organizational intelligence for several decades. Wilensky (1967) discussed organizational intelligence in terms of the gathering, processing, interpreting, and communicating of the information needed in decision making processes. Information is not only a source of power, but a source of confusion—information oversupply has exacerbated the problem of intelligence. The roots of organizational intelligence failures can often be traced to doctrines, structures, and problems and processes that increase distortion and blockage. In Wilensky's analysis, much of an organization's defense against information pathologies lies in managers' attitudes toward knowledge, and in information specialists' capacities to influence strategic discourse.

March and Olsen (1979) believed that organizational intelligence is built on two fundamental processes: "rational calculation" and "learning from experience." Rational calculation is the choice of alternatives based on an evaluation of their expected consequences according to preferences. It looks ahead into the future to anticipate outcomes. Learning from experience is the choice of alternatives based on rules developed from an accumulation of past experience. It looks backwards at history to find guidance for future action. March and Olsen observed that as we have come to recognize the limitations on rational calculation, interest in the potential for organizational learning as a basis for organizational intelligence has increased. Organizations and the people in them learn through their interactions with the environment: "They act, observe the consequences of their action, make inferences about those consequences, and draw implications for future action. The process is adaptively rational." (March and Olsen 1979, 67)

Recently, Quinn (1992, 373) described an intelligent enterprise as "a firm that primarily manages and coordinates information and intellect to meet customer needs." The intelligent enterprise depends more on the development and deployment of intellectual resources than on the management of physical and fiscal assets. Its functions are disaggregated into manageable intellectual clusters that Quinn calls "service activities." Information technology has made it possible to delegate and outsource many of these service activities to other organizations. Instead of focusing on products, the intelligent enterprise excels in a few core knowledge-based service activities critical to its customers and surrounds these with other activities necessary to defend the core. Then it uses advanced information, management, and intelligent systems to coordinate the many other diverse and often dispersed activity centers needed to fulfill customer needs.

Apple Computer Inc. is an example of creating value by leveraging on a few critical knowledge-based service activities. The Apple II computer was primarily a software and marketing breakthrough that helped to launch the PC revolution. The machine retailed for about $2000 but cost less than $500 to build, with 70 percent of the components purchased from outside. Apple did not try to manufacture its computers' microprocessors, circuit boards, housings, keyboards, monitors, or power supplies. All of these components were outsourced while Apple concentrated on concept design, software, logistics, systems integration, and product assembly (Quinn 1992, 42).

Until today, Apple's human-computer interface design guidelines still set the standards for elegance and user friendliness. Outsourcing was not limited to hardware. Apple worked with Dan Breklin to develop Visicalc (the first spreadsheet) and for over a year, Apple II was the only computer to support Visicalc. The Apple brand name and logo was designed by the public relations agency Regis McKenna to help project Apple's image at a time when the company had almost no sales. For product distribution, Apple joined with Bell & Howell, a reputable supplier to the education market, to help place Apple products in schools. As a result of its concentrating on a few knowledge-adding services while developing partnerships in complementary areas, Apple was able for many years, to attain sales per employee figures that were two to four times higher than its competitors.

Haeckel and Nolan define an organization's intelligence as its "ability to deal with complexity, that is, its ability to capture, share, and extract meaning from marketplace signals." (Haeckel and Nolan 1993, 126) In turn, an organization's complexity is a function of how many information sources it needs, how many business elements it must coordinate, and the number and type of relationships binding these elements. According to their analysis, an organization's "intelligence quotient" is determined by three critical attributes: the ability to access knowledge and information (connecting); the ability to integrate and share information (sharing); and the ability to extract meaning from data (structuring). *Connecting* means that information sources, media, locations, and users are linked in such a way that accurate information can be captured and made available to the right users at the right time and place. *Sharing* means that people in the organization can share data, interpretations of the data, as well as their understanding of the core processes of the organization. *Structuring* means that insight or meaning is obtained by matching and relating information from multiple sources so that some form of pattern or trend emerges.

An organization achieves structuring by creating information about information, for instance, how data are organized, related and used. Classification categories, indexes, tables of contents, and data models are some examples of filtering and structuring data. Haeckel and Nolan believe that structuring holds the most potential for the strategic exploitation of information. To illustrate a firm applying the connecting-sharing-structuring loop, they describe the system used by Wal-Mart and its suppliers to replenish stocks. For example, Wal-Mart transmits detailed data about the day's sales to its jeans supplier Wrangler every evening. Sharing is not limited to data: the two firms also share a model that interprets the meaning of the data, and software applications that act on the interpretation to specify quantities of jeans of the right sizes and colors to be sent to particular stores from specific warehouses. As fashion seasons or pricing patterns change, the shared data model is adjusted accordingly, thus allowing both organizations to learn and adapt.

There are two distinct meanings to the concept of intelligence: the possession of knowledge and the creation of knowledge (Gregory 1981, 1994). Possession provides a pool of knowledge that can be called upon to solve problems and give understanding. The creation of knowledge takes place when novelty is generated to solve new problems for which adequate solutions cannot be found in the knowledge base. Indeed, the creation of successful novelty is a convincing mark of intelligent behavior. The context of intelligent behavior is thus problem solving, and problem solving implies the pursuance of goals and objectives. The requirement for novelty is linked to the appearance of new problems, situations, and experiences. Intelligence may be conceived as a quality of behavior: behavior that is adaptive in that it represents effective ways of meeting the demands of environments as they change (Anastasi 1986). We see therefore that intelligent behavior is both goal-directed and adaptive (Sternberg 1982, Sternberg and Detterman 1986), and it will be the capacity of organizations to possess, create, and apply knowledge that will make the crucial difference.

An organization works with three classes of knowledge: tacit knowledge, rule-based knowledge, and cultural knowledge (Choo 1998). *Tacit knowledge* consists of the hands-on skills, special know-how, heuristics, intuitions, and the

Table 1.1. Three Types of Organizational Knowledge

Type	Form	Examples	Use
Tacit Knowledge	–Procedural –Embedded in action	• Know-how • Heuristics • Intuitions	• Ensures task effectiveness, stimulates creativity
Rule-based Knowledge	–Declarative –Encoded in programs	• Routines • Standard operating procedures • Record structures	• Promotes efficiency, coordination, control
Cultural Knowledge	–Contextual –Expressed in discourse	• Stories/metaphors • Mindsets/worldviews • Visions/scenarios	• Assigns significance to new information and knowledge

like that people develop as they immerse in the flow of their work activities. Tacit knowledge is deeply rooted in action and comes from the simultaneous engagement of mind and body in task performance. Tacit knowledge is personal knowledge that is hard to formalize or articulate (Polanyi 1966, 1973). The transfer of tacit knowledge is by tradition and shared experience, through for example, apprenticeship or on-the-job training. Tacit knowledge in an organization ensures task effectiveness — that the right things are being done so that the work unit could attain its objectives. It also provides for a kind of creative robustness — intuition and heuristics can often tackle tough problems that would otherwise be difficult to solve.

Whereas tacit knowledge is implicit, *rule-based knowledge* is explicit knowledge that is used to match actions to situations by invoking appropriate rules. Rule-based knowledge guides action by answering three questions: What kind of situation is this? What kind of person am I or What kind of organization is this? and finally, What does a person such as I, or an organization such as this, do in a situation such as this? (March 1994) Rule-based knowledge is used in the design of routines, standard operating procedures, and the structure of data records. Rule-based knowledge enables the organization to ensure a high level of operational efficiency, coordination, and control. It also facilitates the transfer of learning within the organization.

The third kind of organizational knowledge is *cultural knowledge*. This is knowledge that is part of the organization's culture and is communicated through oral and verbal texts such as stories, metaphors, analogies, visions, and mission statements. Cultural knowledge includes the assumptions and beliefs that are used to describe and explain reality, as well as the conventions and expectations that are used to assign value and significance to new information (Schein 1991). Cultural knowledge assigns significance to new information by supplying values and norms that "determine what kinds of knowledge are sought and nurtured, what kinds of knowledge-building activities are tolerated and encouraged. ... Therefore, values serve as knowledge-screening and -control mechanisms." (Leornard-Barton 1995, p. 19)

All three forms of knowledge can be found in any organization (Table 1.1). The intelligent organization however, is skilled at continuously expanding, renewing, and refreshing its knowledge in all three categories. The intelligent organization promotes the accumulation of tacit knowledge to increase the skill and creative capacity of its employees, takes advantage of rule-based knowledge to maximize efficiency and transfer learning, and develops cultural knowledge to shape purpose and meaning in its community. In effect, the intelligent organization has mastered a fourth class of knowledge – a higher order or meta-knowledge – that it uses to create, integrate, and invigorate all its intellectual resources in order to achieve superior levels of performance.

Is the kind of intelligent organization we have described an unattainable goal or do such firms exist in reality? We believe that examples of intelligent knowledge creation may be found in Japanese companies such as Canon, Honda, Matsushita, NEC, and Sharp. These companies are widely admired for their ability to innovate continuously, recognize and respond swiftly to customer needs, dominate technologies while they are still emerging, and bring new high-quality products to market with impressive speed. For example, Canon reinvented the 35mm camera, pioneered the personal photocopier and color copier, invented the laser printer and ink-jet printer, and is now working on using ferroelectric liquid crystals for large flat panel displays. Judged by the number of United States patents granted, Canon can claim to be the world's most consistently creative company—for a fifth of the R&D budget, Canon has obtained about as many patents as IBM (Johnstone, 1994a). Or consider Honda's history of agile adaptiveness: it gained a late but successful entry into the highly competitive automobile market, won victory in the motorcycle war against an established leader (Yamaha), and developed its own automotive engine that set new standards in fuel-efficiency and pollution control. Many regard Honda as one of the best managed companies in the world (Pascale 1990).

A Japanese scholar explains the success of companies such as Canon, Honda and Matsushita:

> The centerpiece of the Japanese approach is the recognition that creating new knowledge is not simply a matter of "processing" objective information. Rather, it depends on tapping the tacit and often highly subjective insights, intuitions, and hunches of individual employees and making those insights available for testing and use by the company as a whole. The key to this process is personal commitment, the employees' sense of identity with the enterprise and its mission. Mobilizing that commitment and embodying tacit knowledge in actual technologies and products require managers who are as comfortable with images and symbols . . . .
>
> A company is not a machine but a living organism. Much like an individual, it can have a collective sense of identity and fundamental purpose. This is the organizational equivalent of self-knowledge—a shared understanding of what the company stands for, where it is going, what kind of world it wants to live in, and, most important, how to make that world a reality. . . .
>
> In the knowledge-creating company, inventing new knowledge is not a specialized activity—the province of the R&D department or marketing or strategic planning. It is a way of behaving, indeed a way of being, in which everyone is a knowledge worker—that is to say, an entrepreneur. (Nonaka 1991, 97)

The intelligent organization adopts a holistic approach to knowledge management that successfully combines tacit, rule-based, and background knowledge at all levels of the organization. Tacit knowledge is cultivated in an organizational culture that motivates through shared vision and common purpose. Personal knowledge is leveraged with explicit knowledge for the design and development of innovative products, services and processes. Strategic vision and operational expertise are fused in creative action.

Intelligence Through Organizational Learning

An intelligent organization pursues its goals in a changing external environment by adapting its behavior according to knowledge about its external and internal settings. In other words, an intelligent organization is a *learning organization* that is skilled at creating, acquiring, and transferring knowledge, and at modifying its behavior to reflect the new knowledge and insights (Garvin 1993). Learning thus begins with new knowledge and ideas that may be created in-house, or may come from external sources, but must be applied to change the organization's goals and behaviors in order for learning to be complete. Failure to learn often means failure to survive: nearly 30 percent of the corporations in the Fortune 500 list of five years ago are missing today (Pascale 1990); and for every successful turnaround there are two declining firms that do not recover (de Geus 1988).

When the Royal Dutch Shell Group surveyed 30 firms that had been in business for over 75 years, it attributed their longevity to "their ability to live in harmony with the business environment, to switch from a survival mode when times were turbulent to a self-development mode when the pace of change was slow. . . . Outcomes like these don't happen automatically. On the contrary, they depend on the ability of a company's senior managers to absorb what is going on in the business environment and to act on that information with appropriate business moves. In other words, they depend on learning." (de Geus 1988, 70)

Much of an organization's learning is from past experience. After the problem-plagued launch of their 737 and 747 planes, Boeing formed an employee group called "Project Homework" to compare the development of the 737 and 747 with that of the 707 and 727, hitherto two of the firm's most lucrative planes. After working for three years, Project Homework identified hundreds of lessons learned and recommendations. Some group members were moved to the 757 and 767 start-ups which eventually produced the most successful, error-free launches in Boeing's history (Garvin 1993). In another example of learning from the past, British Petroleum established a five-person project appraisal unit that reported directly to the board of directors. Every year, the unit reviewed six major investment projects, wrote them up as case studies, and derived lessons to guide future planning. This form of review is now done regularly at the project level. (Gulliver 1987)

Single-Loop and Double-Loop Learning

Effective learning must stretch beyond detecting and correcting past errors. Sometimes, basic questions about the norms, policies, and goals of the organization need to be answered afresh. In a classic discussion, Argyris and Schon (1978) describe organizational behavior as being governed by the organization's theory of action which includes the norms for organizational performance, strategies for achieving norms, and assumptions which bind strategies and norms together. Organizational learning takes place when members respond to changes in the external and internal environments by detecting and correcting errors between outcomes and expectations. Error correction is through modifying organizational strategies, assumptions, or norms in order to bring outcomes and expectations back into line. The altered strategies, assumptions or norms are then embedded into the organization's memory.

Two modes of organizational learning are possible (Figure 1.1). Learning is *single-loop* when the modification of organizational action is sufficient to correct the error without challenging the validity of existing organizational norms. In other words, there is a single feedback loop between detected outcomes to action which is adjusted so as to keep performance within the range set by organizational norms. The goal of single-loop learning is therefore to increase organizational effectiveness within existing norms. Learning is *double-loop* when error correction requires the modification of the organizational norms themselves, which in turn necessitates a restructuring of strategies and assumptions associated with these norms. Learning in this case is double-loop because a double feedback loop connects error detection not only to organizational action but also to the norms. The goal of double-loop learning is therefore to ensure organizational growth and survivability by resolving incompatible norms, setting new priorities, or restructuring norms and their related strategies and assumptions. While single-loop is adaptive and is concerned with coping, double-loop is generative learning and has to do with creating new mind sets.

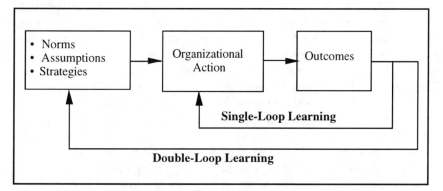

Figure 1.1 Single- and Double-Loop Learning

Many organizations have become quite good at single-loop learning—they measure their performance according to objectives, and correct deviations by changing operational procedures. Far fewer organizations are adept at double-loop learning, and not many organizations challenge their own norms, goals, or policies in relation to their changing environments. If budgeting is the archetypal mechanism for single-loop learning, then strategic planning is the tool for double-loop learning.

Current uncertainty about the value of strategic planning may reflect as much on the inability of organizations and their managers to engage in generative learning as on the inherent difficulty of strategic planning. Royal Dutch/Shell benefited from double-loop learning through its preparedness for the 1973 oil crisis. From its scenario planning exercises, Shell was able to change the conceptual frames of reference that its managers used to perceive reality about the world (Wack 1985a, 1985b). Shell's managers have been assuming that oil demand will continue to grow at rates higher than GNP in a calm political environment where oil supply was unproblematic, a set of norms that the managers had taken for granted for some time. The planning scenarios forced them to challenge these norms and to think about a low-growth world where oil consumption was increasing more slowly than GNP, where oil producers were reaching the limits of their capacities and were reluctant to raise output further because they were unable to absorb the additional revenues. As a result, Shell management was better prepared for the 1973 oil shock, and was able to more quickly revise its assumptions and strategies to respond to the new realities of tight oil supply-demand.

Although many organizations realize that change and learning are needed, they have difficulty stepping out of their existing mental models to learn from the experience of change. Organizational learning should not be equated with organizational change. Incremental change based on existing assumptions and parameters does not constitute learning. Instead, the intelligent organization learns *to* change as well as learn *from* change (McGill and Slocum 1994). The key is to unlearn the past, discard processes and practices that are previously known or believed to be smart. Intelligent organizations learn by assimilating their experiences with customers, competitors, partners, and so on, and using this knowledge to rejuvenate their mental frames of reference.

McGill and Slocum (1994) distinguish between four kinds of organizational intellects: the knowing organization, the understanding organization, the thinking organization, and the learning organization. The knowing organization is dedicated to finding the "one best way" to do business. The understanding organization believes in a "ruling myth" and uses strong cultural values to guide actions and strategies. The thinking organization sees business as a series of problems that need to be solved or fixed. Finally, the learning organization sees every business experience as an opportunity to improve—it models learning, encourages experimentation, and promotes dialogue.

Future Learning

It is not enough to learn from the past, the intelligent organization must also be able to learn about the future. Hamel and Pralahad (1994) call learning about the future developing "industry foresight" and assuming "intellectual leadership." Developing foresight starts by gaining a deep understanding of the trends and discontinuities in technology, demographics, government regulation, and social lifestyles—forces that will draw the competitive space of the future. Developing foresight is creating a point of view of the future that answers three key questions: What new kinds of benefits for customers or clients should the organization provide in the future? What new competencies are needed to offer these benefits? and How will the interface with customers or clients need to be redesigned?

Identifying future opportunities requires not only a profound understanding of the underlying drivers but also the courage and capability to imagine the future. Envisioning possibilities "grows out of a childlike innocence about what could be and should be, out of a deep and boundless curiosity on the part of senior executives, and out of a willingness to speculate about issues where one is, as of yet, not an expert." (Hamel and Pralahad 1994, 82-83) Having the knowledge and imagination to develop industry foresight will establish the organization as intellectual leaders who can influence the direction and form of the industry it is in, and so allow the organization to regain control of its own destiny.

An example of envisioning and enacting the future on a national scale is the National Computer Board (NCB) of Singapore, the agency responsible for designing and implementing the country's national plans to use information technology to move Singapore into the front ranks of the information age (Choo 1995). Singapore is a small island state with a population of 2.8 million that enjoys one of the highest living standards in the world. Devoid of natural resources, Singapore recognized early that information technology must lever the skills and diligence of its citizens. The NCB was established in 1981, and one of its first responsibilities was to manage an ambitious program to computerize the civil service. The future vision was to provide the public with a significantly better and wider range of services while improving productivity. At that time, the missing competency was indigenous expertise for information systems development. The NCB actively promoted a number of joint projects with foreign partners, training centers, overseas education and training schemes, incentive measures, and so on, to quickly build up a critical mass of computer professionals. The civil service computerization is an ongoing success—a recent audit showed that the government had obtained a return of over 2.7 dollars for every dollar spent on information technology in the program, and had avoided the need for some 5000 posts (NCB 1992). In the ensuing National IT Plan (1986-1990), the focus moved to the private sector, where the new vision was to create a strong, export-oriented, local IT industry, and to exploit IT to enhance business performance. The required competencies were to be an awareness and understanding of how IT could be used strategically, and the local technical capabilities to develop world-class IT applications.

Through partnership programs, joint ventures, showcase projects, the innovations of local R&D institutes, promotional activities, incentives and subsidies, and so on, a vibrant local IT industry emerged, growing at a compound annual rate of 30 percent between 1982 and 1990. A number of leading edge IT applications made their debuts, including a national electronic data interchange network (TradeNet) linking traders and government departments, and an expert system for ship planners in the port of Singapore. Both applications are used as case studies of exemplary strategic IT applications in the leading business schools of North America, and have spawned even more ambitious sister projects in Singapore. In 1991, the republic set its sights higher and launched its current IT2000 master plan, to use advanced information technologies to transform the city-state into a networked, intelligent island. According to the IT2000 vision, IT will enable Singapore to turn into a global business hub, boost its economic engine, enhance the potential of individual citizens, link its communities both locally and globally, and improve the quality of life (NCB 1992). The new competencies now include expertise in working with broadband networks, multimedia, and telecomputing; and building an information infrastructure based on technical and legal standards. The role of the NCB as master planner and architect of Singapore's IT destiny has been in defining future visions of Singapore as an IT-enabled society, in acquiring and developing the required competencies, and in reaching out to industry, government, and the public to promote the use and acceptance of IT.

The Intelligence/Learning Cycle

For the intelligent organization, learning and adaptation are behaviors that must paradoxically embrace their own opposites. Organizational learning necessarily includes *unlearning* about the past—the organization should not restrict learning and exploration to its existing markets, products or practices, but should rediscover new goals and responses by stepping out of habitual frames of reference and reexamining norms and assumptions (Hedberg 1981). Similarly, adapting to an environment necessarily includes *creating* an environment that is advantageous to the organization. After all, the external environment consists of other organizations, and every organization is in fact part of larger ecological systems whose members are bound together by common interests and interlocking activities (Moore 1993). In creating the environment, an organization, either by itself or with its partners, develops foresight about future benefits that it can deliver, grows capabilities to provide these benefits and so ensure a future for itself (Hamel and Pralahad 1994). Creating the environment is more than reactively enacting or interpreting the environment, and more than finding a matching fit with the environment. In effect, the intelligent organization can engineer such a fit through its deep understanding of the forces and dynamics that give shape to the future.

The organizational intelligence/learning process is a continuous cycle of activities that include sensing the environment, developing perceptions and generating meaning through interpretation, using memory about past experience to help perception, and taking action based on the interpretations developed (Figure 1.2).

    — *Sensing* is collecting information about the external and internal environment. Because the organization cannot attend to every event or development, it must select areas of priority, filter incoming data according to its interests, and sample events for learning.

    — *Memory* is derived from the experiences of the organization in interacting with the environment, and is expressed formally (documents, procedures) and informally (beliefs, stories). Experience develops rules that are used to match situations with appropriate responses, and frames that are used to define problems and their salient dimensions.

    — *Perception* is the recognition and development of descriptions of external events and entities using the knowledge that is available in memory. Perceptual strategies include developing a representation of an external scene, classifying objects and events according to categories that are known or have been encountered before, and recognizing the identity and main attributes of interested objects. Organizational perception depends heavily on the norms, frames, and rules that members use as lenses to view trends and developments.

    — *Interpretation* is at the center of the intelligence cycle as it attempts to explain "What is really going on here?" in terms that are meaningful to the organization. Interpretation is hard because it must balance conservatism (to interpret data according to existing beliefs) with entrepreneurism (to

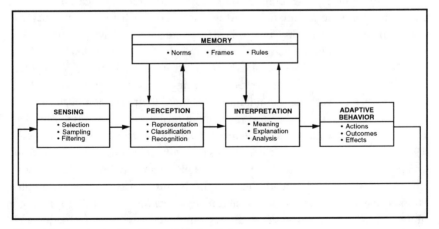

Figure 1.2 Organizational Intelligence/Learning Cycle

interpret data for the exploration of new alternatives). Interpretation leads to understanding and creative insight by which future consequences and opportunities are anticipated and evaluated according to preferences. Ultimately, interpretation is the making of meaning about where the organization was in the past, what it is today, and where it wants to be in the future. Finding meaning is a social process, requiring people to socialize and exchange information.

— Finally, *adaptive behavior* initiates a new cycle of learning as the organization makes decisions and takes actions that result in effects and outcomes. These are fed back into the loop by modifying sensing strategies (adjusting selection and sampling criteria) and by modifying frames and rules in memory (changing existing beliefs, adding new rules).

Building the Intelligent Learning Organization

Building the learning organization requires creating a climate that encourages learning, designing information processes and systems that promote knowledge creation and use, and recognizing and managing intellectual assets. The organization should allow the time and develop the skills for its employees to reflect on their current work practices, analyze customer needs, and think of ways to improve operations. In a learning organization, knowledge creation is everyone's activity, and not the responsibility of a specialized few. Information sharing should be facilitated by dissolving organizational boundaries that block information flow and isolate groups who cling to old perceptions.

Rotation or transfer of staff has been found to be an effective way of sharing knowledge within an organization. Special programs or events such as strategic reviews, system audits, benchmarking, and study missions may be initiated to explicitly provide opportunities for learning (Garvin 1993). From time to time, the organization should engage in double-loop learning by reexamining its basic assumptions and norms. Outside change agents such as consultants may be helpful in synthesizing and putting down on paper the organization's mental models, which may then be critically evaluated.

Information technology should be used to enhance learning. Computer models, for example, can be powerful learning tools because they handle a great number of variables simultaneously, trace their interaction through a large number of iterations, and so reveal relationships that are initially hidden because their cause and effect are widely separated in space and time (de Geus 1988). Computer-based information systems not only process data but also generate new information that describe, explain, and summarize the operations they automate. By rendering visible the rules, assumptions, and constraints that are embedded in the automated operations, this "informating" ability of computerized systems allows employees to learn a broader and deeper view of their work activities (Zuboff 1988).

The organization should also explicitly recognize, measure, and reward its intellectual resources. Many large organizations are developing accounting procedures to measure the value of their intellectual capital, creating new senior staff positions to manage intellectual assets, and building systems to share and retain the expertise of their knowledge workers (Stewart 1994).

Peter Senge, Director of the Center for Organizational Learning at the Sloan School of Management, Massachusetts Institute of Technology, and a man whom *Fortune* magazine has called "Mr. Learning Organization" (Dumaine 1994), prescribes an architectural plan for building a learning organization. The architecture requires three essential building blocks: guiding ideas; theory, methods and tools; and innovations in infrastructure.

Guiding ideas are the vision, values, and purpose shared by people in an organization. Senge maintains that the learning organization sees itself not as collections of objects and people working in networks of contractual commitments for economic transactions, but rather as patterns of interactions between people and activities, where people are part of a community that learn and change together. Using the generative power of language, they interpret and re-interpret their experiences to create new realities and re-examine existing beliefs and values.

Theory, method, and tools are the practical items that help people to learn. Tools must be derived from theory, and only tools that are grounded in important new theories have the power to change the ways that people think.

Innovations in infrastructure supply people with the resources they need in order to learn: time, information, money, management support, contacts, and so on. Innovation examples include learning laboratories where employees can try out new systems and practices in mockups of the workplace, and management flight simulators where managers can hone and rehearse their skills in areas such as new product development and skillful discussions for collective thinking.

With the architectural elements in place, the learning organization must undertake lifelong programs of study and practice in five learning disciplines:

> Personal Mastery—learning to expand our individual capacity to create the results we most desire, and creating an organizational environment that encourages all its members to develop themselves toward the goals and purposes they choose.

> Mental Models—reflecting upon, continually clarifying, and improving our internal pictures of the world, and seeing how they shape our actions and decisions.

> Shared Vision—building a sense of commitment in a group, by developing shared images of the future we seek to create, and the principles and guiding practices by which we hope to get there.

Team Learning—transforming conversational and collective thinking skills, so that groups of people can reliably develop intelligence and ability greater than the sum of individual members' talents.

Systems Thinking—a way of thinking about, and a language for describing and understanding, the forces and interrelationships that shape the behavior of systems. This discipline helps us see how to change systems more effectively, and to act more in tune with the larger processes of the natural and economic world. (Senge, et al., 1994, 6-7)

To Senge's five learning disciplines, we add a sixth: information management. The intellectual bedrock for building an intelligent, learning organization must be laid by information processes and pathways that nourish the many forms of knowledge creation and knowledge use that we have encountered in this chapter. The next chapter discusses the design and management of these information processes.

Chapter 2

A Process Model of Information Management

*A group may have more group information or less group informa-
tion than its members. A group of non-social animals, temporarily
assembled, contains very little group information, even though its
members may possess much information as individuals. This is
because very little that one member does is noticed by the others
and is acted on by them in a way that goes further in the group. On
the other hand, the human organism contains vastly more information, in all probability, than does any one of its cells. . . . One of the
lessons of the present book is that any organism is held together in
this action by the possession of means for the acquisition, use,
retention, and transmission of information.*

(Norbert Wiener 1948, Cybernetics, 158, 161)

INFORMATION. Any difference that makes a difference.

(Gregory Bateson 1979, Mind and Nature, 242)

Bateson's point is that in order for it to generate pattern, thought, and learning, information must be created, processed, and acted upon in an environment
of interconnected social and biological systems. From our discussion of organizational intelligence and learning in the first chapter, it is evident that information creation, acquisition, storage, analysis, and use form the intellectual latticework that supports the growth of an intelligent organization. Indeed, the
organizational learning loop is also the information management cycle of the

intelligent organization. An organization learns if, through its information processing, the range of its potential behaviors is changed (Huber 1991). Thus, information management's basic goal is to harness information resources and information capabilities so that the organization learns and adapts to its changing environment (Auster and Choo 1995).

The organizational learning model of Figure 1.1 may be mapped into a process model of information management shown in Figure 2.1. The process model depicts information management as a continuous cycle of six closely related activities: identification of information needs; information acquisition; information organization and storage; development of information products and services; information distribution; and information use. The process begins at the right-hand end of the cycle when information is created by the organization's actions (adaptive behavior). These actions interact with those of other organizations and systems to alter the environment, generating new messages and information.

In the *identification of information needs*, organization members recognize the volatility of the environment, and seek information about its salient features in order to make sense of the situation, and to have the necessary information to take decisions and solve problems. Information needs are defined by subject-matter requirements as well as situation-determined contingencies—some classes of problems are best handled with the help of certain types of information.

Information acquisition is driven by information needs, and must adequately address these needs. Planning for information acquisition has become a complex function. The fragmentation of human endeavor into pockets of specialization has led to a proliferation of information sources and services that cater to these niche markets. At the same time, organizations increasingly require in-depth treatments of selected issues that are strategic to their growth and survival. Existing sources have to be constantly evaluated, new sources have to be assessed, and the matching of sources to needs has to be regularly re-examined.

In *information organization and storage*, the objective is to create an organizational memory that is the active repository of much of the organization's

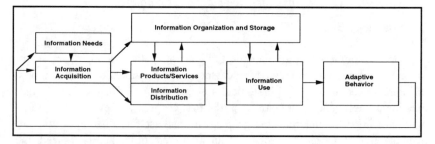

Figure 2.1   Information Management Cycle

knowledge and expertise. The volume of data produced and collected needs to be given structure in ways that reflect the interests and information use modes of the organization and its members. Information technology can raise the efficiency and reliability of the organization's operational activities. Integrated information management policies ensure that significant information concerning the organization's past and present are preserved and made available for organizational learning.

Information acquired and information from memory are packaged into different levels of *information products and services* targeted at the organization's different user groups and information needs. This is not a passive repackaging of incoming data. Information products and services have to add value by enhancing the quality of the information and improving the fit between the information and the needs or preferences of the users.

The goal of *information distribution* is to increase the sharing of information. Widespread information sharing catalyzes organizational learning. Information sharing also creates new insight and knowledge about difficult problems or situations. End users should be given the best available information to perform their work, and the information should be delivered through channels and modes that dovetail well with users' work patterns.

Information use is for the creation and application of knowledge through interpretive and decision making processes. Information use for interpretation involves the social construction of reality, and information representation and delivery should support the multilevel interaction of social discourse. Information use for decision making involves the selection of alternatives, and information provision and content should accommodate the kinetic and non-linear nature of the decision process.

The conceptualization of information management as a cycle of interrelated information activities to be planned for, designed, and coordinated, provides a process-based perspective that complements the more conventional views of information management as information technology management or information resource management. This process view of information management has recently began to gain currency (Davenport 1993; McGee and Prusak 1993). The process model of information management should encompass the entire information value chain, beginning with the identification of information needs, moving on through information acquisition, organization, and storage, products and services, distribution, and closing the cycle with information use (Davenport 1993). Information management frameworks do not always include needs identification and information use.

Although needs analysis may be one of the most neglected processes of information management, the quality of the information that the user receives depends highly on how well the needs have been communicated. Similarly, information use is an essential component, because understanding how information is used (or not used) to make decisions, solve problems, or interpret situations, is essential to a continuous improvement of the other information management processes. To clarify our discussion, Figure 2.1 shows the information management processes as separate boxes arranged in a linear sequence. In reality the processes are not so neatly compartmentalized—the activities overlap and their boundaries are porous. We discuss each information process of the model in the following sections. Many of the themes we introduce here are more fully developed in subsequent chapters.

Information Needs

Information needs arise from the problems, uncertainties, and ambiguities encountered in specific organizational situations and experiences. Such situations and experiences are the composite of a large number of factors that relate not just to subject matter, but also to contextual factors such as organization style, functional constraints, goal clarity and consensus, degree of risk, professional norms, amount of control, and so on. As a result, the determination of information needs must not stop at asking "What do you want to know?" but must also address questions such as: "Why do you need to know it?" "What does your problem look like?" "What do you know already?" "What do you anticipate finding?" "How will this help you?" "How do you need to know it?" and "In what form do you need to know it?" (MacMullin and Taylor 1984) *Information needs are contingent, dynamic, and multifaceted, and a sufficiently complete specification is only possible within a rich representation of the total information use environment.*

MacMullin and Taylor (1984, 98) suggest that problems act as surrogates of the information use environment, and because they encapsulate enough of the more salient demands of the use environment, "defining problem dimensions may allow the information professional to infer needs for information in a more structured, systematic way." They propose a set of eleven problem dimensions that define the information need and use environment and form the user criteria by which the relevance of information to a problem will be judged (Table 2.1). Collectively, these dimensions give a detailed representation of the information use environment surrounding problem situations, and suggest ways of elaborating information needs that include both subject-related needs and situation-related demands.

These problem dimensions are defined as follows:

> 1. *Problems lie on a continuum between design and discovery.* Design problems concern trying to reach a desired state through human effort, while discovery problems concern describing objects and processes in the natural world. Information for design would include a range of options and alternatives, whereas information for discovery would concentrate on a small, detailed set of data.

Table 2.1 Problem Dimensions and Information Needs

Problem Dimensions	Information Needs (Examples)
1 Design	Options, alternatives, ranges
Discovery	Small, detailed sets of data
2 Well-structured	Hard, quantitative data
Ill-structured	Probabilistic data on how to proceed
3 Simple	Path to goal state
Complex	Ways to reduce problem to simpler tasks
4 Specific goals	Goal operationalization and measurement
Amorphous goals	Preferences and directions
5 Initial state understood	Clarify unclear aspects of initial state
Initial state not understood	Soft, qualitative data to define initial state
6 Assumptions agreed upon	Information to help define problems
Assumptions not agreed upon	Views of the world, definition of terms
7 Assumptions explicit	Range of options, frames to analyze problems
Assumptions not explicit	Information to make assumptions explicit
8 Familiar pattern	Procedural and historical information
New pattern	Substantive and future-oriented information
9 Magnitude of risk not great	Cost-effective search
Magnitude of risk great	'Best' available information: accurate, complete
10 Susceptible to empirical analysis	Objective, aggregated data
Not susceptible to empirical analysis	Experts' opinions, forecasts, scenarios
11 Internal imposition	Clarification of internal goals, objectives
External imposition	Information about external environment

2. *Problems lie on a continuum between well- and ill-structured.* Well-structured problems may be solved by logical procedures and require quantitative data, whereas ill-structured problems would tend to seek information on how to interpret or proceed.

3. *Problems lie on a continuum between simple and complex.* In simple problems, a path to reach the goal state is easily defined, whereas complex problems involve many interacting variables and have to be reduced to manageable "subproblems."

4. *Problems lie on a continuum between specific and amorphous goals.* Information is needed to analyze goal states to determine what can be achieved and measured. Specific goals can be operationalized and measured to gauge efficiency. Amorphous goals require information to clarify preferences and directions.

5. *Problems lie on a continuum between "initial state understood" and "initial state not understood."* In the latter case, soft and qualitative data

are needed to help define the initial state and explain interrelationships between causal factors.

6. *Problems lie on a continuum between "assumptions agreed upon" and "assumptions not agreed upon."* Problems in domains such as management and economics are difficult to define because assumptions are contradictory or not universally accepted. Information is needed to explicate underlying perceptions of the world, definitions of terms and concepts, and so on.

7. *Problems lie on a continuum between "assumptions explicit" and "assumptions not explicit."* Information should help surface assumptions made and broaden the range of frames for analyzing problems. By the same token, information provided should include an analysis of its implicit assumptions.

8. *Problems lie on a continuum between familiar and new patterns.* Familiar problems (such as those faced by the professions of engineering, medicine, or teaching) require mostly procedural and historical information, whereas new problems require more substantive and future-oriented information.

9. *Problems lie on a continuum between "magnitude of risk not great" and "magnitude of risk great."* High risk problems justify extensive information searching to locate the most accurate and complete available information, whereas low risk problems may tolerate larger margins of error.

10. *Problems lie on a continuum between "susceptible to empirical analysis" and "not susceptible to empirical analysis."* The former case calls for objective and aggregated data, while the latter is often helped by subjective information from experts or from forecasts.

11. *Problems lie on a continuum between "internal imposition" and "external imposition."* Externally imposed problems usually originate in the environment, and information about the external environment is collected to track particular issues or to keep a general watch in anticipation of future issues.

The organization's information requirements are made up of the information needs of the members of key constituencies that compose the organization. Knowing what information is *not* needed is just as helpful as specifying a long list of information wants. An accurate description of information requirements is a prerequisite for effective information management. Ironically, system designers often take this for granted and assume that information requirements can be quickly determined by examining existing paper flows and data flows. Similarly, senior managers believe that it is the information specialist's job to identify their information needs, and do not assume the "information responsibility" of defining in detail what information they require (Drucker 1994).

In reality, particular information needs will have to be elicited from individuals. Unveiling information needs is a complex, fuzzy communication process. Most people find it difficult to express their information needs to their own satisfaction. Personal information needs have to be understood by placing them in the real-world context in which the person experiences the need, and to the ways in which that person will use the information to make sense of her/his environment and so take action. In her sense-making model, Dervin (1992) describes individuals as moving through space and time, continuously making sense of their actions and the external world. From time to time, a person is stopped in a situation where some kind of cognitive gap prevents movement:the person's internal sense has run out and she/he needs to make new sense. The person then looks for and selects strategies to bridge the cognitive gap, to seek answers to questions. Finally, individuals use the cognitive bridges they built to continue on their journeys.

From the numerous user studies that she and her associates did over two decades, Dervin believes that the ways in which people perceive their cognitive gaps or information need situations and the ways that they want information to help are good predictors of their information seeking and use behaviors. Better yet, the ways in which people perceive their information gaps and the ways in which people want information to help can be coded into universal categories that are applicable over a wide range of users.

Some of the generic information gaps Dervin has found are decision stops (person faces two or more roads ahead), barrier stops (one road ahead but the way is blocked), spin-out stops (no road ahead), perceptual embeddedness (how foggy is the road), and situational embeddedness (how many intersections are on the road). Gaps are operationalized as questions on the timing and location of events, understanding of causes, projected outcomes, and identifying the character of self, others, objects, or events.

The situation-gap-use sequence of the sense-making framework also suggests a line of neutral questioning that could be helpful in determining information needs: "Can you tell me about how this problem arose?" (Situation); "What are you trying to understand about X?" (Gap); and "If you could have exactly the help you wanted, what would it be?" (Use).

Information Acquisition

The organization accumulates a huge amount of information about its internal operations and resources. Much of this information gathering is done according to accepted rules or conventions, or to satisfy stipulated requirements. Accounting practices, company policies, standard operating procedures, government regulations, and so on, help to establish rules about what information to collect about which entities or activities as well as where or how to collect the information. Computer technology has been used for many years to aid the acquisition of internal data, and in these applications there have been dramatic gains in procedural efficiency.

Over and above internal operational data, today's organizations are increasingly concerned with many aspects of their external environment. It is no longer sufficient to track competitors and customers: organizations must also monitor technological innovations, government policies, economic trends, demographic patterns, lifestyle changes, political transitions, international trade—the list goes on. Information and technology are spinning webs that interconnect countries, markets, and many fields of human endeavor. The environment is full of surprises, distant events impinge in unexpected ways, organizations break traditions to dance new moves, and messages hide multiple meanings. Cause and effect associations between parts of the environment are becoming even more entangled over time.

The information needs of the organization's members will rightly reflect this range and diversity of concerns about the environment. At the same time, the attention spans and cognitive capacities of individuals are limited, so that it is not possible nor desirable to acquire information on every development that has possible significance. Because there exists a bewildering variety of methods, sources, and channels that can be deployed to collect information about the environment, selection of sources and sampling of events become necessary. Here we encounter our first difficulty. There is a principle in systems theory, the *Law of Requisite Variety* (Ashby 1956) that states that the internal control mechanisms of a living or social system must vary as much as the environment in which it is trying to survive. A system with the requisite control variety can deal with the complexity and challenges of its environment. A system that tries to insulate itself from environmental variety will become highly unstable. In other words, "only variety can absorb variety" (Beer 1974, p. 30).

According to Beer, an organization is a dynamic system that is characterized by its variety or the number of its possible states. The number of possible states grows daily because of the number of new possibilities generated by the environment through the interaction of markets, technology, education, and so on. To maintain stability, the organization needs to absorb this variety. There are two general strategies (which may be combined): the first is to amplify variety in the organization, the second is to attenuate variety from the environment. In the context of our present discussion, requisite variety suggests an important first principle in information acquisition: *the selection of sources to monitor the external environment must be sufficiently numerous and varied as to reflect the span and sweep of the external phenomena.* An organization that commits itself to a handful of "established" journals and newspapers to sense the environment is probably attenuating variety to an undesirable degree.

There are several ways an organization can improve its ability to absorb variety: take advantage of the specialized knowledge about information resources that is part of the training and experience of librarians; outsource the monitoring of specific issues that are of special importance or for which internal expertise does not exist; and use information technology to both amplify and attenuate variety. Information technology can amplify variety through, for example, systems that let users delineate personal profiles of their areas of interest and then retrieve relevant documents automatically from multiple databases. The same systems can attenuate variety by learning about users' preferences through relevance feedback and other mechanisms, and so become more selective in its trawling for external information.

A powerful way of managing information variety is to involve as many organization members as possible in the gathering of information; in effect, creating an organization-wide information collection network. In any organization, people, not printed sources or electronic databases, will always provide the most valuable information. People read widely; communicate frequently with customers, competitors, suppliers; work on a variety of projects; and accumulate specialized knowledge and experience. Unfortunately, information acquisition planning typically does not include human sources— a serious deficiency, indeed. Human sources are among the most valued by people at all levels of the organization: human sources filter and summarize information, highlight the most salient elements, interpret ambiguous aspects, and in general provide richer, more satisfying communications about an issue.

Information acquisition planning, therefore, should include the creation and coordination of a distributed network for information collection. Complementing the network could be a directory of experts: both the business and subject experts who work within the organization, and the external consultants or professional specialists who have worked with the organization. With the help of human resources and other departments, a database may be created that contains up-to-date information about employees' skills, training, project assignments, customer accounts, conference attendance, site visits, and so on. If employees are willing, they may include additional information about the special interests they pursue outside working hours. The database (or a separate file) may also contain information about consultants, specialists, visitors, speakers, and other external persons who have made contact with the organization. A well-maintained database of internal and external experts can become a prized information asset of the organization, as people seeking information use it to connect with the best available expertise. The database may also be used to locate internal and external experts who can assist in evaluating current information resources, recommending new materials, assigning priorities, and so on.

The requirement for requisite variety in information acquisition implies that most organizations will have to deal with a cornucopia of sources—internal and external, formal and informal. To avoid the risk of saturating the system, information variety must be managed. *The selection and use of information sources have to be planned for, monitored, and evaluated just like any other vital resource of the organization.* An organization-wide plan for information collection is essential.

A *strategic information audit* is a systematic method of diagnosing the strengths and weaknesses of an existing information acquisition and use system. The audit surveys current information uses and needs by functional area, assesses the effectiveness of current information sources, and the effectiveness of information distribution (Orna 1990, Stanat 1990). A questionnaire asks users to identify information sources they use, indicate the frequency of use, and rate the level of usefulness. Users also explain their information needs, both internal information needs (internally generated reports, documents, and so on) and external information needs (published materials such as newspapers, journals, periodicals). The results of the survey will reveal information gaps, inconsistencies, or duplication of effort. Does the audit show a heavy, perhaps lopsided reliance on certain types of sources, such as internal? Is there a relatively low usage of external sources to follow environmental developments? Do sources complement each other and provide multiple perspectives on important issues?

Gaps and deficiencies revealed by the audit could be rectified by the activation of additional sources to cover the required subject areas or by the application of information technology to improve information access and distribution. Users are often able to suggest which information sources would best fill the identified gaps. The use and value of the sources need to be monitored continuously. People should be encouraged to give feedback as part of their information use routine. Feedback should be analyzed with other data on information quality to evaluate source effectiveness in satisfying needs. The information environment is changing so rapidly with the proliferation of new sources and services that analyze and package information in many different ways, that an organization which has not revised its portfolio of sources for the past six months is probably missing out on relevant information.

The lability and interconnectedness of the environment make it increasingly difficult to decide the degree to which an item of information is relevant. The situation is akin to searching for pieces of a picture puzzle with no idea of what the completed scene looks like, but only general clues about how big and detailed the picture should be, the places to look, and the shape and color of the pieces that are likely to fit. So much is happening in the environment that events have to be sampled and news filtered according to their potential significance to the organization. *Such sampling and filtering can best be done by humans— it is an intellectual activity that requires sensitive judgment based on an adequately detailed knowledge of information resources and of the organization's business.* While information technology can and should be used to extend the reach of information foraging, human processing through sampling, filtering, noise reduction, and other value-adding services remains an indispensable link in the information chain.

Information Organization and Storage

Information that is acquired or created has to be organized and stored systematically in order to facilitate information sharing and retrieval. The organization's frames of reference, procedural rules, and decision premises are all ensconced in the methods and criteria by which the organization configures information for storage. Stored information represents a significant and frequently consulted component of the organization's memory. As mentioned in Chapter 1, an organization's rule-based knowledge is used in structuring information for storage and designing routines that access and process this information. Information is retrieved from this knowledge base to make decisions, answer questions, interpret situations, or solve problems.

Organizational decisions vary in complexity and may be categorized as programmed or nonprogrammed (Simon 1977). Programmed decisions are repetitive and well defined, and may be resolved by existing procedures. Nonprogrammed decisions are novel and ambiguous, with no existing procedures to handle them. The capacity to make intelligent nonprogrammed decisions is crucial for an organization that is seeking constant innovation in mercurial environments.

Storage is an area where information technology could have a large impact, partly because the huge volume of data cries out for automation, and partly because most documents today are prepared on computers. So far, we have become quite proficient at organizing structured data in computer databases that are used to support programmed decision making. Structured data such as customer and inventory records generally consist of predefined fields that hold determinate data values that fall within known ranges. For example, customer records contain fields such as customer account numbers and credit status while inventory records have product numbers and stock levels. The semantics and pragmatics of the information use are known beforehand and are used to define record and file structures. The overall design goal here is systems and procedural *efficiency*. Optimized file structures and access methods in the database system can maximize use of computer resources and yield fast response times (system efficiency), and at the same time ensure accurate, up-to-date records that can be processed to complete transactions without error and undue delay (procedural efficiency).

Unfortunately, online transaction processing systems, so efficient at handling transactions, are quite inadequate when it comes to answering queries and providing information that end users need to make decisions. Because transaction data becomes so voluminous over time and because transaction databases are structured to give fast response times rather than to anticipate future user queries, data for decision making becomes buried under mountains of transactional data and great effort has to be expended to mine for the required information. For example, in a financial company's large databases, it can take more than several *days* to process the data for a customer's complete account history.

One way out is *data warehousing*; that is, setting up a separate database of cleaned-up versions of the transaction data specifically to support end user queries and decision making. Data warehouses contain information from several sources throughout the enterprise that is organized and indexed around subjects and data models that are meaningful to the end user, such as customers, products, and orders. End users then access and manipulate warehoused data through decision support tools such as spreadsheets, statistical analysis programs, and executive information systems. In order to analyze, forecast, and plan, end users need the ability to look at the data from many vantage points. Software for *online analytical processing* allows users to create multidimensional views of large amounts of data as they slice and dice the data in various ways for the desired insight.

Structured data form only a fraction of the organization's data store—most of the information is actually "unstructured" so that it is not amenable to the sort of design procedures described above. Most office desks are cluttered with facsimiles, memoranda, minutes of meetings, proposals, reports, requests, messages, and so on. Much of this consists of textual or written information, but also likely includes charts, diagrams, maps, photographs, and audio recordings. Generally, unstructured information contains variable fields that hold indeterminate data values that might have unpredictable ranges. The semantics and pragmatics of the information use are not known beforehand: the same information can be used in a variety of ways, perhaps to trace the rationale of a decision, compare alternatives, locate past precedents, or recall former evaluations.

Due to their sheer volume, and lack of structural homogeneity and procedural clarity, these items are often allowed to fall into neglect. They may not be recorded at all, mistakenly discarded, stored without thought to future use or need, or simply forgotten about. As a result, subsequent retrieval and reference becomes extremely difficult and the sharing of information is severely restricted. Vital facts or proof are hidden or lost, opportunity to learn from history is denied, duplication of effort becomes common, and time spent on searching for documents is wasted. *The organization must establish an integrated records management and archival policy to enable it to create, preserve, and leverage its corporate memory.*

Records management is the application of systematic and scientific control to *all* of the recorded information that an organization needs to do business (Robek, et al., 1987). A formal records management program comprises many of the following functions: records inventory; records appraisal and retention; vital records management; active files management; micrographics management; inactive files management; archives management; forms management; correspondence management; mail management; reports management; directives management; and reprographics management. A records inventory identifies individual records series (group of related records filed and used as a series), determine where they originate, how they are used, and how they interrelate (Schwartz and Hernon 1993). The records inventory is appraised to assess the value of records series to the organization according to their primary values (administrative, legal, fiscal, and research values) and secondary values (evidentiary and informational values).

A records retention policy is then developed that specifies when records will be destroyed or transferred from active to inactive storage, and when certain records will be retained permanently. Vital records are those that preserve the financial and legal standing of the organization and which the organization would need to restart or continue in the event of an disaster. Vital records should be safeguarded by a program that provides adequate levels of protection relative to the evaluated potential risks.

To manage the different types of active records and files in the organization (correspondence, transaction records, project records, case files, and specialty files), a variety of filing methods must be designed to reflect the requirements of information content, information use, format, and media. For example, correspondence records and project records may be filed according to subject classification, whereas transaction records are typically arranged by name or a number identifier. Subject filing is used when a record is requested by subject matter (such as correspondence) rather than by name or number. Subject file systems need to be developed with great care. Users' information needs and uses, their search habits and search objectives, and the types of anticipated retrievals, are some of the factors to guide system design. Users' vocabulary should be considered in selecting subject headings, and these should be applied consistently and with a minimum of ambiguity. A subject authority file, controlling headings and references, is vital to the success of subject filing. Designing subject file systems requires the specialized knowledge of subject classification principles and methods, as well as a thorough grasp of the organization's functions and information needs.

While the historical motivation for records management is to streamline paperwork and so reduce the cost of records creation and storage, for the learning organization, the real value of records management is its facilitating the finding of specific information items that would best address a particular purpose—locating the proverbial needles in the information haystack (Schwartz and Hernon 1993). In developing courses of action to respond to the environment, having accurate information about where the organization stands (current activities, resource levels, internal strengths and weaknesses), and the ability to review past experiences involving similar situations, is as important as understanding the details of the external change.

The correspondence, contracts and agreements, directives, memoranda, minutes of meetings, planning documents, press releases, reports, and the tumble of other documents produced in day-to-day operations form a textual trail by which the organization's decisions, actions, and rationales may be retraced. By re-examining these records, one is able to understand why certain decisions were made, projects initiated, actions adopted, and so on. A learning organization should be able to study the organization's history so that, in planning for the future, it has the full benefit of having looked carefully and learned from its past: ". . . managers can look at the history of an organization to find ways it adapted in the past. A company's history contains its heritage and traditions, which managers need to understand if they are to see the present as part of a process rather than as a collection of accidental happenings. Perceiving a company in this way can enhance a manager's ability to plan for the future. Managers need to learn how to develop historical resources and how to put them to use." (Smith and Steadman 1981, 164)

Perplexingly, the preservation and management of organizational memory is among the most neglected tasks of the modern organization. To make matters worse, current tendencies towards mergers and acquisitions, high-turnover work forces, appointments of managers and directors from the outside, and the emphasis on oral communications, have all resulted in a dilution of organizational memory (Mooney 1993).

Today's organizations, swamped with information, must arrest this threat of organizational amnesia:

> While corporations are being overwhelmed by a burgeoning volume of records, they are, paradoxically, too often unable to locate truly vital information. Without an adequate archival program, important records may be misplaced; without proper preservation measures, many valuable documents will literally self-destruct; without precautions, an unanticipated disaster can wipe out irreplaceable information. Even when the records have been kept, and eventually can be located, the lack of an effective archival program may make it difficult for the corporation to respond promptly and accurately not only to its own information needs but to legitimate outside queries—from government agencies, consumers, and the media. Corporations will grow increasingly unable to solve these challenges without an efficient, comprehensive archival program. (Neal 1993, 1-2)

Smith and Steadman (1981) propose three basic steps towards making the organization's history useful. First, establish the high value-added uses of the organization history. For example, at Citibank, the payoffs are seen as improving the process of corporate planning; at Wells Fargo, corporate history is a marketing tool that gives the bank a distinctive character; and at AT&T, historical research illuminates organizational issues. A learning organization should use organizational memory to ensure that assumptions about the past and present are correctly based and so avoid embarking on irrelevant or misguided courses of action. Second, the organization identifies and rationalizes its historical resources for current and future use. The basics of a good archival collection include executive correspondence files, minutes of board meetings, records of major committee decisions, and summary financial data (Mooney 1993). Third, the organization develops specific programs and studies. Archival holdings will represent less than one per cent of all organization records. The appraisal criteria used to select records must be based on a clear understanding of the organization's history and its information needs.

The potentially severe consequences of the loss or inability to find vital documents are driving organizations to seek more versatile information storage and retrieval systems that can capture, store and retrieve text and other unstructured data. Instead of efficiency, the overall system requirement now becomes *flexibility*—the system should capture hard and soft information, support multiple user views of the data, link together items that are functionally or logically related, permit users to harvest the knowledge that is buried in these resources, and so on. Because the same information can be relevant to a range of different problem situations, it becomes necessary to represent and index the unstructured information by several methods including context-related attributes (e.g., dates, locations, names of senders/recipients, names of committees and members); content-related keywords (e.g., topics, subjects, diagram captions, graph titles, project titles, product names, technologies); abstracts or summaries; and the full-texts themselves.

The development of automated indexing systems makes it increasingly feasible to adopt a user-centered approach to indexing, over and above document-oriented indexing that represents the document's content. In the user-centered approach, indexing can be done on two levels: the first reflects topic and other predetermined features; the second is tailored to situational requirements such as the level of treatment, whether general or specific (Fidel 1994). User-centered indexing may also be request-oriented, in which case the index language is built from an analysis of user requirements and is then used as a checklist to index documents (Soergel 1985, 1994).

The underlying idea is to anticipate user requests and check each document when it is being indexed against a list of anticipated requests. A combination of document-oriented and user-oriented indexing approaches has the potential to significantly improve information retrieval performance as well as user satisfaction. Commercially, a growing number of technologies are becoming available to help materialize a vision of electronic document management: optical character readers and scanners read in text and images; standardized markup languages tag and describe the logical structures of documents; work flow applications regulate document flow according to life cycle phases; text engines automatically identify important themes and concepts, and generate abstracts and summaries; and work group systems simplify and coordinate information sharing, and machine-index stored messages which may then be retrieved with search tools.

Given the amount of textual material in any organization, text information management will become as important as database management, and text retrieval applications will one day be as commonplace as word processing or spreadsheets. Today's text retrieval engines and development tools have attained new levels of functionality and versatility. Some of the newer systems make use of semantic networks of word meanings and links derived from dictionaries and thesauri to allow users to search by querying in natural language, choosing concepts and specific word meanings, and controlling the closeness of match. Other systems simplify the development of text retrieval applications across heterogeneous database environments, using a common access and programming interface based on industry standards.

Information Products and Services

To stay well informed and build up its knowledge base, the intelligent organization needs to feed on a balanced diet of high quality information supplied through a varied menu of information products and services. These products and services should cover a range of time horizons and provide different levels of focus or detail (Figure 2.2). Some information products disseminate urgent news that require immediate attention; others report developments that would take time to unfurl over the short term; while others still peer into the more distant future. For each of these time horizons, the information provided may be sharply focused, describing particular events, objects or organizations; or the information

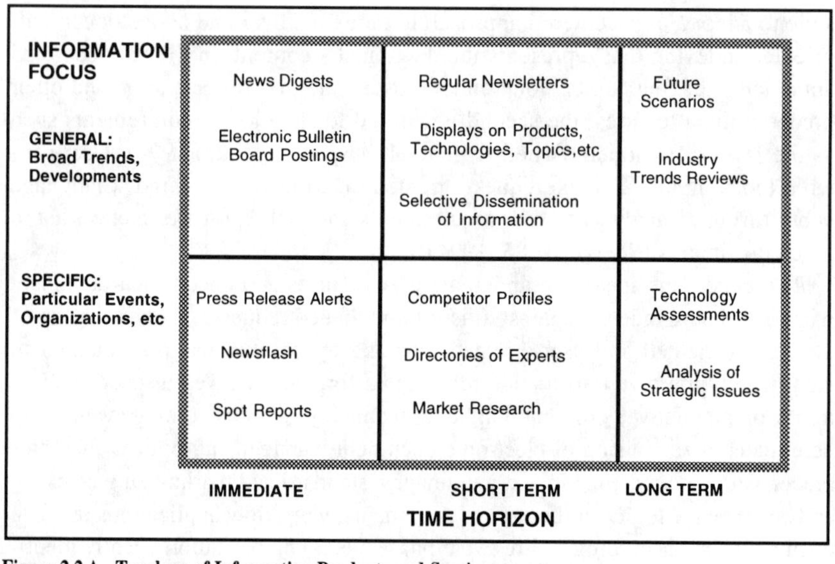

INFORMATION FOCUS	IMMEDIATE	SHORT TERM	LONG TERM
GENERAL: Broad Trends, Developments	News Digests / Electronic Bulletin Board Postings	Regular Newsletters / Displays on Products, Technologies, Topics,etc / Selective Dissemination of Information	Future Scenarios / Industry Trends Reviews
SPECIFIC: Particular Events, Organizations, etc	Press Release Alerts / Newsflash / Spot Reports	Competitor Profiles / Directories of Experts / Market Research	Technology Assessments / Analysis of Strategic Issues

TIME HORIZON

Figure 2.2 A Topology of Information Products and Services

may be general and broad, surveying the terrain on which the organization's future will make its course. The guiding principle is that each information product must provide value to the end user. Information products or services should not rely only on information that happens to arrive in "convenient" packages— where it adds value to the user, incoming information may have to be reassembled, summarized, cross-referenced, compared, and so on.

Users want information not just to give answers to questions (What is happening here?) but also to lead to solutions for problems (What can we do about this?). Moving from questions to problems means moving from a subject-based orientation in which knowing is a sufficient end state to an action orientation in which information is being used to formulate decisions and behaviors. To be relevant and consequential, information products and services should therefore be designed to address not only the subject matter of the problem but also the specific contingencies that affect the resolution of each problem or each class of problems.

Information products and services, and indeed information systems in general, should be developed as sets of activities that add value to the information being processed in order to assist users to make better decisions and better sense of situations, and ultimately to take more effective action (Taylor 1986). Value-added activities are those that signal, enhance, or otherwise strengthen the potential usefulness of system messages. Taylor identifies more than twenty value-added activities that may be classified into six categories of user information selection criteria (Table 2.2): ease of use, noise reduction, quality, adaptability, time savings, and cost savings.

Ease of use reduces the difficulty in using the product or service, and includes the capability to let users scan an information neighborhood (browsing); presenting and arranging data to facilitate scanning and selection (formatting); assisting users in getting answers and in gaining understanding and experience with the system (interfacing); dividing or grouping subject matter (ordering); and making physical access easier (physical access).

Noise reduction is achieved by excluding unwanted information, including information of conceivable value, and focusing information where appropriate on specific items or facts. Noise reduction includes the values added by applying intellectual technologies such as indexing systems or database management systems to assist users in narrowing the information universe to a set of potentially useful data (intellectual access); setting up pointers to related information, thus expanding users' information options (linkage); helping users to find exactly what is wanted by ranking output or providing signals on attributes such as language, and level of subject treatment (precision); and selecting input information that is likely to be of interest to the user population (selectivity).

Quality is a user criterion on the general excellence of the information product or service, and includes the values added by the error-free transfer of information (accuracy); completeness of coverage on a topic or subject (compre-

Table 2.2   Values Added in Information Products and Services

User Criteria	Values Added	Value-added Activities/Features (Examples)
1. Ease of Use	*Browsing*	Table of contents
	Formatting	Charts and tabulations
	Interfacing	Help in using service
	Ordering	Grouping information by subject, date, etc
	Physical access	Document delivery
2. Noise Reduction	*Intellectual access*	Indexing
		Database management systems
	Linkage	References to other related information
	Precision	Ranking of output
		Detailed description of items
	Selectivity	Selective input of information
3. Quality	*Accuracy*	Error-free transmission
	Comprehensiveness	Complete coverage
	Currency	Recent information
		Access vocabulary reflects current usage
	Reliability	Trust in consistent performance of service
	Validity	Soundness of data provided
4. Adaptability	*Closeness to problem*	Responsive to specific needs of person/problem
	Flexibility	Multiple ways of manipulating data
	Simplicity	Most lucid data selected for presentation
	Stimulatory	Activities that raise the profile of the service
5. Time Savings		Speed of response
6. Cost Savings		Money saved for users

hensiveness); recency of data and access vocabularies (currency); trust a user has in the consistent quality performance of the service (reliability); and inclusion of signals about the soundness or otherwise of the data (validity).

Adaptability refers to the ability of the service to be responsive to the needs and circumstances of the users in their work environments. Most of the adaptability value is added by human intermediaries because they can reshape information to better fit users' problem settings. Adaptability includes the values added by providing products and services that meet the specific needs of a person in a particular situation with a particular problem (closeness to the problem); supporting a variety of ways for users to work interactively with the data (flexibility); presenting the most lucid data, explanations, hypotheses, or methods from among several within quality and validity limits (simplicity); and increasing goodwill and visibility through activities such as organizing seminars, editing speeches and papers, and so on (stimulatory).

Time savings and *cost savings* are the perceived values of the service based on the speed of its response and the amount of dollars saved for the users. The value-added framework enhances the design of information products and services by increasing their relevance and responsiveness to end users' needs. The user-centered framework looks beyond content and technology to the requirements arising from users interacting with their information use environment.

After a detailed analysis of four areas of inquiry—innovation as a phenomenon, organizations as information processing systems, effects of technological change, and information user behavior, Maguire, et al., (1994) recommend several principles for the design and management of information services:

1. *Information services need to be flexible and multifaceted.* Flexibility involves the integration of data on various media from internal and external sources, as well as the integration of computer-aided search capabilities with the existing indexing in bibliographical databases. Because the same data can convey different meanings in different use contexts, indexing and abstracting may require a certain amount of necessary redundancy.

2. *No information service has a monopoly; all need to develop both competitive and collaborative strategies.* Competition among information services is inevitable and healthy. In-house services have to coexist and complement outsourced information services and external information brokers.

3. *Intermediary roles need to be translated at the microlevel into transparent systems that empower users, and at the macrolevel to be expanded to perform training and education functions.* Empowering users involve the identification, development and provision of tools that simplify access and interpretation. At the same time, tools and techniques have to be learned, and intermediaries will have to play the role of trainers and consultants.

4. *The information service needs to accept responsibility for performance of some monitoring functions and to assist gatekeepers and their relatives in the performance of others.* While selective dissemination of information is well established and automatic retrieval based on interest profiles will be more common, the initial creation of search profiles and subsequent modification and fine-tuning still require the skilled mediation of the information specialist who combines knowledge about the organization with that about information resources. Gatekeepers and their related

boundary spanners will continue to act as important channels for disseminating information.

5. *The information service must be client-centered rather than collection-centered or system-centered, be continually aware of user needs, and have a marketing orientation.* The call for client-centered service, though widely supported, is often defeated in the physical, organizational, and procedural structures that are erected to offer the service. Awareness of user needs may be heightened by market research techniques such as focus groups and interviews, and by strategic planning activities that define user responsiveness as a central goal.

6. *The information service itself needs to be constantly innovating.* Sources of innovation include the use of information technology to enhance service, staff development to broaden and enrich professional skills, reward schemes to encourage creativity and experimentation, and entrepreneurial ventures with other organizations to share risk and prototype new services.

Information Distribution

Information distribution is the process by which the organization disseminates and shares information from different sources. A wider distribution of information can yield many positive consequences: organizational learning becomes more broadly based and more frequent; retrieval of information becomes more likely; and new information can be created by piecing together disparate items (Huber 1991). In our process model, information distribution and sharing is a necessary precondition of perception and interpretation. Distribution is, in the first instance, about the dissemination or routing of information according to that famous credo, "the right information to the right person in the right time, place, and format."

A general principle here suggests that the mode of information delivery should mesh well with the user's information habits and preferences. The chief executive who prefers information presented face-to-face may want a personal briefing in order to ask specific questions rather than read lengthy reports. The professional staff member who receives electronic mail, facsimiles, and documents via a universal mailbox on a personal computer may prefer to get information electronically through the same interface. Hence, it is the user's criteria of ease of use and physical accessibility that should decide the dissemination modes.

It is well known that certain individuals perform catalytic roles in sustaining and nourishing communication networks in organizations. Allen (1977), after more than a decade of research on communications flow in science and engineering organizations, shows that information from the outside world does not move directly into the organization. Instead, the information flow is indirect and involves two or more steps. External information passes through *technological gatekeepers* who read more, including research-oriented journals, and who have a broad range of personal contacts both outside and inside the organization, which they maintain on a continuing informal basis. It is the gatekeepers who keep their colleagues informed, and who are often consulted about current, external developments.

Tushman and Scanlan (1981) identify a similar phenomenon. Because organizations limit their scope and specialize in certain activities, they evolve local norms, languages, and conceptual frameworks. While this specialization increases the efficiency of internal information processing, it also creates obstacles to information transfer from the external environment. As a result, it becomes necessary to recode information messages at the firm's boundaries. Boundaries can be spanned effectively only by individuals who understand the coding schemes used on both sides of the boundary, enabling them to recognize significant information on one side and disseminate it on the other side. Tushman and Scanlan name this process *informational boundary spanning*.

The phenomenon of information gatekeeping or boundary spanning is not limited to scientific organizations, but can be found among a spectrum of social communication patterns, including voting behavior and the diffusion of innovations (in both cases, opinion leaders influenced the votes of friends, the adoption of innovations such as hybrid seed corn and new drugs). Allen summarizes:

> The phenomenon of the gatekeeper is not an isolated one. Rather it is one example of a much more general class of phenomena. There will always be some people who, for various reasons, tend to become acquainted with information sources outside their immediate community. They either read more extensively than most or develop personal contacts with outsiders. A large proportion of these people in turn attract colleagues from within the community who turn to them for information and advice. (Allen 1977, 150)

The implication seems to be that organizations could enlist the help of gatekeepers to smooth the flow of external information into the organization. In some situations, gatekeepers could be identified, and information targeted at these communication stars. The intention is not to create an information elite. The need for information targeting follows from a recognition that information flow about external new developments is sometimes problematic and requires the intervention of gatekeepers and boundary spanners. Having been alerted by gatekeepers to important items, we may expect more people in the organization to access sources and become better informed on their own. Issues that are complex, technical, or discussed in specialized languages may benefit from such a two-step communication approach.

The point of distribution is information sharing, and an objective of sharing is to enable information from multiple sources and processed by multiple users to be synthesized to generate deeper insight. Gregory Bateson supplies a useful analogy in his discussion of binocular vision. He asks what is to be gained by comparing the data collected by one eye with that collected by the other when, after all, both eyes are typically aimed at the same region in the external space. In fact, the *differences* in the information from each retina is processed in the visual cortex to create a qualitatively new kind of information—about *depth*. Bateson suggests that the principle is general, that extra "depth" in some metaphoric sense can always be obtained by combining information for multiple descriptions that is collected and coded differently (Bateson 1979, p. 80-81). How might information distribution be designed to induce the creation of new knowledge? One answer may be to dismantle the wall between information providers and end users, to co-opt users themselves into the distribution network as active, contributing participants.

For a model of how this could work, we might look at a hugely popular form of information sharing—Usenet newsgroups on the Internet (Krol 1994). In newsgroups, information is posted onto what is essentially an electronic bulletin board that is seen by everyone in the group. Each article has a subject heading, and users can scan these titles quickly to pick out items to read. After reading, users themselves participate by posting new messages that answer questions, add commentary, suggest interpretations, and so on. Related messages are sewn together into threads of discussions about particular topics. From time to time, replies and discussion threads may be summarized and then re-posted. It is tempting to consider a similar model for organizational information dissemination. New items are given informative subject titles and broadcast promptly. Users scan, read, and discuss each other's messages. Multiple perspectives and representations are likely to emerge that reflect users' different experiences and knowledge. Discussion threads may then be summarized by a user or moderator with special knowledge or interest. Information digests of the discussion threads may be posted electronically, or packaged into information products in their own right. Electronic exchanges may occasionally lead to face-to-face focus group discussions or the forming of special interest groups.

The electronic bulletin board serves as the shared collaboration space in which participants actively create shared understandings (Schrage 1990). Unlike meetings and formal gatherings, the electronic collaborative space and its tools are interactive and responsive, many participants have equal and voluntary access, conversations are spontaneous, multiple conversations develop in parallel, and the focus is on the content of the messages on the communal space rather than a competition of personal egos. As a medium for information distribution and sharing, well managed discussion groups of motivated users seem capable of adding considerable depth to the organization's knowledge base.

Information Use

In organizational learning, individuals use information to create knowledge, not just in the sense of data and facts but in the form of representations that provide meaning and context for purposive action. People in organizations therefore behave as sense makers who use information in action (Weick 1979), and information use becomes a hermeneutic process of inquiry, in which understanding is realized through interpretation and dialogue (Winograd and Flores 1987, Boland, et al., 1994). The theory of hermeneutics (Gadamer 1975) describes the interpretive process by which an individual gives meaning to organizational experience, while the theory of inquiring systems (Churchman 1971) describes how a community of inquirers build and test knowledge through dialogue. The hermeneutic interpretive process is an interplay of the part and the whole in a hermeneutic circle (Gadamer 1975): we depend on our comprehension of the whole to identify and understand the parts, but at the same time, we depend on our knowledge of the parts to validate our comprehension of the whole (Boland, et al., 1994). As a result, we continually move back and forth between theory and details, and between vision and specifics, in our attempt to construct interpretations.

How is the validity of these interpretations to be judged? By drawing together the ideas of Leibniz, Locke, Kant, Hegel, and Singer, Churchman (1971) portrays human inquirers as producers of knowledge who test their interpretations through dialogue and debate. In a community of inquirers, individuals see the same situation through different weltanschauungen shaped by their beliefs and values. Inquiry then proceeds by vigorous debate as thesis and antithesis confront each other. The inquiry changes its direction and style frequently as new concepts and elements are introduced from outside the presently accepted ways of understanding a situation. Like the hermeneutic circle, there is constant movement between views of a situation that simplify and views that complicate, between close-up examination of details and reflection about general assumptions, categories, and concepts (Boland, et al., 1994).

Information for knowledge creation is therefore ambivalent and vacillating. Organizational information sustains multiple meanings, each representation being the result of the subjective cognitive and affective interpretations of individuals or groups. Organizational information continuously fluctuates between the fine-grained and the broad-brushed, between components and the whole, between immediate instances and general policies. In the act of knowledge creation, organizational information is transformed into tacit, rule-based, and cultural knowledge that constitute the cognitive fabric of the organization (we discussed the three classes of organizational knowledge in Chapter 1). For much of its life, organizational information cannot be objectified or reified, but resides and grows in the minds and hearts of individuals.

The use of information for knowledge production is unfurled through social interactions dispersed over space and time. In the organizational community of human inquirers, multiple interpretations are exchanged and contested in conversations. Assumptions are made visible, challenged and revised. The process of inquiry swings between representations that reduce complexity and representations that compel a rethinking of existing concepts and categories. Again we see a weaving in and out between the layers of tacit, rule-based, and background knowledge as the organization engages in generative, double-loop learning. Convergence may result in shared interpretations and understanding, but where consensus is not achieved, finding better questions to ask becomes more important than finding answers.

In summary, information use for the making of meaning and understanding requires information processes and methods that provide for a high degree of flexibility in information representation and that facilitate the vigorous exchange and evaluation of multiple representations among individuals. Labeling or naming of concepts and categories has to be relevant to the users' interpretive discourse, and be flexible and easy to change. Information is needed about specific events and instances as well as about new theories and frameworks that dispute current norms and beliefs. Assumptions made should be surfaced for review. Information is to be shared easily but without loss of cognitive richness. Through the exchange and interpretation of information, the organization blends its tacit and explicit knowledge to extract new meanings for action.

The second category of information use is for the making of decisions. Information use is particularly intense in strategic decision processes where the decisions are consequential but there are no predetermined responses that may be recalled from the organization's memory. Based on their analysis of twenty-five strategic decision processes, Mintzberg, Raisinghani and Théorêt (1976) propose a model that describes the structure and dynamics of the decision processes. According to the model, strategic decision making entails three phases (Table 2.3). In the *identification* phase, problems, opportunities or crises are recognized and their cause and effect relationships explicated. Identification thus involves the two routines of decision recognition and diagnosis. In the *development* phase, the alternative solutions to the problem are developed or the opportunity the organization wishes to exploit is elaborated. Development involves the search routine when ready-made solutions exist, and the design routine when a custom-made solution is required. Finally, in the *selection* phase, the decision is made by screening out infeasible alternatives (screening routine), evaluating and choosing an alternative (evaluation-choice routine), and obtaining authorization for the commitment to action (authorization routine).

The decision routines in the three phases are supported by three other routines that provide for control of the process, communication, and the exercise of political influence. The entire process is affected by dynamic factors in the form of interruptions, delays, and repeated cycles. Overall, ". . . the process is dynamic, operating in an open system where it is subjected to interferences, feedback loops, dead ends, and other factors. . . . We find in our study that dynamic factors influence the strategic decision process in a number of ways. They delay it, stop it, restart it. They cause it to speed up, to branch to a new phase, to cycle within one or between two phases, and to recycle back to an earlier point in the process." (Mintzberg, et al., 1976, 263)

Information seeking and use is active throughout the decision process as participants scan the environment, search for diagnostic information and for information about alternatives and their consequences, send information to higher levels for authorization, and monitor the decision process itself. Mintzberg and associates discern three information routines: exploration, investigation, and dissemination. *Exploration* is the general scanning of information, including the review of unsolicited information, that is used to recognize decision situations and build conceptual models. *Investigation* is the collection and analysis of specific information that is required during the diagnosis, search, and evaluation-choice activities. *Dissemination* is the communication of information about the progress of the decision process.

Information is sought and used throughout the entire decision process, not just at the start or during a few narrow activities. The intensity of information use, however, does vary according to the decision phase, with the greatest amount of information resources being consumed during the development phase in working out solutions or elaborating opportunities. Information use is also intense during the early stages of the identification phase, and again during the early stages of the selection phase.

Information is also used in qualitatively different ways during the various decision phases and decision routines (Table 2.3). For the identification phase, information is used to help frame the problem situation and explain causal relationships. The main purpose is to provide enough *comprehension* of an issue so that the decision process can start. For the development phase, alternatives and solutions have to be found or generated, and options have to be described in sufficient detail. Development usually begins with a vague image of the ideal solution, which is then progressively fleshed out into one or more specific alternatives. Because the process is iterative and cyclic, information gathering is greatest during development. Here, the main purpose is the *design* of viable solutions. For the selection phase, the consequences of various alternatives will have to be predicted, and the criteria for choosing alternatives will have to be defined, clarified, and reconciled. Research is often needed to filter out impractical options, and to provide a factual database upon which judgment can be exercised. The main goal now is rational *evaluation* using the best available information, so that the decision is acceptable and can be authorized for action.

Although broken down into three logical phases, the entire decision process is in fact cyclic and nonlinear, with many interferences, interrupts,

Table 2.3 Information Use in Decision Phases

Decision Phase	Decision Routine	Information Use
1 Identification	*Recognition*	Recognize a need for decision making; recognize situation as opportunity, problem or crisis.
	Diagnosis	Understand causes; establish cause and effect relationships.
2 Development	*Search*	Search for ready-made solutions: Search existing organizational memory (memory search); Wait for unsolicited alternatives to appear (passive search); Activate search generator to produce alternatives (trap search); Direct seeking of alternatives (active search).
	Design	Design custom-made solution or modify existing solution: information use is usually focused on one fully-developed solution.
3 Selection	*Screen*	Eliminate alternatives that are infeasible or inappropriate.
	Evaluation-Choice	Choice of alternative is made by: Judgment (an individual makes choice in own mind); Bargaining (selection by a group of decision makers, each exercising judgment); Analysis (factual evaluation, may be followed by judgment or bargaining).
	Authorization	Justification of choice; explanation of rationale; summary of supporting data.

and delays. New information must be injected into the process in the form of external interrupts or new options when the environment changes, when outside forces block the selection of a solution, or when new alternatives are discovered late in the process. The probability and frequency of information interruption increases with the duration of the decision process and with the volatility of the external environment. Our discussion here suggests that the information manager or specialist should be a proactive participant in the decision process, be sensitive to the open, dynamic nature of the decision process, and be well prepared to address the different kinds of information needs that characterize each decision phase and routine.

Summary

Our model of information management outlines six information processes that bootstrap the intelligent organization's capacity to learn and adapt: identifying information needs, acquiring information, organizing and storing information, developing information products and services, distributing information, and using information.

In discussing needs, our central message was that the elaboration of *information needs* should not be confined to subject-related concerns but should also address the situational demands of the information use environment in which the users are immersed. This user-centered perspective requires that we broaden our understanding from *what* the users want to know, to *why* and *how* the users need and will use the information.

On *information acquisition* , we urge that the selection and use of sources be planned systematically and purposefully, just as one would do with any other vital organizational resource. New sources proliferate and existing sources evolve so rapidly that continuous monitoring and evaluation become necessary. A general planning premise is that sources should have sufficient variety to reflect the range and diversity of external phenomena. Information acquisition planning could consider the creation of an organization-wide information gathering network and a database directory of experts that includes people and specialists from all levels and functional areas. Where information needs to be filtered this may best be done by humans—filtering is an intellectual activity that requires detailed knowledge of the organization's business.

Computer-based systems for *information organization and storage* should not only be efficient in terms of resource utilization and response times, but could also provide greater flexibility and information relevance. Users should be able to mine for the insights they need to make decisions from the accumulated operational data. Textual and other unstructured data are key information resources and should be stored and structured so that users can search for them using multiple representations and criteria. Text information management and text retrieval applications are likely to become as important as data management. An integrated records management and archival policy should enable the organization to create, preserve, and learn from its corporate memory and organizational history.

In the development of *information products and services*, we shift our goal from answering questions to helping users solve their problems. To do so, information services should provide information whose content, format, and orientation address the contingencies that affect the resolution of each problem or class of problems. Our main recommendation is for a value-added approach in which information products and services are designed so that they amplify the potential usefulness of the messages they deliver through greater ease of use, noise reduction, improved data quality, greater adaptability, and so on.

Information distribution and sharing is the precondition for perception and learning. A wider distribution of information promotes more widespread and frequent learning, makes the retrieval of information more likely, and allows new information to be created by combining or relating disparate items. Information dissemination should integrate well with the work habits and preferences of the users. Users themselves could be encouraged to become active partners of the distribution system—it should be easy for them to evaluate, comment on, and share the information they have received.

Information use may result in the making of meaning or the making of decisions. In either case, the use of information is a social process of inquiry that is fluid, reciprocal, and iterative. The inquiry cycles between consideration of parts and the whole, and between consideration of practical specifics and general assumptions; participants clarify and challenge each other's representations and beliefs; and choices may be made by personal intuition or political bargaining rather than rational analysis. Our main message is that organizational information structures and processes must be as flexible, energetic, and permeable as the process of human inquiry and decision making that they are supporting.

The process model of information management we have presented in this chapter is based on a user-centered, situational perspective that emphasizes the cognitive and social dimensions of information seeking and use. Information is given meaning and action is given purpose through the sharing of mental representations and emotional resonances by the organization's members. It is only proper that information management begins and ends with the information user.

Chapter 3

Managers as Information Users

*An enlightened ruler does not worry about people not knowing him,
he worries about not knowing people. He worries not about outsiders not knowing insiders, but about insiders not knowing outsiders. He worries not about subordinates not knowing superiors,
but about superiors not knowing subordinates. He worries not
about the lower classes not knowing the upper classes, but about
the upper classes not knowing the lower classes.*

(Zhuge Liang, ca. 200 AD, The Way of the General)

Everyone in an intelligent organization participates in learning and con-
tributes to knowledge creation. Front line employees and lower-level supervisors and managers develop tacit knowledge and specialized know-how. Their
knowledge is closely bound up with the intuitions and heuristics that they
bring to their tasks. Their knowledge is all the more valuable because it is
often impossible to verbalize and hard to transfer. They work at the boundary
between the organization and the outside world, and it is through their actions
that the organization ultimately attains its purpose.

Top management, on the other hand, combines its knowledge about the
competencies of the organization and the exigencies of the environment to
envision goals and directions. As leaders of the organization, they are well
connected, having many outside information sources. Good senior managers
are skilled at winnowing the wheat from the chaff of noisy information. Their
knowledge is for the refinement of mental models and the unification of organizational purpose.

Between top management and the operatives are the line and staff managers who occupy intermediate levels of the organization. Their knowledge bridges the requirements of the broad, long-term visions of top management and the detailed, tacit knowledge of the front line workers. Their knowledge fills the divide between strategic intent and operational reality.

In this chapter, we look at managers at all levels of the organization—chief executives, marketing managers, finance managers, public sector officials, and so on. A better understanding of their information dispositions can aid the design of information management processes that quicken their learning and knowledge building.

What do managers do? This seemingly innocent question has proved to be surprisingly difficult to answer well. For a long time, students of management have sought to piece together the mosaic of activities that make up a manager's work day. After a comparison of eight major studies completed over the past thirty years, Hales (1993) observed both common elements and variations in the content and execution of managerial work. In terms of content, managers engage in specialized technical work as well as general administrative work. Managerial work is ill-defined, so much so that part of it is concerned with negotiating its own boundaries. Within these flexible boundaries, common work elements include the following:

- Managers act as figureheads or leaders who represent their work units.
- Managers monitor and disseminate information flowing into and out of the units.
- Managers negotiate with subordinates, superiors, other managers, other work units, and outsiders.
- Managers handle disturbances, solve problems, and deal with disruptions.
- Managers allocate resources in the form of money, materials, and personnel.
- Managers direct and control the work of subordinates.
- Managers form contacts and liaise with others.
- Managers innovate by seeking new objectives and new methods of operation.
- Managers plan what is to be done and when.

In terms of how they go about doing their work, research has revealed consistent patterns in the ways managers divide their time. Generally, managers spend most of their time reacting to day-to-day problems, and much less time on planning or thinking about strategies. They use face-to-face meetings or telephone calls to deal with operational problems. Most of these activities are short and subject to frequent interruptions. Managers commute swiftly from one problem to the next, splintering the work day into little packets of concentrated activity. Hales (1993) describes the frenetic character of managerial work as being fragmented, reactive, ad hoc, eclectic, and highly interactive. Whatever thinking that takes place happens as decisions and plans that are developed while the managers are still engaged in other activities. Although it may appear to be inefficient or superficial, this form of managerial work is one way of coping with ambiguous, unstructured problem situations for which solutions have to be found promptly, and which have to be acceptable to different groups of stakeholders.

Management as Conversations

A hermeneutic interpretation of "what managers do" is offered by Winograd and Flores (1987). In their view, the essence of managerial work centers on the conversations in which managers engage. The role of these conversations is to create, take care of, and initiate commitments in an organization. Management, after all, has to do with getting things done, especially through cooperative action; and getting things done requires the performance of linguistic acts that include requests for action and commitment, promises to fulfill commitments, reports on the conditions of commitments, reports on external circumstances, declarations of new policies, and so on.

As the organization as a whole fulfills its external commitments, its members are participating in networks of conversations. Most managerial activities are therefore concerned with the fulfillment of commitments by activating networks of recurrent conversations. The networks are recurrent because their general structures remain the same while the detailed content of individual conversations may vary. For Winograd and Flores, these networks of recurrent conversations are the core of the organization. Managerial conversations also generate the contexts in which effective action can be realized. To do this, managers participate in "conversations for possibilities" that explore new contexts for the conversations for action. They ask questions such as "What is it possible to do?" and "What will be the domain of actions in which we will engage?" (Winograd and Flores 1987, 151) Conversations for possibilities require reinterpretations of past activities that include not only past requests, promises, and deeds, but also the complete situations in which these acts take place.

Eccles and Nohria (1992) expand on the role of language in managerial activity. Managers work in a rhetorical universe in which language is used to communicate, to persuade, and to create. Almost every situation or artifact that a manager is involved with has a rhetorical element: committee meetings, group discussions, project plans, written memos, progress reports, newspaper articles, and vision statements are but some examples. In all these situations, managers use language and rhetoric to prod action; to coax, inspire, demand, or otherwise persuade individuals to apply their best efforts. The rhetorical nature of management discourse and practice arises because "the way people talk about the world has everything to do with the way the world is ultimately understood and acted in, and that the concept of revolutionary change depends to a great extent on how the world is framed by our language." (Eccles and Nohria 1992, 29) Without the right words used in the right ways, it is unlikely that the right actions will occur. Without words there is no way of expressing strategies, structures, or systems. Action and rhetoric are tightly coupled at the center of managerial work.

Managers as Information Users

We may now summarize the main contingencies that characterize the information use milieu of managers:

1. Most managerial work is action-oriented. When managers make a decision, they are actually making a commitment to action. When managers make sense of a situation, they are actually interpreting a context for negotiating the possibilities for action. The handling of disturbances, breakdowns, or conflicts all involve the taking of actions that allow the work in an organization to continue to move along. The need to act prevails even when the information available is known to be incomplete or ambiguous.

2. Both the internal and external environments of the manager's work unit are complex and dynamic. Internally, organizational action is played out in an intricate web of personalities, interests, and long-held beliefs. Each issue may be structurally familiar, but is particularized with layers of emotion and history. Externally, the organization joins an environment in which competitors, customers, suppliers, shareholders, regulators and others maneuver for advantage or control. The trajectories of cause and effect are hidden in a crisscross of relationships and dependencies that are never fully revealed. In short, managers grapple with messy problems in fuzzy settings.

3. The need to take prompt action in a rapid stream of ill-defined situations challenges the cognitive capacity of individual managers. Each manager copes by making simplifications and applying heuristics. They do not try to develop a complete representation of the problem situations they face, but work with a simplified model that captures the most salient features. They search for solutions using procedures and rules of thumb that have worked before. The search objective is to find a course of action that will work well enough to solve the problem at hand—each manager "satisfices" rather than optimizes. (Simon 1976)

The special contingencies of their information use environments modulate the information behaviors and preferences of managers. Their orientation towards action suggests that they prefer concrete information to abstract information. Concrete information about specific individuals, organizations, or relationships provides managers with the details and nuances that they need to evaluate the relevance and applicability of the information. Because they deal with messy problems where particulars can make a crucial difference, managers look for information in the form of cases and examples that are sufficiently fine-grained for them to develop a personal feel for the situation. Because they face ambiguous situations where facts and preferences are obscured, managers look for sources and use modes of communication that allow them to probe the hidden dimensions of a situation. For these reasons managers' most important information sources are the other people in the organization, and they tend to interact with these sources in face-to-face communications.

The complexity of the work environment and the need to respond quickly often mean that managers cannot afford a thorough or systematic search of the available information. Information search starts with the recognition that a problem exists, and ends when good enough alternatives have been found. Search is also heuristic and local: familiar and habitual information sources are used first, and solutions are often sought in the neighborhood of the problems. Ultimately, managers use information to choreograph effective action. Action is effective when it is robust, that is, when it accomplishes short-term objectives while preserving long-term flexibility (Eccles and Nohria 1992). Since external circumstances change even as the planned actions unfold, present actions should not restrict a manager's options to adapt to new situations as they evolve.

Implications for Information Management

Our process model of information management consists of six sets of activities: identifying information needs; information acquisition; information organization and storage; developing information products and services; information distribution; and information use. Our portrayal of managers as information users suggests implications for each set of activities. In terms of needs, managers require information that is sharply focused and finely detailed. They are interested in learning about the informal, unspoken codes that can help decipher a fuzzy problem situation. They prefer to receive their information face-to-face so that they can ask questions and get feedback.

Despite these demanding needs, when it comes to information gathering, managers seem to rely heavily on a relatively small number of accessible, familiar, personal sources. Managers exchange information frequently and consult with each other through meetings and telephone calls. More recent research indicates that managers do read or scan printed information sources, and are likely to share interesting news from these sources with others. Managers rarely maintain or use a system to organize and store their information, and instead depend on their own memory or personal lists of data. As a result, managers are sometimes unaware that others in the organization are also working on the same or related problems, or that the same kind of problem has been encountered before. In using information, managers tend to satisfy by choosing alternatives that appear to deliver good enough (but not necessarily the best) results.

In designing information products and services for managers, the starting premise should be to recognize and address the action-orientation and problem-solving contingencies of the managers' information use environment. Information provided needs to be salient, and should be responsive to the special conditions that define the potential usefulness of information. Where possible, information should include actual examples and cases described in some detail in order for managers to develop their own spin of the situation. Information has to be timely, and should be presented in a format that facilitates rapid browsing and uptake. Information delivery should integrate well with the managers' work habits, requiring little additional effort to access the information and to share it with others. Where necessary, information may have to be presented personally in face-to-face briefings.

Managers' information seeking may be limited by their time-saving biases and heuristics: they search for information in familiar places, use information in satisficing modes, and rely on personal memory to organize and store information. Information services may be used to extend the reach of managers' data gathering in various ways. A broader, more complete, and more accurate search of information sources that the manager would not have the time to explore could provide local additional alternatives or helpful background. Other organizations' experiences could be benchmarked to suggest new criteria by which alternatives may be evaluated. Pointing to past solutions of similar problems or related work in other parts of the organization may save managers from reinventing the wheel. Effectual information services for executives depends upon a comprehension of managers' information needs and use environments. Towards this goal, in the next section we review past research on managers as information users.

Research on Managers as Information Users

This section presents a representative selection of the research from the management and information science literatures that examine the information behavior of managers. Because we are interested in how managers gather and use information, we have chosen studies that touch on both these aspects. Past research seems to cluster around a few dominant sets of variables (Figure 3.1). Information seeking and use are driven by information needs and they in turn create new information needs, so these three elements (information needs, seeking, use) together compose the information behavior of managers.

Information behavior as a whole is seen to be influenced by the problem situation, managers' organizational roles, and their personal traits. Problem situation refers to those dimensions of the internal and external environment such as organizational norms and external uncertainty that determine the use and use-

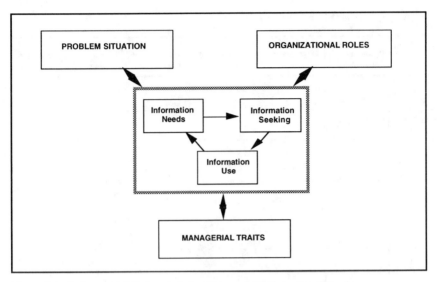

Figure 3.1 A Conceptual Framework for Managerial Information Behavior

fulness of information (MacMullin and Taylor 1984). Organizational roles are ways of grouping related managerial activities into larger categories or functional roles. For example, research has suggested that it is instructive to differentiate between the informational roles and decisional roles of managers (Mintzberg 1973). Finally, managerial traits refer to such personal characteristics as the functional specialization of the manager or his cognitive style. Figure 3.1 depicts these research elements but does not imply casual relationships between them. Table 3.1 relates the reviewed research to these elements. We then introduce the studies in chronological order.

Based on data from observing five chief executives at work over a period of one week, Mintzberg (1973) conceptualized managerial work into three sets of interlocking organizational roles: interpersonal, informational, and decisional (Figure 3.2).

— The manager performs three *interpersonal roles* by virtue of the formal authority vested in his position. As figurehead, he represents the organization in formal matters. As leader, he defines relationships with subordinates. Finally, as liaison, he interacts with external persons to gain information and favors.

— Interpersonal roles give the manager access to many internal and external sources of information and so enable three *informational roles*. As monitor, he taps a variety of sources to understand relationships between the organization and its environment. As disseminator, he transmits special information into the organization. As spokesman, he broadcasts the organization's information to the outside world.

Table 3.1 Summary of Research on Managers as Information Users

	Problem Situation	Organizational Roles	Managerial Traits	Information Needs	Information Seeking	Information Use
Mintzberg 1973		Interpersonal Roles		Informational Roles	Informational Roles	Decisional Roles
Blandin & Brown 1977	Environmental Uncertainty				Relative use of source types	
Stabell 1978			Integrative Complexity		Number of sources used	
O'Reilly 1982	Task complexity/ Uncertainty		Motivation, tenure, education		Source traits source use	
Kotter 1982		Agenda Setting; Network Building			Information seeking to set agendas	Cultivating networks
Daft & Lengel 1984					Information richness & media choice	Uncertainty/ equivocality reduction
Jones & McLeod 1986		Decisional Roles			Relative use of source types	Decision making
White 1986 White & Wilson 1988			Functional Specialty	Internal & external data, sources		
Luthans, Hodgetts & Rosenkrantz 1988		Categories of Managerial Activities				Information use by effective managers
Achleitner & Grover 1988				Task-related needs	People as main sources	
Eisenhardt 1989 1990	High-velocity Environments			Real-time information	Meetings; performance measures	Develop intuition
Fletcher 1991	Problem Situation Dimensions			Problem dimensions -> Needs		
McKinnon & Bruns 1992				Operational tasks -> Needs	Main sources: observation, work itself	Interpersonal information exchange
Tank 1993				Information needs for strategic decisions		Strategic information management
Browne 1993	Structured Decision Process		Bounded rationality		Information seeking patterns	Information use & preferences
Auster & Choo 1994	Environmental Uncertainty			External information needs	Source accessibility, quality; source use frequency	Decisional Roles

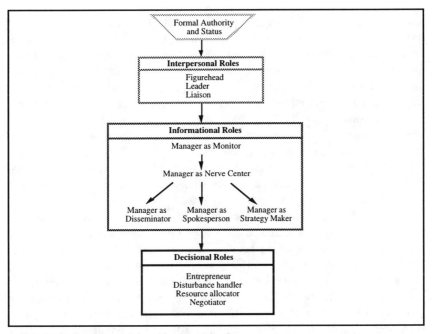

Figure 3.2. The Manager as Information Processing System
(adapted from Mintzberg 1973, 59, 72)

— The unique access to information combined with authority empowers the manager to discharge four *decisional roles*. As entrepreneur, he initiates "improvement projects" that exploit an opportunity or solve a problem. As disturbance handler, he deals with unexpected but important events. As resource allocator, he controls the distribution of all forms of resources. Finally, as negotiator, he engages in major negotiations with other organizations or individuals.

The three sets of ten managerial roles meld into a portrait of a manager as an "information processing system":

> In essence, the manager is an input-output system in which authority and status give rise to interpersonal relationships that lead to inputs (information), and these in turn lead to outputs (information and decisions). One cannot arbitrarily remove one role and expect the rest to remain intact. (Mintzberg 1973, 58)

In fact, "it is the manager's informational roles that tie all managerial work together—linking status and the interpersonal roles with the decisional roles" (Mintzberg 1973, 71).

Blandin and Brown (1977) examined the relationship between a key problem situation dimension—perceived environmental uncertainty—and the information search behavior of top-level managers. Data was collected via seventy questionnaire responses from managers in four electronics firms and four wood products firms. They found significant positive correlations between the level of uncertainty perceived by managers and (1) their reliance on external information sources, (2) their use of informal sources of information, (3) their frequency of use of all information sources, and (4) the amount of time they allocate to environment-related information gathering activities. Blandin and Brown maintain that the interaction between uncertainty and information search is bidirectional. Information search may initially be motivated by an attempt to reduce uncertainties surrounding strategic choices. As information is acquired, however, new uncertainties associated with previously unforeseen issues may arise and require further investigation. In this way, uncertainty and information acquisition are dynamically linked.

Stabell (1978) investigated the effect of a manager's cognitive trait of integrative complexity on the choice and use of information sources. An integratively simple person choosing between sources might use only a single rule such as "leave out quantitative information." An integratively complex person, however, would use many rules based on multiple conceptual dimensions, and relate these rules to specific decision situations. Thus, the integratively complex person recognizes several source attributes and varies the weights of different attributes according to the situation. Complexity theory predicts that the manager with the more integratively complex perception of the information environment will sample a larger number of different sources, will sample more information, and will sample these sources more evenly. Data to test this hypothesis were collected by sampling the actual investment decision making of thirty portfolio managers in a large United States bank. Stabell found significant support for the hypothesis within the category of impersonal sources, and weak support within the category of personal sources.

The study by O'Reilly (1982) focused on information seeking by 163 decision makers in four branch locations of a county welfare agency. Specifically, he looked at the relationship between source accessibility/quality and source use. Results showed that the reported frequency of use of the four major information sources is explained in three of the four cases by the accessibility of the source. The exception is the "group" source, consisting of sources within the work unit, including superiors and peers, which is highly accessible to all respondents. Although the rated importance of the sources was related to their perceived quality, the reported frequency of use was found to be mainly a function of the perceived source accessibility.

In an oft-cited study, Kotter (1982) analyzed the information behaviors of fifteen successful general managers of nine corporations in various industries in cities across the United States. Data were collected over a few years through interviews, observation, and questionnaires. Kotter concluded that successful general managers are especially effective in "agenda setting" and "network building." In agenda setting, the managers develop loosely connected goals and plans that address their short- and long-term responsibilities. They evolve their agendas over time by gathering information continuously. They seek information aggressively, often by asking incisive questions that would provide answers useful for agenda-setting. They rely more on information from discussions with individuals rather than on printed sources. In network building, the managers develop cooperative relationships among those people whom they feel are needed to implement their emerging agendas. They cultivate relationships with people and sources both inside and outside the firm, mainly through face-to-face contact. The most successful managers create networks with many talented people in them and with strong ties binding the members.

Daft and Lengel (1984) introduce the concept of *information richness* as a basis for understanding managerial information seeking. Managers essentially handle two sets of information tasks: processing sufficient amounts of information, and reducing information equivocality. The accomplishment of these tasks requires managers to balance the use of sources with different information richness, defined as the capacity of the communication to change mental representations within a specific time interval, that is, to change or provide substantial new understanding. Richness depends on the variety of cues and the rapidity of feedback that the communication can provide. Among the information media used in organizations, face-to-face communications are the richest because they allow feedback and the use of multiple cues and language variety. Conversely, numeric, formal reports such as computer printouts are the least rich because they lack these capabilities. Top managers need rich information when they are trying to reduce the equivocality of ambiguous messages about unclear situations, such as events in the external environment. The interpreted information then moves down the organization through communications of progressively lower richness. Media of lower richness are used to define goals, policies, and procedures at lower levels in order to provide the clarity and certainty the organization needs to function efficiently. Overall, the balanced use of information richness enables the organization to learn about an uncertain environment, while providing direction for participants to do their work.

In an example of the application of managerial roles, Jones and McLeod, Jr (1986) compared the use of sources by senior managers in the four decisional roles proposed by Mintzberg (1973). Data was collected by interviews, questionnaires, and logs of the information transactions of five senior executives over two weeks. A large proportion of the executives' information came from the external environment and was divided equally between people and organizational sources. Information from first- and second-level subordinates was frequently obtained and valued highly. When engaged in the entrepreneurial decisional role, the executives preferred internal sources and verbal messages. In the resource allocator role, they preferred internal information but did not care if it was verbal or written. In the disturbance handler role, they preferred internal to external information, and preferred internal sources that use verbal media. Finally, in the negotiator role, they did not rate negotiating information highly and were indifferent about where it came from or how.

The Department of Information Studies at the University of Sheffield completed a number of studies in the 1980s that examined business information needs and uses (Roberts and Wilson 1988). A 1984 study investigated the demand and supply of business information of sixty manufacturing firms in three selected geographical areas in the U.K. (Roberts and Clifford 1984). The study found that the main demand for external information was in the areas of marketing, products, exporting, finance, and competitors, although the demand was spread over all the areas provided. Demand for information resulted mostly from responding to current, immediate events rather than longer-term issues. Information gathering was unsystematic, intermittent, and eclectic. The five most important sources of external information were trade associations, sales force, customers, suppliers, Chambers of Commerce, and public libraries. More than half of the respondents, at some time or another, made use of pubic library services for business purposes.

In a pair of related studies, White (1986) and White and Wilson (1988) examined the relationship between managers' functional specialties and their information needs and uses. Theories of organizational structure would suggest that these needs would be dictated by the functional role of an individual in the organization. Data were collected by interviewing eighty-two managers of ten manufacturing firms in the South Yorkshire/Derbyshire region of Britain. Five main functional divisions were identified: production, sales, marketing, finance, and personnel. The general conclusion is that no simple correlation exists between functional specialty and information needs. When asked to rank categories of information important to their work, significant numbers from all five functional divisions ranked financial information as "very important." A significant number of operational managers reported marketing information as "very important." Marketing and sales managers, who are typically considered to be external-oriented, were found to use large amounts of internally-produced data. Conversely, managers who mostly handle internal data could encounter a problem requiring outside information. In summary, "information-need and information-seeking behaviour was based more on contingent reality, and immediate problem solving, than on some notion of set functional roles and responsibilities." (White and Wilson 1988, 15)

Respondents ranked personal contacts, journals, trade literature, and libraries most often as "useful" or "very useful" information sources. Trade journals and newspapers were seen as useful to 'keep up with the outside world,' or for information about specific developments. Local libraries were useful for specific needs that could be addressed with relative ease, such as specifications and statistics. The manager's major information resource, however, were the personal contacts, who were seen as the best sources of vital market and competitor intelligence.

In another large-scale study of managers, Luthans, Hodgetts and Rosenkrantz (1988) analyzed the activities of 457 managers from organizations of all sizes in both private and public sectors over a period of four years. They concluded that managers engage in four categories of activities: traditional management (planning, decision making, and controlling); routine communication (exchanging routine information and handling paper work); human resource management (motivating, disciplining, handling conflict, staffing, and training); and networking (socializing or politicking, and interacting with outsiders). Activities in all four categories were done relatively frequently, with traditional management and communications each taking up about 30 percent of the managers' time and effort, and human resource management and networking each taking up about 20 percent. For managers who were effective (as measured by unit performance, and subordinate satisfaction and commitment), communication activities, human resource management, and traditional management appeared to be the most important activities that accounted for their effectiveness. Among these, the relative contribution of communication activities to effectiveness was by far the largest. Communications were most frequent with subordinates, outsiders, others in the organization, and superiors. Somewhat in contradiction to earlier studies, Luthans and his associates found that managers do spend time and effort on planning and decision making, as well as a considerable amount of their energies on human resource management.

Achleitner and Grover (1988) examined information transfer patterns in the finance department of a major defense/commercial contractor. All ten managers in the department identified people as the sources of information for their work. Over 90 percent of the managers' work time was spent in oral communication. People were major sources of data, procedural information, interpretive information, source (who to see) information, current information, and some external information. Task-related information dominated daily activities; that is, procedures, meeting objectives, and problem solving. The information workers requested information from trusted human sources in an informal network. Communication patterns generally followed the organization's hierarchy.

How do managers seek and use information in fast-moving environments? Eisenhardt (1989, 1990) studied the information behaviors of top management teams in twelve microcomputer firms operating in "high-velocity" environments where the market and technology are moving so rapidly that the information available is poor, mistakes are costly, and recovery from missed opportunities is difficult. In such dynamic environments, the ability to make fast decisions was found to be linked to strong performance. Contrary to expectations that fast decision makers would limit their information gathering and analysis to save time, the study found that fast managers used as much, and sometimes more, information than do their slower counterparts. Nonetheless, fast managers concentrated on real-time information about current operations and current environment that is reported with little or no time lag, whereas slow decision makers relied on planning and future-oriented information. Real-time information is gathered in several ways: fast managers tracked operational measures of performance, shared information in frequent operational meetings, and sought advice from experienced, trusted managers. Again, surprisingly, fast managers used the information to develop a larger number of alternatives than the slower decision makers. They analyzed the information quickly, however, by comparing the alternatives with each other, rather than examining each alternative in depth. Fast managers have learned information strategies to accelerate their decision making without compromising decision quality.

For her doctoral research, Fletcher (1991) studied the information behaviors of upper-level general managers in both the public and private sectors. Most information systems concentrate on only the subject matter aspect of information need, but subject matter is just one dimension of an information user's problem situation, one aspect of the information need. Identifying the range of situational dimensions would help clarify information needs, and reveal characteristics beyond subject matter that determine the usefulness of information for a given problem situation. After analyzing interviews with twenty-six managers, Fletcher developed a scheme of eighteen broad categories of situational dimensions that may be used to describe what the respondents perceive as being present and salient in their problem situations. The situational dimensions were grouped into three components: part of the problem, part of the outcome, and part of the process. Most of the situational dimensions occurred as being "part of the problem." Among these, the *Familiarity* dimension (whether the problem is familiar), has the highest frequency, and emerges as a potentially important category.

In a study of line and staff managers, McKinnon and Bruns (1992) examined how middle- and upper-level managers in six Canada and six United States manufacturing firms obtain and use information they need to control daily operations. The firms are involved in heavy manufacturing of basic materials and products, high technology manufacturing, and consumer branded product manufacturing. The seventy-three respondents interviewed were mostly plant managers, sales directors, accountants, and other managers. The study found that these managers' information needs are determined by operational requirements: production managers need information to order materials and manage production facilities; sales and marketing managers seek information about orders, prices, competitor actions, and customer needs. For them, "yesterday's information is of little interest, and tomorrow's is hard to come by. It is today that must be managed, and only today's information will do." (p. 19) The two most important sources of information that the managers value and use are personal observation and management work itself. Other people are a third important source, especially when they have proved themselves to be reliable. Another frequently used source are reports, including informal as well as formal outputs of a management accounting or information system. The major mode of information exchange is through interpersonal communications that take place in meetings, one-on-one interactions, and unfocused walking through the business.

In 1992, the Conference Board conducted a survey of 200 senior executives representing companies with average annual sales of over US$1 billion who were members of the European Council on Corporate Strategy, the U.S. Council of Planning Executives, and the European and U.S. Councils of Information Management Executives. The executives identified four key needs: for better quality information; for more nonfinancial indicators; for more competitive intelligence; and for a strategic information management facility (Tank 1993).

— Almost three quarters of the respondents were dissatisfied with the information provided, pointing out a shortage of some types and an excess of others. Executives wanted more external information on industrial sector intelligence, market research and market share, and technology trends.

— They expressed a clear demand for information on nonfinancial performance measures, which indicate overall organizational health rather than mere financial survival. These nonfinancial indicators included customer satisfaction and retention; safety and environmental performance; energy efficiency; product defect rates; brand awareness; and employee turnover, motivation and development.

— Executives said they received too much general political and economic background information, but not enough hard, competitive information that is important to the business. Thus, companies were looking for information to benchmark their performance against the "best of the best," and they wanted information about the future of their industries and customers faster than their competitors.

— Finally, many companies were aiming for a "strategic data handling facility" that "allows data of disparate origins to be associated, compared and integrated to support strategic decision making. This is much more than a large, accessible database; it is a powerful tool to access alternative courses of action and make appropriate decisions." (Tank 1993, 13)

How is information sought and used in a protracted, strategic decision process? Browne (1993) followed the decision and information use processes of the Council of the Kuring-gai College of Advanced Education in Sydney, Australia as its members grappled with a single problem for five years: one of "surplus staffing," or how to reduce the number of academic staff in view of falling student enrollments. Much work was done by the council and related groups to examine the implementation and implications of staff retrenchment, but the problem was eventually "dropped" when the chairman of the council announced that "as a result of government policy no retrenchments would occur."

The council's efforts showed many of the features of the structured decision process of Mintzberg, et al., (1976) that we discussed in Chapter 2, including distinct routines for decision identification, diagnosis, search, design, evaluation, and choice; and numerous interruptions, delays, and recycles that affected the pace of the process. Although the information activities did not display any particular patterns of occurrence in relation to the central decision routines, the information behavior of this group of decision makers did reveal a few perhaps surprising features: the decision makers constantly screen, scan, and transmit information; they use information for general enlightenment; they use information to legitimize the decision process; they make few requests for information; they seek information not directly related to the evaluation of alternatives; they depend more on written information than oral information; and they consider more summary, abstract information than impressionistic, concrete information (Browne 1993, 187).

In a national study of over 200 chief executive officers in the Canadian publishing and telecommunications industries, Auster and Choo (1993a, 1993b, 1994a, 1994b) found that the CEOs used an uneven mix of internal and external, as well as personal and impersonal, sources to keep themselves informed about the outside business environment. Interestingly, between perceived environmental uncertainty, source accessibility, and source quality, it is the latter that had the most important relationship with the use frequency of a source.

It seems that when it comes to gathering information about the business environment, CEOs prefer sources that they believe to be reliable and to provide relevant information (Choo 1994). This contradicts expectations that managers search for good-enough data rather than the best information and may be explained by the CEOs' need for high-quality information in order to deal with novel, ill-structured problem situations that are presented by the external environment (Auster and Choo 1993a, 1993b). While the most frequently reported sources were internal and personal, many CEOs also indicated a high usage of printed materials such as newspapers, economic reports, and government documents (Auster and Choo 1994a, 1994b). Interviews with the CEOs to find out how the information was subsequently utilized revealed that mostly it supported entrepreneurial decision making: to initiate business strategies, new products, or improvement projects.

Summary

In their survey of the research on managerial information behavior, Katzer and Fletcher (1992) characterized managerial activities as being dynamic, uncertain, and complex, often involving messy situations that are ill-defined. They take place in an environment that is "informationally overloaded, socially constrained, and politically laden." Partly as a result of this, managers prefer to communicate orally, with little time left over to read long documents. Managers gather information externally to learn what their directions should be and who can help them, and they sometimes make decisions based on intuition, in which case information may be subsequently sought to justify these decisions.

Overall, the authors conclude that the information behavior of managers is a dynamic *process* that unfolds over time, and that the process interacts actively with the information *environment* in which the managers work. The managers' information environment is defined by the organizational setting, the roles they perform, and the activities they undertake. With this as context, managers then seek and use information to deal with a series of "problematic situations" such as hiring staff, developing marketing plans, or preparing budgets. In handling each problematic situation, the manager determines what types of managerial roles and activities are most appropriate, and which dimensions of the situation are most salient. This set of roles, activities, and dimensions then shapes the manager's information behavior. As new information arrives, and as the manager reflects and acts on the problematic situation, the perception of the situation changes, creating new uncertainties and priorities. The problematic situation is redefined in terms of roles, activities, and dimensions that, in turn, leads to revised information behaviors. The process iterates until the problematic situation is considered resolved in the manager's mind.

The Politics of Information Sharing

The concept of an intelligent, learning organization is predicated upon a free flow of information throughout the organization. Unfortunately, an organization is not monolithic, but is divided into separate political domains, each with its own manager-leaders, culture, language, and information resources. Managers recognize that their positions and their ability to get their way depend on the unique information they hold and the deployment of this information to justify courses of action (Pfeffer 1992). Managers have information power when they or their units can cope with or control critical uncertainties faced by the other subunits in the organization (Hickson, et al., 1971). For example, a sales manager who has the information and relationships to secure steady orders despite a volatile market has high power. Managers can also exercise power by controlling the flow of information that shape decision making premises. Pettigrew (1973) describes the case of a senior manager who influenced the board of directors' decision to purchase a large computer system through artfully gatekeeping the information reaching the directors. As information becomes a source of power and indispensability, managers will find it increasingly difficult to just give away what is now the primary unit of organizational currency (Pfeffer 1992).

From their study of information management approaches in more than twenty-five organizations, Davenport and his associates found that the major reason for the inability to create information-based organizations was the failure to manage the politics of information use and definition across an organization (Davenport, et al., 1992). In fact, people were the least likely to share their information freely in the most information-oriented firms. The most common political model of data sharing was a form of *information feudalism*, in which individual managers and their departments control information acquisition, storage, distribution, and analysis. Managers act as powerful feudal lords who not only rule over the creation and circulation of information, but also determine the meanings and interpretations that should be attached to information. This fragmentation of information integrity undermines the organization's efforts to consolidate and cross-fertilize its knowledge assets so that the organization as a whole can learn and adapt.

Instead of feudalism, Davenport, et al., recommend a form of *information federalism* as being the most appropriate model in today's environment. Federalism recognizes that politics is a necessary and legitimate activity for people with divergent interests to work out a collective purpose and the means for realizing it. Under federalism, managers negotiate among themselves the use and definition of information. Managers bargain with each other to cede some of their information assets in return for producing a larger pool of knowledge that they can tap into and exploit to advantage.

Davenport recounts the example of Larry Ford, IBM's chief information officer, implementing a federalist information model. After all the senior managers endorsed a new information strategy that maximizes the value that information can bring to IBM as a whole, Ford and his divisional IS managers had gone out into the field to campaign door to door, negotiating with each senior manager about sharing his information with others in the firm, asking questions such as: "Would you share your product quality data with the service organization?" "How about sales?"IBM found that educating and persuading managers of their information sharing responsibilities was the biggest roadblock to setting up information federalism. To attain this model, the organization needs a strong central leadership, politically astute information management, and a culture that promotes cooperation and learning. At the end of the day,

> no amount of data modeling, no number of relational databases, or no invocation of the "information-based organization" will bring about a new political order of information. Rather, it will take what politics always takes—negotiation, exercising influence, backroom deals, coalition-building, and occasionally even war. If information is truly to become the most valued commodity in the businesses of the future, we cannot expect to acquire it without an occasional struggle. (Davenport, et al., 1992, 64)

Managerial Information Processing and Organizational Learning

Although much of this chapter has been given over to managers as information users, it is important to recognize that managers are not just consumers of information, they are also *creators* of information and knowledge, and it is in this role that they accelerate the organizational learning process. Knowledge creation is an organization-wide activity that involves senior management, middle management, lower management, as well as front line employees.

Senior managers, partly because they are in closest contact with a fast-changing external environment, tend to introduce or create uncertainty in the organization. They seek a large quantity of information from the environment and inject a continuous stream of outside data that is often noisy or confusing. They make general, ambiguous policy statements that are not always consistent with each other, and they declare visions for the organization that are difficult to achieve. By introducing uncertainty, senior managers are stimulating the organization to experience and evaluate as many phenomena as possible. In effect, they are articulating the future of the organization through metaphors, symbols, and analogies that orientate the learning activities of the rest of the organization.

While senior managers increase uncertainty, middle managers reduce variety by spanning the gap between the strategic intentions of top management, and the detailed, tacit knowledge of the front line employees (Nonaka 1988). Middle managers can reduce the noise and chaos in the information creation process and provide starting points for action by the lower and upper levels. They translate and reconcile individual visions and organizational dreams. They lead teams to crystallize the knowledge to transform visions into action. Middle managers act as the organization's knowledge engineers, idea entrepreneurs, and change masters (Nonaka 1994, Kanter 1983).One hopes that in the current haste to restructure and reengineer, organizations do not lose sight of the indispensable facilitating role of its intermediate managers.

Research to compare the management styles of American and Japanese organizations suggests that it is the cognitive skills at carrying out organizational learning that underlie Japanese managerial success (Pascale 1990, Nonaka 1990, Sullivan and Nonaka 1986). Companies such as Canon, Honda, Matsushita, NEC, Sharp, and Sony are well known for their uncanny ability to respond swiftly to customer needs, dominate emergent technologies, and quickly develop new products and markets. According to Nonaka (1988, 1990, 1994), their secret of success is skill in managing the creation of new knowledge through a process in which top management acts as the initial catalyst, front line employees develop the tacit knowledge, and middle management mediate between the upper and lower levels to engender the knowledge needed to move from "what is" to "what ought to be."

Chapter 4

Environmental Scanning as Strategic Organizational Learning

To overcome the intelligent by folly is contrary to the natural order of things; to overcome the foolish by intelligence is in accord with the natural order. To overcome the intelligent by intelligence, however, is a matter of opportunity. There are three avenues of opportunity: events, trends, and conditions. When opportunities occur through events but you are unable to respond, you are not smart. When opportunities become active through a trend and yet you cannot make plans, you are not wise. When opportunities emerge through conditions but you cannot act on them, you are not bold. Those skilled in generalship always achieve their victories by taking advantage of opportunities.

(Zhuge Liang, ca. 200 AD, The Way of the General)

Today's organizations face an external environment that is increasingly complex and volatile. In an international survey by the *Harvard Business Review*, twelve thousand managers in twenty-five countries identify a wide array of forces of change including "globalizing markets, instantaneous communications, travel at the speed of sound, political realignments, changing demographics, technological transformations in both products and production, corporate alliances, flattening organization . . ." (Kanter 1991, p. 151). These forces of change are said to cause the traditional walls of business boundaries to crumble. The managers in the survey indicated that change is a fundamental part of organizational life everywhere, and that fostering closer relationships with customers and suppliers is a critical issue.

From an information perspective, every change or development in the external environment creates signals and messages that an organization may need to heed (Dill 1962). Some of the signals would be weak (difficult to detect), many would be confusing (difficult to analyze), and others would be spurious (not indicative of a true change). In seeking information, the organization would have to attend selectively to a flood of signals created by a dynamic environment, interpret often confusing messages, and make sense of clues in relation to the firm's goals and activities. Weick (1979) suggests that a central information task of organizations is to interpret equivocal information about the external environment.

Environmental scanning is the acquisition and use of information about events, trends, and relationships in an organization's external environment, the knowledge of which would assist management in planning the organization's future course of action (Aguilar 1967, Choo and Auster 1993). The external environment of an organization includes all outside factors that can affect the organization's performance, even its survival. Although many factors exist, it is helpful to divide the external environment into a small number of sectors. For business organizations, the environment may be analyzed as consisting of six sectors: customers, suppliers, competition, socioeconomic, technological, and governmental (Jauch and Glueck 1988). Alternatively, one may distinguish between a macroenvironment comprising social, economic, political, and technological sectors, and a task/industry environment comprising mainly the customer and competitor sectors (Fahey and Narayanan 1986).

Organizations scan the environment in order to understand the external forces of change so that they may develop effective responses that secure or improve their position in the future. Thus organizations scan in order to avoid surprises, identify threats and opportunities, gain competitive advantage, and improve long- and short-term planning (Sutton 1988). To the extent that an organization's ability to adapt to its outside environment depends on knowing and interpreting the external changes that are taking place, environmental scanning includes both *looking at* information (viewing) and *looking for* information (searching). It could range from a casual conversation at the lunch table or a chance observation of an angry customer, to a formal market research program or a scenario planning exercise.

One of the earliest studies on environmental scanning differentiated between four styles of scanning: undirected viewing, conditioned viewing, informal search, and formal search (Aguilar 1967). In *undirected viewing*, the manager is exposed to information with no specific purpose or information need in mind. In fact, the manager is unaware of what issues might be raised. Undirected viewing takes place all the time, and alerts the manager that "something" has happened and that there is more to be learned. For example, the manager converses with business associates during social gatherings. In *conditioned viewing*, the manager is exposed to information about selected areas or certain types of information. Furthermore, the manager is ready to assess the significance of such information as it is encountered. For example, the manager browses through sections of newspapers or periodicals that report regularly on topics of interest. In *informal search*, the manager actively looks for information to address a specific issue. It is informal in that it involves a relatively limited and unstructured effort. For example, the manager regularly keeps an eye on the market to check on the results of some new product pricing policy. Finally, in *formal search*, the manager makes a deliberate or planned effort to obtain specific information or information about a specific issue. For example, the manager systematically gathers information to evaluate a prospective corporate acquisition.

Environmental scanning is also seen to take place at multiple levels of detail. At high-order levels, scanning looks at the total environment, develops a broad picture, and identifies areas that require closer attention. At low-order levels, scanning homes in on the specific areas and analyzes them in detail. Etzioni (1967, 1986) compares this to a satellite scanning the earth by using both a wide-angle and a zoom lens. For an organization, such an approach results in a "mixed scanning" strategy that guides information collection and decision making. We see similarities between Etzioni's multiple levels of broad and focused scanning and multiple modes of scanning through general viewing and purposeful searching.

In their recent study of environmental scanning for the British Library, Lester and Waters (1989) define environmental scanning as the "management process of using environmental information in decision making." The process comprises three activities:

— the gathering of information concerning the organization's external environment

— the analysis and interpretation of this information

— the use of this analyzed intelligence in strategic decision making. (Lester and Waters 1989, 5)

Lester and Waters extend the definition of environmental scanning to include the analysis, interpretation, and use of the information gained in strategic decision making. This definition is in line with current strategic management theory, where the analysis and diagnosis of environmental threats and opportunities typically form the first phase of the strategic management process (see, for example, Glueck and Jauch 1984, Mintzberg 1994).

Is environmental scanning different from information seeking? In a review of the literature of library science, management, psychology, and computer science, Rouse and Rouse (1984) define human information seeking as the process of identifying and choosing among alternative information sources. Information seeking is embedded in a larger process of decision making, problem solving, or resource allocation that provides the context for establishing information needs. It is dynamic in that the methods and criteria for information selection or rejection vary over time and depend on intermediate results. At a conceptual level then, environmental scanning may be seen as a special case of information seeking.

Scanning is part of the process of strategic decision making, and a study of scanning and information acquisition should analyze the selection and use of alternative information sources. Much of the field research, however, particularly in library and information science, deals with the information needs and uses of defined groups of users, and with the search and retrieval of information, often from documentary or bibliographic sources and online information systems. In most of these situations, a problem or information need is articulated or at least made relatively clear, and information is then sought to address the specific question or need. This process may be contrasted with scanning, which not only includes searching for particular information but also simply being *exposed* to information that *could* impact the firm. As we explained earlier, scanning is often undirected viewing without specific purpose or information need, and without awareness as to what issues might be raised.

From Competitor Intelligence to Social Intelligence

In what ways is environmental scanning different from related information gathering activities such as business intelligence, competitor intelligence, competitive intelligence, issues management, and social intelligence? Starting from the most specific, *competitor intelligence* has as its objective, "to develop a profile of the nature and success of the likely strategy changes each competitor might make, each competitor's probable response to the range of feasible strategic moves other firms could initiate, and each competitor's probable reaction to the array of industry changes and broader environmental shifts that might occur." (Porter 1980, 47) Competitor intelligence is therefore highly specific, focusing on the actions, behaviors, and options of one or more existing or potential competitors.

Competitive intelligence is a little broader and refers to the analysis of competitors as well as competitive conditions in particular industries or regions (Sutton 1988). A working definition of competitive intelligence is "an analytical process that transforms disaggregated competitor, industry, and market data into actionable strategic knowledge about the competitor's capabilities, intentions, performance, and position." (Bernhardt 1994, 13)

Business intelligence has a significantly larger scope, and has been defined as "the activity of monitoring the environment external to the firm for information that is relevant for the decision-making process in the company." (Gilad and Gilad 1988) In practice, business intelligence often concentrates on current competitors as in competitive intelligence, but also includes topics such as analysis of potential acquisitions and mergers, and risk assessments for particular countries (Gilad and Gilad 1988, Sutton 1988). *Environmental scanning* casts a still wider net, and analyzes information about every sector of the external environment that can help management to plan for the organization's future (Aguilar 1967, Choo and Auster 1993). Scanning covers not only competitors, suppliers, and customers, but also includes technology, economic conditions, political and regulatory environment, and social and demographic trends.

Issues management evolved from public affairs and its goal is "to develop company policy and supporting action programs to participate in the public policy process in the resolution of sociopolitical and economic problems that will affect the future viability and well-being of the organization." (Ewing 1990) Issues are developments that will impact on an organization's performance and capability to meet its objectives, and are important in terms of resources required or precedents set. Public issues involve multiple stakeholders with competing interest and involve some form of collective action (Bigelow, Fahey and Mahon 1993). Issues management therefore involves the identification of potential issues that may affect the organization and its commitment of resources strategically to influence the course of those issues. Stanley (1985) emphasizes the need to perform systematic scanning in order to anticipate issues. He identifies five arenas in which issues are likely to arise: economic (changes in economic indicators); social (public attitudes); political (government policy changes); technological (inventions or new techniques); and other (such as environmental, health, or safety issues).

Social intelligence is the broadest in scope and approach, and is concerned with the capability of society and institutions to identify problems, collect relevant information about these problems, and transmit, process, evaluate, and ultimately put this information to use (Dedijer and Jequier 1987). It has been used to describe the capability of a country to use information to pursue national strategies. Thus, social intelligence has also been defined as "the organized ability of a country, or any of its components, to adapt to the rapidly changing world by combining the acquisition, evaluation, and use of information with planned operations and activities." (Ventura 1988) More briefly, Radosevic (1991) has called it the analytical-informational capability of a country, where the core of a nation's social intelligence is its knowledge industries and information networks.

We may attempt to differentiate these various forms of external information seeking by comparing the length of the time horizon they adopt and the breadth and depth of the data gathering that they require (Figure 4.1). On the information gathering dimension, *Competitor Intelligence*, *Competitive Intelligence*, and *Issues Management* are relatively focused, concentrating on individual competitors or strategic issues. *Social Intelligence*, on the other hand, has the widest compass, and has been used to analyze the overall intelligence infrastructure and capability of countries. On the planning horizon dimension, Competitor Intelligence has a tactical, short-term orientation, stressing con-

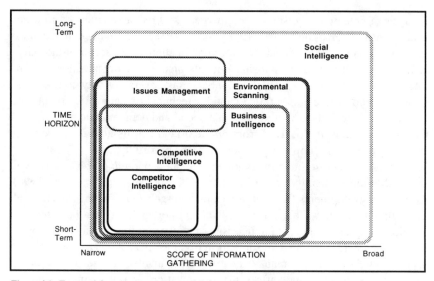

Figure 4.1   Forms of Organizational External Information Gathering

cerns such as pricing, distribution, promotion, and so on. Issues Management
has a longer-term orientation, because it engages in public policy processes
involving multiple players and stakeholders. As the figure indicates, there is
considerable overlap between Competitor and Competitive Intelligence; and
between Business Intelligence and Environmental Scanning, and they are
often used to describe more or less the same activities. In the following sections, we take a closer look at Competitive Intelligence, Business Intelligence,
and Social Intelligence.

Competitive Intelligence

Michael Porter's two books on Competitive Strategy (1980) and
Competitive Advantage (1985) greatly increased the general awareness of
competitor and competitive intelligence, and provided what has become the
widely discussed theoretical framework for competitive analysis. The 1980
volume on Competitive Strategy was subtitled "Techniques for Analyzing
Industries and Competitors," and it devotes eight of sixteen chapters to competitive analysis techniques. Porter's central message is that formulating an
effective competitive strategy requires a deep understanding of the relationship between the firm and its environment. The most important component of
the environment is the industry in which the firm competes, and the intensity
and nature of the competition in an industry may be systematically analyzed
by examining five basic competitive forces: threat of new entrants, rivalry
among existing firms, threat of substitute products or services, bargaining

power of buyers, and bargaining power of suppliers (Porter 1980, 4). Through the analysis of these forces, the goal of competitive analysis is to enable the firm to position itself in the industry where it can best defend against these competitive forces or influence them in its favor.

The *threat of new entrants* depends on the barriers to entry and on the reaction from existing firms that the entrant can expect. Barriers to entry may be erected by exploiting economies of scale, product differentiation, access to distribution channels, and government policies; and by requiring large capital investments or high switching costs. Some cost advantages cannot be replicated by potential entrants regardless of their size or economies of scale. For example, if costs decline as an existing firm accumulates experience in producing a product, and if the firm can keep this knowledge proprietary, then an entry barrier has been raised.

Rivalry among existing firms results in price competition, promotion campaigns, product introductions, customer service innovations, and so on. Rivalry is likely intense when the industry has numerous or equally balanced competitors, industry growth is sluggish, fixed costs are high, the product is viewed as a mass commodity, firms pursue diverse competitive strategies, a few firms have high stakes in achieving success, or when the exit barriers are high.

The *threat of substitute products* limits the potential returns of an industry by capping the prices that can be charged. Potential substitute products may be identified by searching for other products, sometimes in industries that seem far removed from the existing industry, that can perform the same function as the product of the industry. Substitute products are most threatening when they have an increasing price-performance advantage compared with the industry's product, and when they are produced by industries that are earning high profits.

The *bargaining power of buyers* is great when buyers are concentrated or purchase large volumes, the product purchases form a significant fraction of the buyer's costs, the product itself is standard or undifferentiated, switching costs are low, buyers' profits are low, buyers are in a position to produce the product themselves through backward integration, the product is unimportant to the buyers' own products, and the buyer has full information about demand, prices, and costs.

Similarly, the *bargaining power of suppliers* is great when suppliers are concentrated, suppliers do not have to contend with substitute products, the industry is not an important customer of the suppliers, the suppliers' product is critical to the buyer, the suppliers' products are differentiated or have built in high switching costs, and suppliers can threaten forward integration.

After analyzing its industry in terms of these competitive forces, the firm can now assess its strengths and weaknesses relative to the industry, and so develop a defensible position by adopting one or more of the three generic competitive strategies—overall cost leadership, product differentiation, and focusing on a particular product or market segment. While industry analysis provides the competitive strategy, competitor analysis is required to understand and predict a particular competitor's moves and responses. Two fundamental questions need to be addressed in developing a response profile of the competitor: What drives the competitor? and What is the competitor doing and can do? These are answered by examining the competitor's future goals, assumptions, current strategy, and capabilities. Porter's diagnostic framework leading to a competitor's response profile is outlined in Table 4.1

Table 4.1 Components of Competitor Analysis
(adapted from Porter 1980, 49)

1 What Drives the Competitor	**Future Goals**	Goals at all levels of management and analyzed in multiple dimensions
	Assumptions	Assumptions held about itself and the industry
2 What the Competitor Is Doing and Can Do	**Current Strategy**	How the competitor is currently competing
	Capabilities	Competitor's strengths and weaknesses
3 Competitor's Response Profile	• Is the competitor satisfied with its current position? • What likely moves or strategy shifts will the competitor make? • Where is the competitor vulnerable? • What will provoke the greatest and most effective retaliation by the competitor?	

Business Intelligence

Herbert E. Meyer, former Special Assistant to the Director of Central Intelligence during the Reagan Administration and Vice Chairman of the CIA's National Intelligence Council, hails business intelligence as "the most powerful management tool of all (Meyer 1987, 3). For Meyer, finding out what the competitors are doing is necessary, but insufficient, for two reasons:

First, your competitors are moving through the same murky environment that you are moving through. The trick is to grasp the external conditions through which all of you are moving: the emergence of new technologies, shifting demographic patterns, changes in consumer spending and lifestyle trends, political upheavals, the opening of new markets, the broad range of government policies at home and abroad that impact business including budgets, taxes, regulations and the environment. These are the forces that shape events; that put new dangers—and opportunities—in your path. . . .

Second, in today's environment the company that is most likely to do you damage isn't one of your competitors at all. More likely it is a company outside your industry armed with a new technology, or a new idea, that will profoundly change your industry—your company as well as your competitors. (Meyer 1987, xvi)

Business intelligence is an organizational function whose end product is "processed information of interest to management about the present and future environment in which the business is operating." (Greene 1966) Thus, business intelligence is oriented towards the future, and is concerned with exploring possible views of future competitive environments. As a domain, business intelligence has a broader compass than competitive intelligence, and covers the areas shown in Table 4.2 (from Gilad and Gilad 1988, 6).

Table 4.2   The Domain of Business Intelligence

• Current competitors	• Economic environment
• Potential competitors	• Social and community environment
• Growth opportunities	• Demographics
• Markets	• Suppliers
• Political and regulatory environment	• Acquisition candidates

Although business intelligence is collected informally by every organization, the function should be implemented and managed as a formal, systematic organizational activity (Gilad and Gilad 1988). With a coordinated business intelligence system in place, important information is less likely to be lost, gaps in the collection and analysis of information can be identified and filled, duplication of effort can be reduced and, above all, information from various sources can be integrated into a coherent whole for strategic planning.

Social Intelligence

Social intelligence, a still evolving concept, eludes complete definition. Stevan Dedijer of Lund University in Sweden used the term to call for a holistic approach to integrate various branches of the study of intelligence, and taught a course on social intelligence that drew from an eclectic range of disciplines and application areas. Cronin defines social intelligence in a developing nation as "the capability to adapt/respond to changing circumstances in order to achieve preferred development objectives, or, more simply, as the ability to survive and thrive." (Cronin 1992, 104)

Social intelligence has formed the framework for several case studies of the way in which intelligence is used by nations to meet their development challenges. For example, Radosevic and Dedijer (1990) described how the former Yugoslavia was debilitated by a structural blockage caused by its inability to understand changes in external conditions and react to them adequately, and they maintained that a stronger attention to the intelligence capability of government, individuals, and other social factors could have significantly improved the management of available information resources and so accelerated crisis resolution. Onyango (1991) examined Kenya's recent industrialization and technology transfer efforts and concluded that weak social intelligence capability had resulted in errors in technology selection, high costs for its technology acquisitions, and inadequate indigenous technological capacity leading to excessive dependence on foreign technology. Tell (1987) compared the social intelligence capabilities in Sweden and Malaysia for the acquisition and provision of scientific and technical information. Sweden declared STI a national resource, established institutions that developed online STI databases, and generally showed that all the information needed for planning was obtainable from open sources in industrialized countries. The government of Malaysia, on the other hand, was more preoccupied with operational and library-infrastructure building tasks.

A general theme emerges from these and related studies. The knowledge industry and information networks in a society constitutes its social brain, and the ways this brain function may be called social intelligence (Dedijer and Jequier 1987). The effectiveness of the society's social intelligence is therefore related to the size of its knowledge industry and the density and quality of its information networks, although a developing country lacking in both could overcome this through an intelligence policy whereby the needed information and knowledge could be acquired from outside its borders. The ability of a society to survive, develop, and adapt therefore depends to a large extent on its social intelligence.

Cronin and Davenport recently offered an ecumenical vision of social intelligence as:

the process by which a society, organization, or individual scans the environment, interprets what is there, and constructs versions of events that may afford competitive advantage. The distinguishing feature of this approach is that the total environment is explored: what is visible and what is masked, what is stated and what is understood and what is overt and what is covert. . . . It implies skills in gathering, decoding, analyzing, and applying intelligence for effective action and in using techniques and technologies that come from various fields and contexts, some of which can be learned only from experience. Social intelligence also entails knowledge of the environment, proprietary knowledge, and the ability to access stocks of raw and processed intelligence. Finally, social intelligence is synonymous with a high level of social interaction skills, and ability to negotiate the rules of the game, and a high level of self-awareness. (Cronin and Davenport 1993, 8-9, 28)

The tools and techniques of social intelligence range as widely as its definition, but must encompass the key functions of communication, broadcasting, linking, and pattern matching (Cronin and Davenport 1993). The ability to communicate and share information via telecommunications or computer networks is essential, but information exchange must be supplemented by the capability to trap relevant information and to analyze what has been trapped. Analysis requires a context or framework for interpretation, and messages will have to be linked with other messages to reveal their significance. This in turn implies an ability to "broadcatch" (Brand 1988) or collect information from many sources using different formats in order to facilitate pattern detection and matching.

Summary

Substantial overlap exists between competitor and competitive intelligence; and again between business intelligence and environmental scanning. Competitor and competitive intelligence are often used interchangeably, although the latter implies a more extensive analysis that includes the competitive structure and conditions of the industry (Sutton 1988). Nevertheless, in either case the end result is to predict and understand the competitors' moves and responses (Porter 1980). Conceptually, the domain of business intelligence (Table 4.2) is similar to that of environmental scanning—both are concerned with not just the immediate competitive situation, but also the economic, political and social factors that make up the organization's total external environment. Both business intelligence and scanning are also more future-oriented in that they adopt longer-term perspectives and are often concerned with developing a strategic vision for the organization. In practice, business intelligence and scanning programs tend to concentrate heavily on information about the competitive or market environment so that, in a sense, competitor or competitive intelligence remains a major component of most of these programs. In this book, we occasionally use the terms business intelligence and environmental scanning more or less interchangeably, and we acknowledge that the production of competitive intelligence is a primary objective of these activities.

Environmental Scanning and Organizational Learning

The nature and scope of environmental scanning was delineated at the beginning of the chapter. To recapitulate, environmental scanning is the acquisition and use of information about events, trends, and relationships in an organization's external environment, the knowledge of which should assist management in planning the organization's future course of action (Aguilar 1967, Choo and Auster 1993). In the model we presented in Chapter 1, organizational learning is based on five related processes: sensing, perception, interpretation, memory use, and adaptive behavior. Environmental scanning is evidently a critical component of organization sensing and perception, and the information gathered through scanning provides crucial material of interpretation and analysis. In attempting to understand and respond to a dynamic external environment, organizations behave very much as interpretation systems, and this is the position taken by Daft and Weick:

> Organizations must make interpretations. Managers literally must wade into the ocean of events that surround the organization and actively try to make sense of them. Organization participants physically act on these events, attending to some of them, ignoring most of them, and talking to other people to see what they are doing. (Daft and Weick 1984, 286)

Further, they suggest that organizational interpretation of its environment may be divided into three stages that constitute the overall learning process: scanning, interpretation, and learning. During *scanning*, the environment is monitored and data collected on events and relationships. During *interpretation*, the collected data are given meaning by the sharing of perceptions and the collective construction of cognitive maps. During *learning*, a new response or action is invoked based on the interpretation. Through action-based learning, the organization gains knowledge about action-outcome relationships between the organization and the environment. Action generates new data for scanning and interpretation, thus starting a new cycle.

Organizations differ in their modes of scanning-interpretation, depending on management's beliefs about the analyzability of the external environment, and the extent to which the organization intrudes into the environment to understand it (Daft and 1984). An organization that believes the environment to be analyzable, in which events and processes are determinable and measurable, would seek to discover the "correct" interpretation through systematic information gath-

		UNDIRECTED VIEWING		ENACTING
	Information Needs	Nonroutine, informal data. Hunch, rumor, chance opportunities.	Information Needs	Experimentation, testing. Create own environment. Learn by doing.
Unanalyzable	Information Seeking	External, personal sources. Casual information. Irregular contact, reports. No scanning unit.	Information Seeking	External, personal sources. Irregular reports, feedback. Selective information. No scanning unit.
	Information Use	Much equivocality reduction. Few rules, many cycles. Reactor strategy. Coalition building.	Information Use	Some equivocality reduction. Moderate rules and cycles. Prospector strategy. Incremental decision process.
		CONDITIONED VIEWING		DISCOVERY
	Information Needs	Routine, formal data. Based on traditional boundaries.	Information Needs	Formal information. Questioning, surveys. Finding correct answer.
Analyzable	Information Seeking	Passive detection. Internal, impersonal sources. Regular record keeping and information systems.	Information Seeking	Active detection. Internal, impersonal sources. Special studies, extensive information. Scanning unit.
	Information Use	Little equivocality reduction. Many rules, few cycles. Defender strategy. Programmed decision process.	Information Use	Little equivocality reduction. Many rules, moderate cycles. Analyzer strategy. Analytical decision process.

ASSUMPTIONS ABOUT ENVIRONMENT (left axis)

Passive   *Active*

ORGANIZATIONAL INTRUSIVENESS

Figure 4.2 Scanning/Interpretation Modes

ering and analysis. Conversely, an organization that perceives the environment to be unanalyzable would create or enact what it believes to be a reasonable interpretation that can explain past behavior and suggest future actions. An organization that actively intrudes into the environment would allocate resources for information search and for testing or manipulating the environment. A passive organization, on the other hand, takes whatever environmental information comes its way and tries to interpret the environment with the given information. Based on the two dimensions of environmental analyzability and organizational intrusiveness, four modes of scanning-interpretation may be differentiated: undirected viewing, conditioned viewing, enacting, and discovery (Figure 4.2).

Undirected viewing, a term first used by Aguilar (1967) and which we introduced near the start of the chapter, takes place when the organization perceives the environment to be unanalyzable and so does not intrude into the environment to understand it. Information needs are ill-defined, and much of the information is nonroutine or informal, usually obtained through chance encounters.

Information seeking is opportunistic, relying more on irregular contacts and casual information from external, personal sources. Information use is concerned primarily with reducing the high levels of environmental equivocality. To resolve equivocality, organizations use assembly rules to shape data into a collective interpretation (Weick 1979). As suggested by Weick, the greater the equivocality, the fewer the number of rules activated because of the uncertainty about what the information means. At the same time, arriving at a common interpretation requires many information cycles of data sharing. The organization tends to adopt a reactor strategy, reacting to seemingly uncontrollable changes in the environment (Miles and Snow 1978). Decision making takes the form of coalition building to agree on a single interpretation and course of action (Cyert and March 1963).

Conditioned viewing, again from Aguilar (1967), takes place when the organization perceives the environment to be analyzable but is passive about gathering information and influencing the environment. Information needs are routine and formal, based on traditional assumptions and limits held by the organization. Information seeking is based on passive detection, using internal, impersonal sources, with a significant amount of data coming from records and information systems. Because the environment is seen to be knowable, there is less need for equivocality reduction, but a greater number of rules can now be applied to assemble an interpretation. The organization tends to adopt a defender strategy, concentrating on internal efficiency to protect what it already has (Miles and Snow 1978). Decisions are mostly programmed (March and Simon (1958/1992), following standard procedures and regulations derived from past experience.

Enacting takes place when the organization perceives the environment to be unanalyzable but then actively intrudes into the environment in order to influence events and outcomes. Information needs are those required for experimentation, for testing the environment, and for learning by doing. Information seeking is from external, personal sources and emphasizes feedback about the actions that the organization has taken. Information is used to reduce environmental equivocality as well as to challenge existing rules and precedents. The organization tends to adopt a prospector strategy by introducing new products or services to take advantage of opportunities (Miles and Snow 1978). Decision making processes tend to be phased and incremental, involving iterative cycles of design and trial-and-error (Mintzberg, et al., 1976).

Discovery takes place when the organization perceives the environment to be analyzable and it actively intrudes into the environment to collect information extensively in order to find the correct interpretation. Information needs are for hard, formal, often quantitative data, typically from surveys, market research, and forecasts. Information seeking is based on active detection, collecting information extensively and intensively through a variety of sources, including internal, impersonal (formal) ones. Because information is generally unequivocal, information use involves the activation of multiple possible rules but only a moderately small number of cycles to converge on an interpretation. The organization tends to adopt an analyzer strategy, maintaining its core of activities but with occasional innovations based on its reading of the environment (Miles and Snow 1978). Decision making is based on logical, rational procedures, often including systems analysis and quantitative techniques (Leavitt 1975).

Past research on scanning is reviewed in the next section, but for now we can say that the scanning-interpretation model harmonizes well with the empirical knowledge about organizational scanning. As suggested by the model, the amount of information seeking or scanning is related to the perceived analyzability of the environment (Kefalas and Schoderbek 1973, Nishi, et al., 1982, Daft, et al., 1988, Boyd 1989, Auster and Choo 1993a, 1993b, 1994a, 1994b). Furthermore, when the environment is perceived to be difficult to analyze, there is a tendency to use personal sources more heavily (Aguilar 1967, Kobrin, et al., 1980, Ghoshal and Kim 1986, Smeltzer, et al., 1988, Al-Hamad 1988, Auster and Choo 1994a and 1994b, Choo 1994). In introducing the concept of organizational intrusiveness, the scanning-interpretation model emphasizes the dependency between information gathering and the capability to intrude actively into the environment. This is similar to the widespread call to base strategic planning and action on more thorough environmental scanning and analysis, and the dependency is also borne out by field research (e.g., Choo 1994, Subramanian, et al., 1994). In summary, the scanning-interpretation model appears to be a viable framework for analyzing the primary environmental and organizational contingencies that influence environmental scanning as cycles of information seeking and information use activities.

Research on Environmental Scanning

Since environmental scanning includes both looking for information and looking at information, scanning is a form of organizational *browsing*. In this context, browsing is defined as the process of exposing oneself to a resource space by scanning its content and/or structure, possibly resulting in awareness of unexpected or new content or paths in the resource space (Chang and Rice 1993). Scanning or browsing behavior is influenced by external factors such as the nature of the business and the strategy pursued, information factors such as the availability and quality of information, and personal factors such as the scanner's knowledge or cognitive style.

The positive outcomes of scanning are many—finding the desired information, using the information for situational interpretation or decision making, modifying initial information requirements, discovering information serendipitously, and so on—all of which can help to induce and invigorate organizational learning. Poorly managed scanning, however, can also lead to negative outcomes such as information overload, confusion and disorientation, high costs in

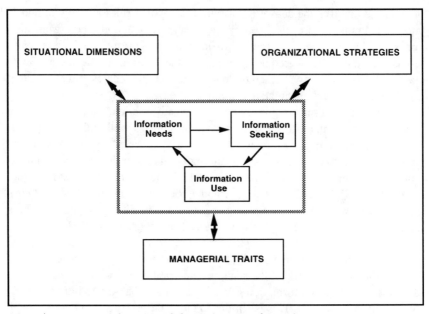

Figure 4.3 A Conceptual Framework for Environmental Scanning

terms of staff time and money, and inaction and increased inertia from adopting a "wait-and-see" attitude.

In this section we review research studies that investigate the effect of situational dimensions, organizational strategies, information needs, and personal traits on scanning behavior (Figure 4.3). *Situational dimensions* are often studied by measuring the perceived uncertainty of the external environment, a concept that is closely related to the perceived environmental analyzability of the scanning-interpretation-learning model that we discussed in the last section. *Organizational strategies* refer to the position or stance or the organization vis-à-vis the outside environment, and two examples of well-known strategy typologies are those developed by Miles and Snow (1978) and Porter (1980). *Managerial traits* that have been studied include the managers' functional specialties, hierarchical levels, and cognitive styles. Scanning as a form of information behavior comprises information needs, information seeking, and information use (see Figure 3.1, Chapter 3). In the context of environmental scanning, *information needs* are often studied with respect to the focus and scope of scanning, particularly the environmental sectors where scanning is most intense. *Information seeking* has been examined in terms of the sources that are used to scan the environment as well as the organizational methods and systems deployed to monitor the environment. Finally, *information use* is usually looked at in relation to decision making, strategic planning, or equivocality reduction.

Situational Dimensions: Perceived Environmental Uncertainty

The measurement of managers' perception of environmental uncertainty would be important to an organizational analysis of the amount of scanning (Achrol 1988, Sharfman and Dean 1991). Perceived environmental uncertainty is often analyzed as the omnibus variable that represents the totality of the scanner's perception of the external environment's complexity and changeability. As an antecedent of scanning, it is closely related to the concept of the believed analyzability of the environment we discussed in the last section.

Duncan (1972) identified dimensions of the environment that would determine its perceived uncertainty. He infers two dimensions from earlier theorists such as Emery and Trist (1965), Thompson (1967), and Terreberry (1968): the simple-complex dimension (the number of environmental factors considered in decision making) and the static-dynamic dimension (the degree to which these factors change over time). Duncan found that decision makers in environments that are dynamic and complex experienced the greatest amount of perceived environmental uncertainty. Perceived environmental uncertainty is conceptualized as (1) lack of information on environmental factors associated with a decision situation, (2) lack of knowledge about the outcome of a specific decision, and (3) inability to assign probabilities with confidence on how environmental factors affect success or failure.

The extant scanning research generally agrees that managers who experience higher levels of perceived environmental uncertainty lend to do a larger amount of environmental scanning. Kefalas and Schoderbek (1973) surveyed the scanning behavior of forty executives from six companies in the farm equipment and meat packing industries. They found that executives in the dynamic environment (farm machinery) did more scanning than those in the stable environment (meat packing), although the difference was not statistically significant. Nishi, et al., (1982) analyzed the scanning behavior of 250 executives in the Japanese computer industry and information processing industry. Again, executives in the dynamic (computer) industry spent more time scanning than did those in the stable (information processing) industry.

Daft, et al., (1988) studied scanning by the chief executive officers of small-to medium-sized manufacturing companies located in Texas. They introduced the concept of *perceived strategic uncertainty* as a predictor of scanning activity. Perceived strategic uncertainty refers to the uncertainty of an environmental sector, weighted by the importance of events in that sector to the firm. Chief executives responded to greater perceived strategic uncertainty with higher scanning frequency using all available sources, implying that they employ multiple, complementary sources to interpret an uncertain environment. Chief executives of high-performing firms did more frequent scanning through all media when strategic uncertainty was high, compared to low-performing firms.

Moreover, their breadth of scanning was wider, and they tailored their scanning according to the amount of perceived uncertainty in each sector.

Boyd (1989) studied the scanning behavior of executives in several industries (banking, health, insurance, and chemicals). He found a strong relationship between scanning of an environmental issue and the perceived importance of that issue, and concluded that "perceived importance is itself the most important predictor of scanning activity." (Boyd, p. 95) This is so even when the issue is experiencing a low rate of change, or when the executive already has adequate information about the issue.

Boyd's work confirms the finding of Daft, et al., (1988) that the perceived importance of environmental developments has a large impact on scanning. Auster and Choo (1992, 1993a, 1993b) examined the environmental scanning behavior of chief executive officers in the Canadian publishing and telecommunications industries, and also found a substantial correlation between the executives' amount of scanning and their level of perceived strategic uncertainty.

Elenkov (1997) examined the relationship between perceived strategic uncertainty and environmental scanning behaviors in a sample of 141 medium-size Bulgarizan companies. All of these companies were operating in a highly constrained external environment and a business culture that was characterized by a low degree of 'calculative' strategic decision making. The results indicated that as perceived strategic uncertainty increased, the use of personal sources would tend to increase, and that the use of external sources over internal sources would also rise. Elenkov proposed a refinement of the perceived strategic uncertainty model to take into account "politically dominated environments" where scanning is not influenced by business rationale, as well as "institutional pressures and demands embodied in political ideologies, unique cultural norms, and social expectations." (Elenkov 1997, p. 290)

In summary, the situational dimension of perceived environmental uncertainty appears to be a good predictor of the amount of scanning. Perceived environmental uncertainty is a function of the perceived complexity (number of factors, opacity of causal relationships) and perceived dynamism (rate of change) of the external environment. Recent research has found that if the perceived sectoral importance of the environment is included as a third functional variable in a measure of perceived strategic uncertainty, the association between environmental uncertainty and scanning is even stronger.

Organizational Strategies

Hambrick (1979, 1981, 1982) analyzed the effects of two sets of strategy-related factors on scanning: the strategy adopted by the organization vis-à-vis the external market; and the nature of the industry to which the organization belongs. Based on a survey of executives from the top three levels of organizations in three industries (higher education, health care, life insurance), he found that organizational strategy alone did not appear to affect the amount of scanning conducted, but that the industry the organization represents strongly affected the content of what was scanned. Thus, hospitals stressed scanning on the engineering environment, insurance firms stressed the entrepreneurial environment, and colleges had mixed patterns of emphasis. Hambrick explains the lack of a connection between strategy and scanning in the following way: organizations adopting different strategies have different propensities and capacities to act on environmental information. They may possess generally equal information, but they act on it in different ways to create their own competitive positions.

Jennings, et al., (1992) explored the relationships between the environmental scanning activities of chief executives in the savings and loan industry and their organizations' strategies. Business-level strategy was differentiated according to Porter's (1980) generic classification between product or service differentiation and cost leadership. The data suggested that savings and loan firms following a differentiation strategy tended to implement scanning activity that places the greatest importance on evaluating opportunities for growth and improving customer attitudes. On the other hand, those following a cost leadership strategy tended to adopt scanning activities that evaluated competitive threats and tracked competitors' policies and tactics. Thus, scanning appeared to be linked to organizational strategy, although the direction of causation could not be ascertained.

As in Hambrick's study, Subramanian, et al., (1993b) examined the relationship between organizational strategy as classified according to the Miles and Snow typology and the firm's environmental scanning focus. The study population was Fortune 500 manufacturing firms. Applying Jain's (1984) classification of scanning systems (discussed below), the study found that of the sixty-eight respondents, the largest majority (one-third) had reactive scanning systems, while only a few had primitive scanning systems. Firms following prospector strategies had the most advanced scanning systems, followed by analyzers and, finally, defenders. According to the authors, defenders had a limited product-market domain and defended their turf by having efficient transformation systems. Prospectors constantly changed their product-market domain to exploit new opportunities. Analyzers shared characteristics of both defenders and prospectors. A majority of the prospectors exhibited scanning systems that were either reactive or proactive (39%); analyzers predominently used reactive systems (42%); and the majority of defenders employed ad hoc scanning systems (44%). Unlike Hambrick's earlier research using the same strategy classification, Subramanian and his associates did find a relationship between organizational strategy and the scanning system adopted.

Miller (1994) investigated the relationship between organizational culture and environmental scanning through a case study of 220 managers with a Fortune 500 manufacturing firm. To differentiate subcultures in the organization, the study applied the competing values framework (Quinn 1988), which proposed four culture types: a Rational Goals mode that stresses order with a focus on the external environmental; an Open Systems model that stresses flexibility and developmental change, again with a focus on the external environment; a Human Relations model that stresses spontaneity and group cohesiveness with a focus on internal organization; and an Internal Process model that stresses predictability and hierarchy, again with a focus on internal organization.

Miller divided the managers into four culture modes. Profile 1 showed balanced scores across all four culture models, but the score for each model was relatively low ("weak comprehensive"). Profile 2 also showed balanced scores, with values that are close to the mean ("comprehensive"). Profile 4, too, showed a balanced culture but with high scores for each model ("strong comprehensive"). The exception was Profile 3, which showed an imbalanced culture dominated by the hierarchical (Internal Process) and rational models ("H-R culture"). The study found that managers in the strong comprehensive culture profile were the most frequent scanners and open-minded managers within the sample. In contrast, managers in the H-R and weak comprehensive cultures were the most infrequent scanners and closed-minded managers in the sample. The study concluded that "a balanced culture positively influences scanning frequency. Specifically, imbalanced cultures sustain rational managers who rarely scan, while balanced cultures develop adaptive managers who frequently scan." (Miller 1994, 194)

Yasai-Ardekani and Nystrom (1996) compared the relationships between organizational context and the designs of environmental scanning systems for organizations with effective and ineffective scanning systems. Their analysis of data from over 100 North American business organizations indicated that organizations with effective scanning systems tended to align their scanning designs with the requirements of their context, whereas organizations with ineffective scanning systems typically failed to show the requisite level of alignment between contexts and scanning design. Thus, for organizations with effective scanning systems, those facing greater task-environment change use a wider scope of scanning, scan more frequently, and assign their top management teams more responsibility for scanning. Furthermore, those operating with more inflexible technologies use a wider scope of scanning (to reduce their technological vulnerability); and those with a low-cost orientation scan more broadly, frequently, and intensively (to protect against competitive erosion).

In summary, recent research suggests that the organization's overall business strategy is related to the sophistication, scope, and intensity of its environmental scanning. An organization that follows a particular strategy, such as product differentiation, cost leadership, or focus (Porter 1980), or adopts a certain strategic stance, such as prospector, analyzer, or defender (Miles and Snow 1978), is likely to operate a scanning mode that provides the required information and information processing capabilities to pursue its goals.

Tentative evidence also exists to suggest that a balanced organizational culture is likely to encourage managers to scan more frequently and take on a more adaptive outlook.

Managerial Traits

The expectation is that factors such as the manager's hierarchical level, functional specialization, and personality or cognitive style would affect the conduct of environmental scanning. Unfortunately, no consistent pattern emerges from the few studies that have investigated the relationship between managerial traits and scanning activity.

Aguilar (1967) found that functionally specialized managers tended to use particular sources (e.g., production managers relied on suppliers), whereas top level managers tended to rely on informal networks of contacts outside the company. Managers of large companies tended to rely more on internal sources. The study of Kefalas and Schoderbek (1973) concluded that executives' hierarchical level was not related to the focus of scanning. Furthermore, there was considerable scanning of the market sector by executives of all functional specialities. Similarly, Hambrick (1979) found that the scanning activities of executives did not appear to vary significantly with their hierarchical levels, nor with their functional specializations. The study of executives in the Japanese computer industry and information-processing industry by Nishi, et al., (1982) concluded that upper level executives spent more time on external scanning than lower level executives. In addition, executives spent a higher proportion of their time scanning the environmental sector closest to their functional specialities. In a study of information needs of managers of manufacturing firms in a region of the United Kingdom, White (1986) and White and Wilson (1988) concluded that their information needs were not confined to their functional specializations. Box (1991) surveyed 300 entrepreneurial manufacturing firms in Tulsa, Oklahoma and found a significant relationship between the entrepreneur's locus of control, prior experience, scanning practices, and the performance of the firm as measured by the average annual employment growth. Furthermore, industry dynamism and environmental hostility moderated the relationship between entrepreneurial years and age and firm performance.

Because environmental scanning requires managers to make sense of an uncertain environment, research on scanning should include the cognitive styles and processes by which managers seek and use scanning information. These processes go beyond job-related functions, and raise research question such as: How do managers know what information they need about the environment? How do they deal with multiple sources that provide information on the same topic? How do they interpret ambiguous messages about environmental change? How do they detect, recognize, and frame problems from within a stream of environmental information?

Cognitive style is a multi-faceted concept, with a large number of dimensions that can potentially influence information seeking and use (Rouse and Rouse 1984, Allen 1991). Paisley (1980) suggested that to understand a person's plan for information use, it may be necessary to understand that person's cognitive attributes in terms of his or her differentiation and labeling of constructs (Schroder 1971), tendency toward field dependence (Witkin 1959), style of serialist or holistic thinking (Pask and Scott 1972), and so on.

In the context of environmental scanning, a few cognitive-personality style variables could be important, for example, ambiguity tolerance, field dependence, and locus of control. *Ambiguity tolerance* is the tendency to perceive ambiguous situations as desirable, whereas ambiguity intolerance is the tendency to perceive or interpret ambiguous situations as sources of threat (Budner 1962). This suggests that for a given level of perceived uncertainty, people with higher tolerance for ambiguity would do more scanning than their low tolerance counterparts. *Field dependence* is the reliance on external cues for orientation to situations: people who are field-dependent respond uncritically to environmental cues, while those who are field independent orient themselves correctly in spite of environmental cues. Field-dependents seem to gather more information and use more sources than the field-independents, who seem to have more analytic ability (Allen 1991, Paisley 1980). *Locus of control* refers to the perception that people have about the factors responsible for what happens to them: people with an internal locus of control view what happens to them as being under their own control, while people with an external locus of control view what happens to them as determined by circumstance and event beyond their influence. The expectation would be for the internals to seek information more actively than the externals.

Only very few past studies have investigated the effect of cognitive factors on scanning. Boyd (1989), in his study of executives in several industries, found tentative support for the hypothesis that managers with a higher tolerance for ambiguity will engage in higher levels of scanning activity. Box (1991), discussed above, analyzed the entrepreneur-manager's locus of control as part of scanning behavior that was related to the firm's growth performance. An early attempt to include cognitive factors was made by Stabell (1978), who found that how a manager chooses between impersonal information sources is associated with the manager's cognitive ability to apply multiple source selection rules in a selective way (the manager's "integrative complexity").

Vandenbosch and Huff (1977) examined environmental scanning by executives in relation to Executive Information Systems (EIS). The data collected from interviews with 36 executive EIS users indicated that three-quarters of the respondents did not use the EIS for scanning, but instead used the EIS to seek answers to specific questions. The study concluded that a personal predisposition towards scanning, strong organizational support for scanning, and the characteristics of the EIS all interacted to determine how an EIS would be used for scanning. Disposition toward scanning was linked to the individual's tolerance for ambiguity and innovativeness. Organizational support depends on whether scanning was encouraged or expected in the organization — the influence of senior management and colleagues may be significant. EIS which are flexible and can combine information from different sources would also promote scanning.

In summary, the effect of the manager's job-related and cognitive traits on scanning is an area in need of further research. There is tentative evidence to suggest that managers scan widely, covering not just their functional specializations but also other areas; and the upper level managers scan more and more broadly than lower level managers, but on the whole, much more research needs to be done on cognitive and personality factors.

Information Needs: Focus of Environmental Scanning

The external environment of a business enterprise includes all outside factors that can affect the performance or survival of the organization. Although there are many factors, students of strategic management often divide the external business environment into a few *environmental sectors*. For example, Jauch and Glueck (1980) identify six environmental sectors: customers, suppliers, competition, socioeconomic, technological, and governmental. Fahey and Narayanan (1986) distinguish between a macroenvironment comprising social, economic, political, and technological sectors, and a task/industry environment comprising mainly the customer and competitor sectors.

The research studies on which environmental sectors form the primary focus of environmental scanning show general agreement. The market-related sectors of the external environment, with information on customers, suppliers, and competitors, appear to be the most important.

— Aguilar's 1967 scanning study involved interviews with managers in over forty companies in the United States and western Europe. The study found that for these managers, the importance of information on "market tidings" was overwhelming—it was three times as important as the next area of concern ("technical tidings").

— Similarly, Nishi, et al., (1982) found that for both the Japanese computer industry and information-processing industry, the marketing sector was the major environmental sector, followed by the technology sector.

— Jain (1984) studied scanning in Fortune 500 U.S. corporations through interviews and questionnaire surveys. He found that scanning was directed at four areas: economic, technological, political, and social. Scanning the economic area was the most significant, followed by the technological area.

— Ghoshal (1988) surveyed the scanning practices of managers in the largest companies in the Republic of Korea (South Korea). The most important kinds of environmental information are those concerning the market, competition, technology, regulatory policies, resources, and broad issues.

— Johnson and Kuehn (1987) studied the scanning behaviors of managers and owners of small and large businesses in the southwestern United States. Small business respondents spend almost a third of their information seeking time looking for market-related information on sales, products, and customer problems. Next in importance is information about technology.

— Lester and Waters (1989) investigated the environmental scanning activities by corporate planning departments of seven large U.K.-based companies. The study found that the planners put most effort into acquiring information on the competitive sector, information concerning competitive industries, companies, products and services, and markets. Relatively little attention was given to macro-environmental influences such as economic, political, social/cultural factors.

— In their study of Canadian chief executives in the publishing and telecommunications industries, the customer and technological sectors were seen to be the most important and uncertain, followed by the competition and regulatory sectors (Auster and Choo 1993a, 1993b). For telecommunications executives separately, the technological sector was perceived to be the most strategically uncertain, followed by the customer, competition, and regulatory sectors (Choo 1993).

— Olsen, et al., (1994) surveyed the scanning practices of fifty-two chief executives of multinational hotel chains. For these executives, scanning concentrated on addressing short-term concerns in the competitive environment such as pricing strategies, customer needs, and competitor offerings. Interestingly, the overall environment was seen to be relatively stable, with the technology sector being the most volatile, albeit mildly so. The authors recommended that the executives should broaden their scanning to include emerging trends that could affect the industry in the longer term.

In summary, environmental scanning by business organizations is focused on the market-related sectors of the environment. Information about customers, competitors, and suppliers is seen to be the most important. In industries where other sectors of the environment, such as technology or demographics, are perceived to be having a very large impact on the structure and dynamics of the industry, these sectors would also be considered high scanning priorities.

Information Seeking (1): Use and Preferences

Almost every study on scanning seeks to identify which information sources are used most frequently or are most important in environmental scanning. Because managers have access to a large number of information sources, those sources are commonly classified according to whether they are internal or external to the organization, and whether they are personal or impersonal. The internal and external source categories are self-explanatory. Personal sources communicate information personally to the manager, whereas impersonal sources are often defined as sources that communicate information to broad audiences, or through formalized, group-communication activities (e.g., Aguilar 1967, Keegan 1974). By this definition, impersonal sources would include publications, conferences, company library, and online databases. The pattern of source usage in scanning that emerges from the literature is that while both internal and external sources are frequently used, personal sources such as customers, associates, and staff members appear to be more important. Furthermore, sources such as the library and online databases are not often used directly by managers when scanning the environment.

— Aguilar's 1967 study found that personal sources greatly exceeded impersonal sources in importance. The most important personal sources were subordinates and customers, and the most important impersonal source was publications. Managers of large companies tended to rely more on internal sources. Information from outside sources was mostly unsolicited, whereas information from inside sources was mostly solicited.

— Keegan (1967, 1974) was one of the first to focus on the environmental scanning of multinational companies. He interviewed executives in thirteen multinational companies based in the United States about recent instances when they received external information. The study concluded that sources outside the organization were more important than sources inside the organization, with the former accounting for 66 percent of information from all sources. Furthermore, the flow of information within the company was strongly constrained by intra-organizational, departmental boundaries.

— O'Connell and Zimmerman (1979) compared how policy level executives and planning staff managers in fifty U.S. and fifty European multinational corporations scanned the international environment. Both groups identified persons in their own positions as the chief sources of environmental information. The most important sources were the categories "home office top management" and "home office staff"—both of which are internal sources.

— Kobrin, et al., (1980) studied how large international firms based in the United States assessed foreign social and political environments through a survey of nearly 500 firms. The information sources considered important by a majority of the firms were internal—subsidiary and regional managers, and headquarters personnel. Banks were clearly the most important external source. There was a preference for obtaining environmental assessments directly from people whom they know and trust. They rely on their subordinates, colleagues in other firms, banks, and personal observations during frequent trips to foreign countries.

— Smeltzer, et al., (1988) analyzed the scanning practices of small business managers in the Phoenix and Kansas City metropolitan areas in the United States. Personal sources were significantly more important than impersonal sources. Family members and customers were the most prevalent personal sources, while magazines and journals were the most prevalent impersonal sources.

— The study of large United Kingdom companies by Lester and Waters (1989) found that traditional sources, such as libraries, were felt to be tedious and frustrating to use. Respondents were also skeptical about the value of information-brokering services, and they preferred raw to refined data. There was great interest in, and in some cases considerable use of, online information services. Generally, the use of formal, published resources was ad hoc, informal, and low key.

— In her study of environmental scanning by sixteen chief academic officers of community colleges in Pennsylvania, Gates (1990) found that they relied on personal sources within the organization and written sources outside the organization. Interviews suggested an overall dependence on personal networks. The administrators scanned demographic, economic, and technological sectors most frequently. Scanning, however, was driven by issues that had become salient because other individuals raised them. Scanning was then used to plan institutional responses and implement curriculum changes.

— Mayberry (1991) looked specifically at the effects of a selective dissemination of information service on the environmental scanning process of an academic institution (Langston University). After six months of using the SDI service, the administrators indicated continued reliance on personal sources but showed a significant increase in the overall satisfaction level for the use of library-type sources.

A few studies have attempted to examine some of the factors that might explain the selection and use of certain types of information sources in environmental scanning.

— Culnan (1983) looked at the scanning behavior of a few hundred professionals in a bank holding company and a diversified natural resources manufacturing firm. She examined the effects of perceived source accessibility and perceived task complexity on the use of various information sources. The study found that information acquisition was not entirely a function of perceived source accessibility: information needs associated with the complexity of the task to be performed were related to the use of sources perceived as less accessible.

— The study of large South Korean firms by Ghoshal and Kim (1988) concluded that information about the immediate business environment (competitors, existing technologies, and product markets) required daily for operational decisions is usually obtained from business associates such as customers, suppliers, trade associations, and bankers. On the other hand, for information about the broader environment (general social, economic, political, and technological changes) printed sources in the public domain are more important: general and trade journals, special government publications, reports from academic institutions, think tanks, or consulting organizations.

— The study of Canadian chief executives by Auster and Choo (1992, 1993a, 1993b) revealed that executives use multiple, complementary sources when scanning the environment. Personal sources (managers, staff members, customers, associates) are among the most frequently used, while the company library and electronic information services are not frequently used. Perceived source quality is the more important factor in explaining source use than either perceived source accessibility or perceived environmental uncertainty. The study suggests that the turbulence of the external environment, the strategic role of scanning, and the information use contexts of managers, combine to explain why information quality is more important than source accessibility when managers scan the environment.

In summary, the general pattern of source usage for scanning suggests that although managers use a wide range of sources in scanning, they prefer personal sources that communicate information directly rather than impersonal sources that communicate information formally or to broad audiences. This preference for live information from personal sources is particularly strong when seeking information about market-related environmental sectors that are highly fluid and equivocal. There is some evidence to indicate that source selection for scanning is influenced by the perceived quality of the source, and not just its perceived accessibility.

Information Seeking (2): Scanning Methods

Several studies have attempted to classify different modes or methods of environmental scanning practiced by organizations. Scanning activities in business corporations can range from being ad hoc and informal to being highly systematic and formalized. Field research seems to suggest that the size of the firm, the experience and proficiency with long-term planning and analysis techniques, and the perception of the external environment, are some of the factors that influence the choice of scanning method.

— Aguilar's case studies found that in the small firms, scanning was done by top management in the course of normal business operating activities, and the information obtained tended to be concerned with the immediate industrial milieu. In the medium-size firm "a number of distinct scanning systems were loosely linked at the top management level through internal communication characterized by an element of bargaining." (Aguilar 1967, 175) In the large firms, there was an increased amount and complexity of internal communications, a greater use of institutionalized scanning units, and an increased reliance by top management on staff assistants to filter information.

— In the study by Keegan (1974) of multinational companies, there was little evidence of any systematic method of information gathering: computer-based systems were not being used, and even manual systems did not play a significant role.

— Thomas (1980) surveyed the scanning activities of nine very large corporations in the United States and Europe through published sources. He concluded that the practice of scanning for planning has taken firm root among these large firms. According to Thomas, the scanning process was characterized by its permanence (continuity over time), periodicity (linkage with planning), and pervasiveness (spread over multiple levels and units). Thus, some of the firms studied had operated scanning systems for several years, integrated scanning into their corporate planning, and involved many functional units at various organizational levels in their scanning process.

— Klein and Linneman (1984) conducted an extensive international survey of the environmental assessment practices of large corporations. Approximately half of the respondents had formalized environmental assessment as part of the planning process. The increased importance of environmental assessment was attributed to greater environmental turbulence, longer planning time horizons, use of futures forecasting techniques, and greater experience with long-range planning processes. Trend extrapolation was the most widely used form of judgmental technique.

— Preble, et al., (1988) analyzed the scanning done by ninety-five multinational corporations based in the United States. They found that:

- Over half of the firms were conducting continuous in-house international scanning.
- Nearly half of the executives reported some degree of computerization used in scanning processes.
- The executives relied on internal sources of international environmental information much more than external sources.
- Half of the firms had formal procedures where executives were regularly involved in the scanning of publications.

Comparing these results with the study by Keegan (1974) fourteen years earlier, it appears that, at least among multinational companies, there has been a shift towards more formalized scanning systems and sophisticated scanning techniques. A recent study of environmental scanning in large United States firms examined current scanning practices in Fortune 500 companies (Subramanian, et al., 1993a). Results indicated a trend toward increased sophistication and specialization in the type of systems used for scanning, with about 60 percent of the sample firms exhibiting advanced scanning systems. Other trends include an increased amount of specialization in the scanning function, greater use of industry-specific sources of information, and an increased concern with the economic and technological sectors of the environment.

Choudhury and Sampler (1997) propose using the concept of information specificity to address the question of how an organization should allocate its environmental scanning resources and choose to outsource aspects of the scanning effort. Information specificity consists of knowledge specificity and time specificity: information is high in knowledge specificity if it can be acquired only be individuals possessing specific knowledge, while information is high in time specificity it must be captured when (and not after) it originates. Applying the information specificity concept within the economic framework of transaction cost theory, they propose that: (1) resources be directed first to acquire knowledge low in knowledge specificity but high in time specificity; (2) acquisition of information low in knowledge specificity be outsourced; and (3) acquisition of information high in knowledge specificity be accomplished by: the user when time specificity is high, a subordinate when time specificity is moderate, and a central unit when time specificity is low.

A small number of studies looked at scanning in nonprofit organizations.

— Wilson and Masser (1983) explored the environmental monitoring activities of County Planning Authorities in England and Wales. They discerned two stereotypes: those authorities that defined information as "hard data" and those that defined it more widely as "qualitative data." The latter group was more likely to have a policy of comprehensive information acquisition and to regard information retrieval, processing, and evaluation as serious information management issues. Information management, however, is seen as a technical task undertaken by specialists, and is to some extent divorced from organizational characteristics.

— Al-Hamad (1988) studied the scanning behavior of sixty-seven executives from seventeen colleges, universities, and hospitals in the United States. Two methods of scanning emerged from the data analysis. In a stable, certain environment, scanning tended to be an unstructured process in which information was obtained from nonformalized sources such as irregular contacts and social occasions, and trial-and-error experimentation was attempted. In a dynamic, uncertain environment, scanning tended to be a structured process in which information was obtained formally through information systems, record keeping, and so on, and information was analyzed through procedures such as trend analysis.

— McIntyre (1992) reported case studies of three school districts each with its distinct scanning conditions—active scan, directed scan, and passive scan [similar to the scanning-interpretation modes of Daft and Weick (1984) described earlier]. The study found that the history, values, and political context of the school district were important factors influencing scanning and planning. Directed scanning of the school environment provided the most useful data for strategy formulation. According to the author, the turbulent school setting and the unsophisticated background of the school planners favor a more proactive mode of scanning, while passive scanning was a valuable supplement to the directed process.

A few researchers have proposed theoretical classifications of the various modes of environmental scanning that they have observed in the field. Thus, Fahey and King (1977) suggested that corporate environmental scanning may be differentiated according to three distinct models: the irregular model, periodic model, and continuous mode. In the irregular model, scanning is ad hoc and driven by some external occurrence or crisis. In the periodic model, scanning is regular, and is directed at decisions or issues in the near term. Finally, in the continuous model, scanning is structured and integrated with corporate planning processes, and usually involves a central scanning unit. From their structured interviews with planning officers of twelve large corporations they found that scanning in most of the firms was ad hoc and event-driven. None of the firms had successfully integrated environmental scanning into their strategic planning.

From his study of United States-based corporations that make up the Fortune 500, Jain (1984) proposed that organizational scanning systems go through four phases as they evolve: primitive, ad hoc, reactive, and proactive phases. As the firm progresses through the phases, its intensity of scanning increases, the time horizon of the scanning lengthens, and the level of confidence in the scanned information rises. A scanning system needs time to evolve and adapt to the organizational culture, and to gain the confidence of top management.

There is some research data to support the evolutionary nature of organizational scanning. Jain's 1984 study found that only 8 percent of his sample of Fortune 500 firms had the most evolved proactive scanning systems. A similar study in 1993 on Fortune 500 companies determined that 25 percent of the new sample had proactive scanning systems, with only 10 percent of the firms exhibiting primitive scanning systems (Subramanian, et al., 1993a).

In summary, organizations scan in a variety of modes, ranging from the irregular, ad hoc scan to continuous, proactive information gathering as part of an institutionalized scanning-planning system. The size of the organization, its industry category, its dependence and perception of the environment, and its experience with scanning and strategic planning, are some of the factors that affect the choice of scanning method.

Information Use

The most widely discussed use of information gained from scanning is in strategic planning and decision making. According to the doctrine on strategic management, environmental scanning and analysis is a necessary early stage of the strategic planning process. Information about the external environment is analyzed and interpreted to reveal trends and illuminate potential threats and opportunities. These interpretations then form the cognitive framework for managers to make decisions and develop responses. Thus, research by Thomas (1980), Jain (1984), Preble, et al., (1988), Ghoshal (1988), Lester and Waters (1989), Stanat (1990), Tomioka (1990), Hedin (1993), and several others have established that environmental scanning is formally linked to the strategic planning process, especially among the larger enterprises in the United States, western Europe, Japan, and the newly industrialized countries of Asia. At the individual manager level, Auster and Choo (1993a, 1993b, 1994a, 1994b) found that chief executives in two Canadian industries most frequently used environmental information in the entrepreneurial decisional role, that is, in the initiation of new improvement projects and strategies.

Does environmental scanning improve organizational performance? Several studies suggest that this is the case.

— Miller and Friesen (1977) analyzed eighty-one detailed case studies of successful and failing businesses, and categorized them according to ten archetypes—six for successful and four for unsuccessful firms. The study found that the intelligence-rationality factor, which comprises environmental scanning, controls, communication, adaptiveness, analysis, integration, multiplexity, and industry experience, was by far the most important factor in separating the successful companies from the unsuccessful, accounting for more than half of the observed variance. The environmental scanning and intelligence activities in all but one of the successful archetypes were judged to be "substantial" or "concerted," whereas the intelligence efforts in the failing firms were described as "poor" or "weak." Miller and Friesen observed that "one fact is particularly worth noting. That is that the highest intelligence/rationality score amongst the failure archetypes is lower than the lowest intelligence/rationality score amongst the successful archetypes. The intelligence factor discriminates perfectly amongst failure and successful archetypes." (Miller and Friesen 1977, 269).

— Newgren, et al., (1984) compared the economic performance of twenty-eight United States corporations that practiced environmental scanning with twenty-two nonpracticing firms. Performance was measured over a five-year period (1975-1980) using the firms' share price/earnings ratio, normalized by industry. Data analysis showed that scanning firms significantly outperformed nonscanning firms. The average annual performance of the scanning firms was also consistently better than the nonscanning firms throughout the period. The study concluded that environmental scanning and assessment has a positive influence on corporate performance.

— Scanning also benefits small businesses. Dollinger (1984) analyzed the performance of eighty-two small firms and concluded that intensive boundary spanning activity was strongly related to an organization's financial performance, where boundary spanning was measured by the number of contacts with outside constituencies such as customers, competitors, government officials, trade associations, and so on.

— West (1988) examined the relationship of organizational strategy *and* environmental scanning to performance in the United States food service industry. Data was collected from sixty-five companies over the period 1982 to 1986. Strategy was classified according to Porter's (1980) typology of differentiation, low cost leadership, and focus. The study found that strategy and environmental scanning had a substantial influence on the firm's return on assets and return on sales. High performing firms in both differentiation and low cost strategies engaged in significantly greater amounts of scanning than low performing firms in those two strategic groups.

— Daft's, et al., 1988 study of scanning by chief executives found the leaders of high performing firms (those with higher return on assets) increased the frequency, intensity, and breadth of their scanning as external uncertainty rose.

— Subramanian and his associates studied scanning and performance in U.S. Fortune 500 companies and found support for a relationship between performance, measured by profitability and growth, and advanced scanning systems: firms using advanced systems to monitor external events showed higher growth and profitability than firms that did not have such systems (Subramanian, et al., 1993a).

— Subramanian led another recent study of over 600 hospitals of the American Hospital Association, which concluded that hospitals with the more sophisticated scanning functions performed significantly better than hospitals that used less advanced or basic methods to monitor the environment (Subramanian, et al., 1994). The sophisticated scanners scored high in their capability to obtain information *and* their capability to use the scanning information in the strategic planning process. These hospitals performed better in terms of occupancy rates and per bed expenditures.

The benefits of scanning were not solely economic or financial. In a in-depth case study of environmental scanning at the Center for Continuing Education, Murphy (1987) concluded that scanning is an important component of the organization's strategic planning process, improving the Center's ability to react to and implement change in response to external factors. Furthermore, scanning has also contributed to increased communication among the line and staff personnel of the organization, and greater employee involvement in the decision making process. Ptaszynski (1989) examined the effect of the introduction of environmental scanning in another educational organization. The study found scanning to have a positive effect on the organization in these areas: communication, shared vision, strategic planning and management, and future orientation. The most significant effect was that scanning provided a structured process that encouraged people to regularly participate in face-to-face discussions on planning issues. As a result, the organization was able to develop a number of strategic options that could be used proactively to cope with external change.

To recap, information derived from environmental scanning is increasingly being used to drive the strategic planning process by business and public sector organizations in most developed countries. Research evidence shows that environmental scanning is linked with improved organizational performance. Nevertheless, the practice of scanning by itself is insufficient to assure performance—scanning must be integrated with strategy, and scanning information must be effectively utilized in the strategic planning process. An important effect of scanning is to increase and enhance communication and discussion about future oriented issues by people in the organization. Coupled with the availability of information on external change, scanning can induce the kind of strategic, generative (i.e., double loop) organizational learning discussed in Chapter 1.

Summary

What may be gleaned from the research that has been completed so far on environmental scanning as a mode of strategic organizational learning? A summary may include the following observations:

1. *Situational dimensions: the effect of perceived environmental uncertainty.* Managers who perceive the environment to be more uncertain will tend to scan more. Environmental uncertainty is indicated by the complexity, dynamism, and importance of the sectors comprising the external environment.

2. *Organizational strategy and scanning strategy.* An organization's overall strategy is related to the sophistication and scope of its scanning activities. Scanning must be able to provide the information and information processing needed to develop and pursue the elected strategy.

3. *Managerial traits: unanswered questions.* Little is known with confidence about the effect of the manager's job-related and cognitive traits on

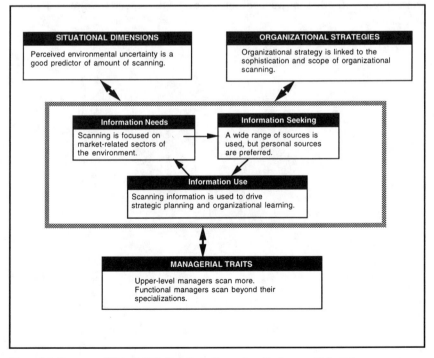

Figure 4.4 Summary of Principal Findings from Research on Environmental Scanning

scanning. Upper level managers seem to scan more than lower level managers. Functional managers scan beyond the limits of their specializations.

4. *Information needs: the focus of environmental scanning.* Business organizations focus their scanning on market-related sectors of the environment. In industries where developments in other environmental sectors are considered highly strategic, these sectors would also be scanned intensively.

5. *Information seeking: source usage and preferences.* Although managers scan with a wide range of sources, they prefer personal sources to formal, impersonal sources, especially when seeking information about developments in the fluid market-related sectors.

6. *Information seeking: scanning methods.* Organizations scan in a variety of modes, depending on the organization's size, dependence on and perception of the environment, experience with scanning and planning, and the industry within which the organization operates.

7. *Information use: strategic planning and enhanced organizational learning.* Information from scanning is increasingly being used to drive the strategic planning process. Research indicates that effective scanning and planning is linked to improved organizational learning and performance.

Figure 4.4 outlines these principal findings, using the conceptual framework (Figure 4.3) that introduced our review of the research on environmental scanning.

Chapter 5

Environmental Scanning in Action

The future was predictable; but hardly anyone predicted it.

(Attributed to Alan Kay, Apple Fellow)

Therefore those who do not know the plans of competitors cannot prepare alliances. Those who do not know the lay of the land cannot maneuver their forces. Those who do not use local guides cannot take advantage of the ground. The military of an effective rulership must know all these things.

(Sun Tzu, ca. 500 BC, The Art of War)

Perspectives from Neurobiology

Environmental scanning is about seeing, perceiving, and making sense. Therefore, it is only natural that we turn towards the most sophisticated perception mechanism that we know, the human visual system, to understand how nature has solved this rather daunting problem. In a sense, environmental scanning is the visual and perception system that feeds information about the outside world to the strategic planning and management functions that constitute the brain of the organization.

We can find many parallels between how the human visual system processes information from external scenes and how environmental scanning processes information about the external milieu.

1. First and most basic, humans use the information from the visual system to perform a number of tasks that are essential for survival, such as foraging for food, avoiding dangers, or planning movement from point to point. For an organization, having timely, accurate information about external change is, in much the same ways, just as critical to its survival: securing resources, spotting threats and opportunities, and setting long term plans.

2. Second, the visual information that enters our eyes is vast and ambiguous. We are easily deceived by our own visual systems—each of us experience frequent errors in perceiving objects or recognizing people, and ingenious optical puzzles have been devised to show up how the visual system copes with inconsistent or incomplete visual cues. In fact, relying on only any one aspect of visual information from the eyes usually leads to ambiguity in trying to understand an external visual scene—the brain needs to synthesize visual information on many features of the visual scene (shape, color, motion, texture, etc.) in order to come to an interpretation. For an organization, the flood of information about the outside environment is so marked by equivocality, inaccuracy, and incompleteness that settling on an acceptable interpretation becomes an organization-wide challenge.

3. Third, and this follows logically from the last observation, seeing is the result of an active construction process involving many levels and subsystems in the visual system. The eye and retina do not function at all like a camera that passively registers the effects of incoming light signals, which are then decoded in the visual cortex, a view that held sway until the mid-1970s. Instead, interpretation is an inseparable part of seeing, and interpretation is achieved through a complex division of labor in a cross-linked network of discrete cortical areas and subregions that specialize in particular visual functions. In the last chapter, we presented the symmetrical point of view that organizations behave very much like interpretation systems, where scanning/perception is intimately linked with interpretation as part of the organization's overall learning process.

Over the last few years, we have made great leaps in our knowledge and understanding of how mammalian visual systems function, including the anatomical structures and neuronal processes that make up the human visual system (Gazzaniga 1995, Koch and Davis 1994). Light entering the eye is focused by the lens onto the retina. Nerve cells in the retina, called *ganglion cells*, receive signals from other neurons in the retina and send signals to the brain. Each of the retinal ganglion cells will fire most rapidly to a small spot of light in just the right position but will respond only weakly to uniform illumination over that general area. In this way, the retina is already processing information by sending to the brain interesting parts of the visual field, where the light distribution is not uniform. The early parts of the visual system are therefore highly parallel, and the visual information is mainly relayed through a small part of the thalamus (the lateral geniculate nucleus) to the visual cortex.

Five visual areas have been found in the visual cortex (V1 to V5), each specialized in function: the neurons in V1 and V2 operate together as a kind of post office that parcels out signals to the other visual areas for further independent but parallel processing; the neurons in V3 specialize in form; V4 in color; and V5 in visual motion. Altogether, four parallel but distinct perceptual pathways connecting these five visual areas have been identified, one for motion, one for color, and two for form (Zeki 1992, 1993), shown schematically in Figure 5.1. The four perceptual pathways follow a similar sequence, signals from the retina and geniculate nucleus are projected onto V1, which together with V2, segregates and distributes to the specialized visual areas for independent parallel processing. For example, in the motion pathway, the main visual area is V5. Input originates from the retina, is relayed through the geniculate nucleus, and projected on the V1. From here signals pass to V5, both directly and through V2.

Based on research of the macaque monkey, Crick (1994) suggests that it is possible to represent the five visual areas and their connections in a quasi-hierarchy of visual information processing. Starting with retinal ganglion cells at the lowest level, signals are relayed through the lateral geniculate nucleus at the

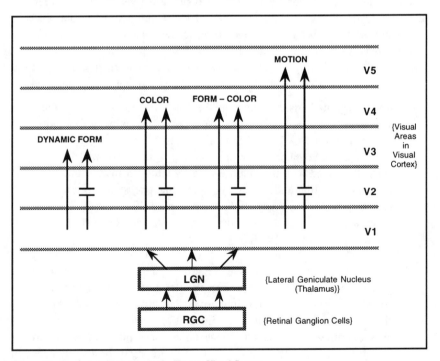

Figure 5.1 Perceptual Pathways in the Human Visual System

next level, then projected onto the V1 level. V2 at the next level works with V1 to distribute signals to V3, V4, and V5 at higher levels. As we move up the hierarchy, the features to which the neurons respond become more complex, and the sizes of the receptive fields increase, so that they cover a progressively larger part of the visual field. The arrangement is quasi-hierarchical because connections can and do skip levels, nearly all connections are reciprocal, and there are many cross-connections between cortical areas at the same level.

Despite this extensive division of labor in the visual cortex, none of the specialization and subdivision is evident at the perceptual level. How does the brain produce a unified picture of the seen world? Anatomically, there is no master area in the visual cortex to which all the other areas converge and where a unified image might be generated. Instead, the specialized visual areas connect with each other, either directly or indirectly through other areas, forming a massively parallel and reciprocal network of links between the four parallel perceptual systems at every level.

Zeki (1993) hypothesizes that signal integration is achieved not in a single step but at different stages, including the stages where functional specialization is first established in the visual cortex (V1, V2). This multistage integration depends on the ubiquitous re-entrant connections between the visual areas. Re-entrant connections allow information to flow both ways between visual areas in a kind of two-way feedback that resolves conflicts between differently specialized cells responding to the same stimulus, and correlates neuronal events across different visual areas without the need for a supervisory function (Edelman 1992). According to this theory, the integrated visual image is an emergent property of the complex network of activated cortical structures and neuronal connections:

> [the] integrated visual image in the brain is the product of the simultaneous activity of several visual areas and pathways, including areas such as V1 and V2 which receive their input from the LGN, distribute them to the specialized visual areas and are re-entrantly linked with the latter. As the re-entrant pathways are diffuse, non-modular and not easily localizable, and the opportunities for integration are many and integration itself is a multi-stage process, it follows that integration is a diffuse and not easily localizable process. (Zeki 1993, 334)

In summary, the brain's visual perception system employs a number of information processing strategies to turn the flood of incoming visual signals into understandable visual scenes: functional specialization; parallel but quasi-hierarchical pathways; and multistage integration through re-entrant connections. It is tempting to consider to what extent these information processing strategies might be applied in organizations to improve the effectiveness of environmental scanning.

Functional specialization in environmental scanning makes good sense in today's environment where the interpretation of complex, ambiguous events and developments necessitate the use of in-depth (tacit) knowledge. The tracking of customer issues should involve the sales personnel, competitor issues the marketing staff, technology issues the production and R&D departments, and so on. Already some organizations have chosen to outsource the monitoring of critical issues or sectors to outside specialists, usually because there is no in-house expertise to do so or because a more thorough analysis is desired. In the human visual system, this functional specialization begins very early, in the first two visual areas of the visual cortex. This phenomenon suggests that specialized processing of the incoming scanning information should begin as close to the source as possible in order to grasp the incoming information in all its original richness and detail.

The human visual system is so rich in connections that it behaves both as a *parallel* and as a *hierarchical* information processing system. Thus, the first visual area (V1) separates and distributes signals on different attributes of the visual scene to the other visual areas for further, independent processing that is done in parallel. At the same time, information also flows up serial connections between visual areas so that progressively more complex representations are built up.

The implication for environmental scanning seems to be that an organization can benefit by simultaneously balancing the advantages of the parallel and hierarchical processing of scanning information. Parallel processing would tolerate a certain amount of positive redundancy among groups in the organization analyzing scanning information, and encourage them to produce multiple, competing hypotheses about the incoming data. Hierarchical processing requires cross connections between these groups as well as with upper-level management to attempt to progressively broaden interpretations by combining insights from different groups.

The notion of *multistage integration* suggests that the brain has solved the problem of integration in a unique way—there is no master area in the visual cortex, no "Cartesian Theatre" (Dennett 1991), where a unified visual image is staged. Instead, the brain has been able to gain flexibility and speed of response by distributing the information integration process across multiple stages of parallel perceptual pathways.

The suggestion for environmental scanning could be that an organization should not attempt to integrate its scanning information at a single locus, such as in the mind of the president or chief executive. Integration and interpretation of scanning information should be a shared activity, distributed across multiple levels, and taking advantage of specialized knowledge workers wherever they may be found in the organization. Where a high level committee exists to translate scanning information into plans, the group should include knowledgeable staff from various functional areas *and* organizational levels, co-opt experts with special insights, introduce outside opinions, and so on.

Re-entrant connections are the mechanism by which the brain achieves multistage integration. In organizations, this suggests that the flow and sharing of scanning information should be two-way: A sends a message to B, B processes the message and sends a return message to A. This form of bidirectional feedback and general information sharing could be facilitated by the use of electronic bulletin board systems (see discussion on Usenet newsgroups in Chapter 2), and the new generation of workgroup application systems exemplified by products such as Lotus Notes.

Overall, the ultimate goal for organizational scanning is to emulate nature's trick for the biological visual system. This can be done by mobilizing, networking, and synthesizing the information gathering and processing capabilities of the organization to construct a unified interpretation of the external environment as a guide to action and planning.

Environmental Scanning in Action in U.S. Corporations

Do real organizations practice scanning and interpretation in ways that approach the design principles we have observed in the human visual system: distributed information processing, functional specialization, and multistage integration? Consider the experiences of firms such as AT&T, Motorola, Kraft, General Motors, and Eastman Kodak.

AT&T

AT&T divides its environmental scanning function into three services: an electronic directory of experts; an intelligence database; and a competitive analysis group (Sutton 1988, 1989; Teitelbaum 1992). The online *experts directory*, known as AAA (Access to AT&T Analysts), connects technical experts, intelligence analysts, and users seeking information. Staff members are invited to fill out questionnaires detailing their areas of expertise. Users enter keywords describing a topic of interest and get a list of company experts including their job titles, electronic mail addresses, and telephone numbers. In 1993, the AAA network was still operative, with several hundred subscribers (Gilad 1994).

By spreading the net as widely as possible, the best information can sometimes be found in unexpected places. Martin Stark, competitive information manager at AT&T, recalls how two maintenance workers who had signed up for the AAA program proved to be the best sources when a team designing a home alarm feature needed information on fire codes. The network also serves as a broadcast medium for disseminating significant news by electronic mail. Thus, someone who has just picked up information on a topic (such as a competitor) can use the network to send a message to everyone who has previously expressed interest in that competitor.

The *intelligence database* has three components: a market database, a financial database, and a competitive digest. In the online market database, users can find information on 1,400 products, 580 companies, 180 industries, and 65 geographic areas, as well as five-year product market forecasts prepared by the business units themselves. Data are gathered and input by employees in the various business units. Updated news from the database may be routed to users based on keywords they have given in their profiles.

According to Blaine Davis, corporate vice president, strategic and marketing planning,

> the members of the network chose to collect this information and to make it available. . . . The network includes both hourly employees and executive level employees at 110 company locations worldwide. Their functional titles range all the way from strategic planning to product and market management, competitive analysis, engineering, administration, manufacturing, service, development, market research, library services, and training. We average about 110 to 120 log-ins per month, from 50 to 60 users. Those log-ins produce roughly 500 queries. (Davis, quoted in Sutton 1988, 22.)

Although the network is centrally administered by the corporate planning department, each business unit collects its own data, and the 800 users are encouraged to exchange information with each other. In effect, the network is being used to share and synergize the competitive analysis work that is going on in parallel among the various business units.

Martin Stark, competitive information and analysis manager, illustrates:

> For example, one of our competitors is Northern Telecom, and several of our units keep track of that company. The switching group looks at Northern Telecom, and so does the PBX group. We try to find out what kinds of studies they're doing so that when we have a question we're in a position to respond without doing extra work. That's what we mean by "distributed" information. (Stark, quoted in Sutton 1988, 23.)

The financial database reconciles standards and conventions used across the globe, cleaning up and consolidating the data so that users may retrieve meaningful financial data according to accounts, companies, ratios, or years. Finally, the competitive digest is based on published news from all over the world. A unit translates these clippings into daily reports, which include strategic impact statements prepared by internal experts on the news items. The digest and impact statements are sent to senior managers and are then systematically archived to facilitate future access and retrieval.

The third set of services is provided by the central *competitive analysis group*. The group coordinates the scanning that is done by the various business units, and responds to information requests.

From our sketch of the scanning and intelligence function in AT&T, we can discern some of the features that we derived in our discussion of the human visual-perception system. The company attempts to promote distributed information gathering and analysis at many levels of the organization, to ensure that the rich internal store of specialized expertise is well exploited, to encourage information sharing and two-way information flow, and to coordinate these activities from a central locus.

Motorola

Motorola's strategic intelligence system was initiated by Chairman and Chief Executive Officer Bob Galvin, who had become convinced of the need for such a program after serving on the U.S. President's Foreign Intelligence Advisory Board during the 1970s. To develop the system, he hired Jan Herring, a professional intelligence officer who had worked 20 years with the Central Intelligence Agency. Herring explains the final design for the system thus:

> The design is best described as an intelligence community, where there is a clear division of responsibility between the corporate intelligence office and the operational divisions—each organization contributing its part to make up the whole system. Only the intelligence database would be centralized. But because Motorola has a superb worldwide communications network, with some 5,000 electronic mail terminals, all intelligence collectors and users would be able to access the database. . . . One of the major objectives in any intelligence system is to create a sharing culture in the company. Being able to come online and read information that others have put in is an incentive to contribute. Then it becomes a self-sustaining database. (Herring, quoted in Sutton 1988, 10, 28.)

The division of labor worked out as follows: the corporate intelligence office maintained the central database; coordinated collection and served as the clearing house for strategic intelligence reporting; led the corporate-wide analysis projects; and supported the operational divisions' intelligence activities. The operating divisions, on the other hand, ran their own operational or tactical intelligence collection; performed division-level analysis; and supported corporate collection and analysis efforts.

From the start, the corporate office was dedicated to serving the information needs of top management only, both the corporate and the operational. A high-level policy committee, comprising all group vice presidents and chiefs of headquarters functions, assigns intelligence priorities to the unit. The staff of the corporate office are highly trained, some with both intelligence and business experience, and they analyze the information collected to arrive at and recommend alternative courses of action. Strong emphasis is placed on foreign intelligence. Motorola is one of the few U.S. companies that systematically monitors technology developments in Japan, making large investments in obtaining technical literature, learning the language, and developing long-term relationships with Japanese researchers and organizations.

The payoff? Here's an account put together by Gilad from open sources:

> During a meeting in 1985 between Motorola's top management and its European managers, top executives queried the European people about the Japanese in Europe. The Motorola-Europe guys were not impressed. They reported that the Japanese were not really that aggressive in Europe. That did not fit with the character of Motorola's Japanese rivals. Motorola then sent a Japanese-speaking intelligence analyst to Japan to dig out information on the Japanese competitors' capital budgets. After researching for a while, the manager turned out the numbers. They showed that the Japanese planned to double their total capital investment in 1987, but not in their TV and VCR factories, as everyone expected. Instead, they were going after the semiconductor market in Europe. Based on that information, Motorola changed its strategy: it aligned several European partners and worked closely with customers. Despite the Japanese attack, Motorola either retained or increased its market share. (Gilad 1994, 126)

The common element of the environmental scanning systems in AT&T and Motorola is a distributed network of specialists who are called upon to participate in information scanning and analysis. Several teams or subunits monitor different issues in parallel. A central office integrates the processed intelligence and undertakes strategic, corporate-level analysis. The network of experts need not require computer-based communications.

Kraft Inc., for example, identifies a network of competitively knowledgeable employees throughout the firm, each with a specialty, by asking department and division heads for nominations. They name thirty or forty people, generally middle managers, from all functional areas, including manufacturing, operations, R&D, and marketing. These individuals scan selected journals, newspapers, and magazines; send clippings for the research analysts; and create a browse list of articles for managers that include two-sentence summaries and estimated reading times.

Or consider *General Mills*. According to Smith and Prescott (1987), General Mills trained all members of the organization to recognize and collect information of potential competitive interest. The analysis of the collected information was highly distributed—internal focus groups were formed periodically to discuss issues such as the changing industry climate, and competitors' strategies and success factors. Participants in the focus groups were drawn from various functional areas to ensure a diversity of background and specialization.

General Motors, Eastman Kodak, and other Fortune 500 Companies

By comparing the competitor analysis systems of General Motors, Eastman Kodak, and British Petroleum, Ghoshal and Westney (1991) found that all three corporations adopt a dispersed and interconnected system rather than a single analysis unit. Each firm had formal, multimember analysis units at the corporate level, and additional units or specialized individual analysts at the group and business unit levels. Analysis was also linked to specific functional areas, so that, for example, the R&D organization had its own formal analysis unit monitoring technology and product development. In order to integrate the activities of such a dispersed system, the three firms use a mix of coordination mechanisms, including special project teams, ongoing competitor assessment teams, joint theme-related presentations, and support groups.

All three companies formed project teams comprising people from all over the corporation who had particular expertise to focus on specific issues or competitors. Ongoing competitor assessment teams also drew members from all over the corporation, but they were given the task of tracking a single issue or competitor continuously. From time to time, joint presentations were organized around a specified theme or competitor. Analysts from various parts of the organization presented their own views of the issue, with little or no prior coordination, thus stimulating debate and discussion. Finally, the support groups did no analyses, but brought together specialists from all over the company to exchange information, share expertise, and jointly deal with problems such as competing definitions.

Overview

A recent survey of Fortune 500 corporations by Subramanian, et al., (1993) profiled the degree of sophistication and the extent of specialization in the environmental scanning activities of U.S. firms. The survey found that 60 percent of the 101 respondent firms had scanning systems that could be classified as being in the advanced stages of development. Using a classification scheme proposed by Jain (1984), the scanning systems of firms are thought to evolve over time through four distinct stages: primitive, ad hoc, reactive, and proactive, with the last two stages being considered advanced. In the *primitive mode*, scanning is done without an impetus; in the *ad hoc mode*, scanning is done to increase understanding about a specific event; in the *reactive mode*, the objective is to make an appropriate response to the market situation; and in the *proactive mode*, scanning aims at predicting the environment for a desired future.

The current survey found that 25 percent of the respondents had proactive scanning systems, while another 35 percent had reactive systems. Only 10 percent were considered to be working with primitive systems, with the remaining

30 percent scanning in the ad hoc mode. Comparing these results with those of Jain's similar survey a decade ago indicates a movement towards more advanced scanning systems—the proportion of firms scanning proactively (the most evolved mode) tripled from 8 percent in the 1984 survey to 25 percent in the 1993 study, while the proportion of firms scanning with primitive systems shrunk from 31 percent to only 10 percent. The new study also measured the sophistication of the scanning systems by scoring three attributes: the existence of a distinct and separate group of people involved in environmental scanning, the continuity of the scanning as an ongoing, year-round activity, and the number of staff dedicated to performing the scanning function. Results showed that 52 percent of the firms studied had specialized scanning systems, where scanning was continuous and the responsibility of a separate unit. An average of eight employees were dedicated to the scanning activity.

Environmental Scanning in U.K. Corporations

Lester and Waters (1989) studied the environmental scanning activities of seven large, well-known, but unnamed U.K. corporations. The companies range in sales from £600 million to £41 billion, and employ between 9,000 and 130,000 people. Their businesses are in industrial gases and health care, oil supply, refining, and marketing; construction, energy, engineering, and transportation; confectionery and drinks; automotive and electronic component distribution; telecommunications and electronic systems; and motors, defense, and aerospace.

Table 5.1 summarizes the scanning modes in these firms, and compares the roles of the strategic business units with the central corporate planning department. (The seventh company is not reported in detail for reasons of confidentiality.) As can be seen from the table, with one exception these firms perform scanning in a decentralized, bottom-up mode, in which the business units do most of the information gathering and analysis, and the information is then consolidated centrally. Two firms emphasize that their scanning is also done through project groups or teams that carry out in-depth analyses of particular issues, an approach that is advocated by Prescott and Smith (1987). The central planning department typically sets the scene by identifying key issues in the external environment for business units to consider, coordinating the planning-scanning efforts, and consolidating information, that is, combining the information "to grow a wider interpretation."

The relationship between the planning department and business is two-way: business units do most of the detailed scanning and analysis; the planning department assists, challenges, and cross-checks the former's assessments. Some degree of duplication is necessary so that the central planning department can effectively discuss issues with the business units. Scanning information is used for long-term strategic decision making at two main levels—the executive

Table 5.1   Environmental Scanning in Six Large U.K. Corporations

	Scanning/Planning Mode	Role of Business Units	Role of Planning Dept
Company 1	• Decentralized • Bottom-up • Continuous	• Do most of information searching • Discuss strategic issues continuously	• Identify key environmental issues • Consolidate views from SBUs • Coordinate planning [1 planner]
Company 2	• Top-down • Continuous and ad-hoc scanning	• Produce own competitive analysis • Provide information on short-term trends to CPD	• Initiate planning, including trends analysis • Review SBUs' analyses, grow to wider interpretation [Director + 3 planners]
Company 3	• Decentralized • Bottom-up • Ad hoc, project work on specialized, detailed investigations	• Do most of information searching • 2-way informal information flow with CPD	• Define planning scope for SBUs • Critique, cross-check SBU assessments • Consolidate information [Director + 3 planners]
Company 4	• Decentralized • Teams formed to do intensive strategic reviews • Continuous	• Market scanning by SBUs, continuously and in detail • SBUs produce own plans from scans	• Sends planners to work with SBUs in teams • Act as consultants [2 managers + 5 planners]
Company 5	• Decentralized • Bottom-up	• Each SBU has own scanning system • Technical specialists do the scanning • Initiate new ideas upwards	• Identify themes for SBUs to consider • Summarize SBU assessments [Director + 3 planners]
Company 6	• Decentralized • Bottom-up	• SBUs montior, analyze own environment • Supply information and analysis for Databook	• Identify key environmental issues • Prepares computerized Databook of consolidated information from SBUs [3 planners]
		(CPD: Corporate Planning Department SBU: Strategic Business Unit)	

board level and business unit level, with the central planning department providing the link between these levels.

In summary, the overall impression is that scanning in these large U.K. organizations is distributed and bottom-up, with most of the detailed, specialized searching and analysis done by the business units. Scanning is both continuous and ad hoc, with a few companies forming project teams to investigate key environmental issues. Information integration is done in stages at both the board and business unit level.

The pharmaceutical industry is highly information intensive. Companies derive their revenue streams from a relatively small number of products, which are the result of long and intensive research and development. Because sales may be quickly and drastically jeopardized by competitor products, it becomes imperative to know as much information as possible about competitors' activities.

Desai and Bawden (1993) surveyed competitive intelligence practices in Britain's pharmaceutical industry, with special reference to the role of the information professionals and the collection and use of information. Managers of information units at ten pharmaceutical companies were interviewed. The study confirmed that the competitive intelligence function is taken very seriously within the U.K. research-based pharmaceutical industry. Information gathering emphasized traditional sources such as journals, newsletters, printed directories, and electronic databases. More unconventional sources were underused— sales representatives, patents information, and external experts were three potentially useful sources that were not well exploited.

Most information units provided competitive intelligence only reactively, in response to information requests. Any proactive information provision was limited to general current awareness services. Information analysis, evaluation, and integration were done more by end users than by the information staff. The three groups of users who used the information unit most intensively were the R&D and clinical research staff, managers and team leaders, and senior management. Feedback from users seems to be lacking, and many information units made no formal attempt to assess the value of the information they provide or the information technologies that were applied.

Environmental Scanning in Swedish Corporations

According to Herring (1992), more than five hundred Swedish firms in the banking, insurance, electronics, furniture, automotive, and defense industries are actively practicing environmental scanning and business intelligence. At least fifty of the major corporations, including L.M. Ericsson, Volvo, and ABB, can claim world-class business intelligence systems, where information collection and analysis are well integrated and closely linked to corporate planning and operations. Information is collected through the effective use of their own employees as well as through consulting firms, Swedish diplomats, and banks' overseas offices. The capabilities in business intelligence are the result of collaboration and coordination between companies, the government, and the education sector.

Historically, the Swedish banks have always been considered the leaders in the country's development of business intelligence. At the beginning of this century, Wallenberg Bank was the first to establish its own highly successful intelligence program. In the late 1970s, the major banks came together to support the forming of UC Research, a fee-based company that provides database services consisting of published information; gathers intelligence proactively using the participating banks' foreign offices to answer specific requests; and communicates with some three thousand business agents around the world who may be approached for their expertise or information.

Government is also active in business intelligence activities. Sweden's overseas embassies often support the information gathering needs of Swedish companies. As much as 60 percent of the government's intelligence coverage is given to economic and technological matters.

In leading universities such as the Stockholm School of Economics and the University of Lund, full-time courses in business intelligence are regularly taught. (The former is soon expected to graduate the world's first PhD students in the field of business intelligence.) Herring attributes the strong educational base to the efforts of Professor Stevan Dedijer, who had served in World War II as an OSS officer and later as advisor to several developing countries. Dedijer began teaching and preaching business intelligence at the university of Lund in the early 1970s. Over the past two decades, Dedijer "has created not only a body of educational knowledge concerning intelligence and its application in the business world but has produced hundreds of well-trained intelligence officers for the Swedish business community." (Herring 1992a, 45).

Hedin (1993) studied the environmental scanning and business intelligence activities of ten large Swedish corporations: Volvo (automobile), Astra-Draco (pharmaceutical), SAS (airline), Electrolux (appliances), Telia (telecommunications), Ericsson Radio Systems (telecommunications), Insurance Group (insurance), SCA Graphic (forestry), Gambro (medical technology), and Celsius Tech (defense electronics). Three of the companies had the intelligence staff function located at corporate headquarters level, three had the function at the business unit or area level, while the remaining four had units or personnel in the marketing or product-planning department. Several of the firms have had their systematic intelligence function in the present form for three to eight years. The number of people in these functions ranged from one to fifteen.

The companies consider market information from their internal sources to be of paramount importance, and that much of the information about competitors already exist within the organization, being regularly obtained by the sales force, technical staff, managers, and others. Unfortunately, the information is scattered and unorganized, and has to be centrally coordinated through an internal network.

At Ericsson Radio, for instance, a Business Intelligence Coordinator establishes contact with and coordinates the intelligence activities of the various divisions and business units. Internal sources are also used when the information from external sources needed to be verified or when in-depth analysis was required. The most commonly used external sources were, in order, newspapers, industry press, online databases, trade shows, and annual reports. Informal contacts with the employees of competitor firms are a way of obtaining information, especially about other competitors they have in common. This form of information sharing takes place mainly at trade shows and conferences. In analyzing the information collected, the most common methods used are SWOT analysis, financial model analysis, scenarios, and benchmarking. In situations when the lack of time prevented formal analysis, the information was sent on directly to managers for their own use. For disseminating intelligence, the most commonly used products are reports and newsletters.

At Electrolux, the public affairs unit issues about twenty different newsletters. Reports and memos are prepared for ad hoc or specific project work. One firm outsourced its market intelligence database to an external consultancy and ordered reports when necessary. Two firms strongly preferred verbal intelligence briefings at meetings.

Displaying competitors' products is also a way of presenting intelligence. Telia organizes an annual "The Week of the Competition" during which switchboards and other products from competitors are displayed. Volvo has a center where employees may test-drive cars produced by competitors.

Overall, the most frequent users of business intelligence are top management, the marketing department, and the sales force. Newsletters, however, are distributed to almost everyone in the firm, and so reach a much wider audience. Among managers and other personnel, interest is growing about the importance and use of business intelligence. From 1992 to 1993, six of the ten firms had obtained more resources for their scanning functions, either a larger budget, more computer support, or more staff. Three firms had their resource support unchanged, and only one firm decreased its resources.

Hedin concludes his study with this observation:

> A successful intelligence function does not seem to be dependent upon a large centralized staff or sophisticated computer systems. What seems to be required is an "intelligent" intelligence system, where the parallel intelligence process is recognized and where internal information is shared between different units in a network of formal as well as informal contacts. The future of formalized business intelligence functions lies perhaps not only in improving the relationship with top management, but also in the function of an

internal information clearing-house or a network coordinator, whose mission it is to educate and assist other units regarding intelligence activities. The "spider-in-the-web" metaphor may in this case illustrate the role of the function. (Hedin 1993, 135)

Environmental Scanning in Japanese Corporations

Corporations headquartered in Japan are ahead of United States and European corporations in the area of environmental scanning and business intelligence. Several scholars, intelligence professionals, business executives, and government officials have observed that it is the relentless pursuit of information, intelligence, and knowledge that is the single most important factor in explaining Japanese economic growth since World War II. Harvard-based Japan scholar Ezra Vogel (1979) wrote that "if any single factor explains Japanese success, it is the group-directed quest for knowledge. When Daniel Bell, Peter Drucker and others hailed the coming of the post-industrial society in which knowledge replaced capital as society's most important resource, this new conception became a great rage in Japan's leading circles. But these leading circles were merely articulating the latest formulation of what already had become conventional Japanese wisdom, the supreme importance of the pursuit of knowledge."

Through tracing the historical development of intelligence activities in Japan, Dedijer (1991) supports and extends Vogel's hypothesis by further suggesting that it is the Japanese skills in social intelligence that gave Japan its crucial edge: "Japan since 1868 had among the best economic, trade, technological transfer, and cultural intelligence in the world." (Dedijer 1991, 15; see also discussion on social intelligence in Chapter 4.)

Intelligence professionals such as Jan Herring and Herbert Meyer have similarly noted that information and intelligence gathering is endemic to Japanese culture. It seems that everyone at every level takes an active role, and is often given explicit instructions on what information to collect. "Really, there's no such thing as a Japanese entity that doesn't have intelligence gathering built in . . . . Pulling in information is part and parcel of what the Japanese are paid to do. You will not find that in the job description of most American managers." (Meyer, quoted in Martin 1992, 44)

Environmental scanning as practiced by different Japanese corporations share a surprisingly common pattern (the same isomorphism has been observed in the scanning activities of large South Korean companies, in a 1988 study by Ghoshal). Information gathering is typically achieved through six channels and sources: the planning division, individual specialists, patent department, advisory boards, individual employees, and technology attachés (Lagerstam 1990).

— The *planning department* specializes in collecting and directing the collection of information in the firm. It has a very high status and reports directly to the vice president of technology.

— Information gathering and analysis is often organized into research project groups, consisting of *individual specialists* with expert knowledge in their fields. The companies consider them to be the supreme information collectors.

— In the *patent department*, as much as one-fifth of the staff may be engaged in information collection, that is, scanning other competitors' patent applications to monitor their technological progress.

— Companies generally invite retired professors to sit on their *advisory boards*, with the intention of transferring information from academia to the firms.

— Apart from formalized units, every *employee* is expected to participate actively in information gathering. Their efforts often result in written suggestions submitted to managers. The Japanese average eight suggestions per employee per year, the highest rate in the world.

— *Attachés* are stationed abroad to catch the latest news and developments. Biotechnology companies, for example, typically have over ten attachés each, stationed mainly in New York, Dusseldorf, and Los Angeles.

The same six methods of gathering information are used in most Japanese companies. Such a multiplicity of methods must lead to a certain amount of duplication, but the Japanese firms encourage this information redundancy, allowing more than one unit to gather and analyze the same information, in order to ensure that everything important has been included and to speed up the process (Lagerstam 1990). (In the chapter on information sources, we will elaborate on specific sources and techniques that Japanese firms have been known to exploit.)

In business, the superpowers of information and intelligence gathering are the Japanese trading companies, or *sogo shosha*. The total revenue of the nine major sogo shosha make up approximately 30 percent of Japan's GNP—together they handle nearly 50 percent of Japan's total exports and 60 percent of its imports. The nine corporations (C. Itoh, Kanematsu Gosho, Marubeni, Mitsubishi, Mitsui, Nichimen, Nissho Iwai, Sumitomo, Toyo Menka) employ more than 60,000 people in their 2,200 offices throughout the world, and have total annual sales in 1990 ranging from US$45 billion to $160 billion. According to Juro Nakagawa, a general manager of Nichimen Corporation,

> Japan's economic development after World War II owes much of its success to trading companies. Their employees have cultivated and established contacts within government circles, international agencies, trade circles and research institutions. They regularly attend innumerable conferences, exhibitions and social gatherings and they have developed a corporate culture based on gathering information from a variety of sources including trade magazines, newspapers and business associates in order to establish new businesses. (Nakagawa 1992, 42)

Each sogo shosha invests huge amounts of resources to create its own far-reaching network for data gathering. The Mitsubishi intelligence staff in New York, for example, takes up two entire floors of a Manhattan skyscraper. It is reported that Mitsui's business intelligence unit, the Mitsui Knowledge Industry Corporation, is superior to the CIA in collecting information, so much so that the Japanese government was said to have used Mitsui's network during World War II (Teitelbaum 1992). At the Tokyo headquarters of Marubeni (a trading company serving the Fuyo keiretsu, which includes Canon, Fuji Bank, and Nissan), row upon row of clerical workers could be seen diligently filing away slips of paper, photographs, charts, and reports sent from far-flung employees on competing businesses and businesspersons (Duggan and Emenstodt 1990). The sogo shosha's voracious appetite for information has been described vividly:

> To serve their broad commercial interests, the Japanese trading com-panies—the sogo shosha—have created vast overseas data-collection networks. Indeed, every branch office of every trading company operates like an information vacuum cleaner, sucking in statistics, documents, brochures, articles from technical and current events magazines, reports delivered at industrial and scientific conferences attended by one or another Japanese executive, and even gossip picked up at dinner parties or on the golf course. . . . Raw informa-tion collected by Japanese executives stationed overseas is transmit-ted daily—sometimes hourly or even by the minute—back to Japan. There, at company headquarters, a senior intelligence staff collates this raw material and shapes the finished intelligence products for key policy makers within the trading company. And, yes, in one form or another—informally as well as formally—much of this intelli-gence is shared with executives at the trading companies' manufac-turing partners and with selected Japanese government officials, who move the information around still more. (Meyer 1987, 58-59)

Through diligence and tenacity, the sogo shosha have become masters of gathering vast quantities of business intelligence information by tapping the most public, boring sources, and cultivating legitimate, open human contacts. Juro Nakagawa, then general manager of the new ventures development divi-sion of the Nichimen Corporation (now a business professor at Aichi Gakuin University), relates a few personal examples of intelligence gathering during his thirty years with a Japanese trading company.

> 1. One Sunday in 1971 in New Delhi when I was reading the *Hindustan Times*, I came across an article reporting that there was a shortage of antibiotics in India. I immediately transmitted this information to Japan. After six months of negotiations with the State Trading Corporation of India, we got the first contract for the sale of

antibiotics such as penicillin and streptomycin. The current annual sales of this business ran between US$3 million and US$5 million.

2. In 1978, we exported 40,000 Japanese cars to Chile, amounting to US$400 million—the lion's share among the Japanese competitors. This success was due to information received from our agent in Santiago to the effect that the import duty on cars with a maximum of a 1,000 cc engine was only 10 percent in comparison with 100 percent on cars with larger engine capacity. Our manufacturer had confidence in our information and expanded production capacity of its 800 cc engines. Here again, human intelligence was vital in establishing new business.

3. In 1984, I made a contact with BC Telephone of Vancouver for importing database management know-how for video text (Telidon) to Japan. This business materialized after one year of negotiations during which time we learned from an article in a trade magazine that our Japanese competitor had imported similar technology from Canada.

4. Another example of success in business based on information collected from newspaper articles is from my work in Canada. In Calgary in May 1987, I read an article in the [Toronto] *Globe and Mail* about a revolutionary 3D medical imaging system invented by a Canadian medical doctor in Toronto. Upon contacting him, I learned that three Japanese companies had already approached him. Nevertheless, after three years of enthusiastic and hard negotiations with the inventor, we were made the sole exporting agent for Japan. (Nakagawa 1992, 43-44)

In summary, there is much to suggest that environmental scanning and business intelligence is the vital key to the strategic success of Japanese organizations in the international arena (Tomioka 1990). The Japanese energy that drives the information gathering, the diligence with which information is communicated and shared in a timely fashion, the universal commitment to acquire and accumulate knowledge, and the strategic use of information to create new businesses, enter new markets, and strengthen existing positions—these are the defining traits of intelligent organizations that have learned to collect, organize, analyze, and use information to beget competitive advantage. Recall the rows upon rows of clerks filing away slips of paper, the coordinated teams of businessmen swarming trade shows, the eager employees on study tours perpetually firing their cameras, the endowment of professorial chairs and the establishment of affiliation programs at top U.S. universities, and what we are witnessing is a "massive human 'infrastructure' that sends in bits and pieces of competitive data in a continuous flow, like a giant net that makes sure very little can and will be missed. . . . This is the infrastructure that almost guarantees competitive learning." (Gilad 1994)

Scanning for Future Learning

In Chapter 1 we saw how the National Computer Board of Singapore, master planner of the country's series of ambitious and successful information technology plans, is an organization skilled at learning about the future. How does such a future-oriented organization scan its environment?

One of the special features of the Board's scanning system is a strategic information outpost based in the San Francisco Bay area, close to two world class research universities with excellent libraries and the knowledge-rich Silicon Valley. For the period 1990-1994, Seng Hon Wong, one of the Board's most senior staff, worked in Stanford and Berkeley as the Board's full-time environment scanner. Wong tracks more than 100 sources continuously—daily newspapers, weekly trade publications, monthly periodicals, industry newsletters, conferences, reports from market research companies, Internet newsgroups, and many other sources. Wong was a frequent user of the business libraries of the universities at Stanford and Berkeley.

Wong tries to meet the one key person in a leading edge corporation who has the overall technological picture and can provide insights that go beyond the media hype. Such a person is likely to be, for example, the chief multimedia technologist or equivalent at Apple Computer or Bell Atlantic. They are prepared to give objective accounts, because they can differentiate between information that is strategic to their own organizations, and information that would benefit from sharing and discussion. Also, Wong finds that the exchanges in Internet newsgroups are a useful barometer of the level of interest in specific issues, and act as an antenna of shifting directions and emerging concerns.

Information collected from these various sources is given time to solidify in Wong's mind. Every four to six weeks, the accumulated material is processed to pick out the best or most significant items. A short commentary is added to each item, and the material is then faxed back to targeted senior managers at the Board's Singapore office. These items and their commentaries are stored in a microcomputer database that is also indexed by keywords.

About twice a year, Wong returns to Singapore to guide the corporate planning exercise, explore the feasibility of new strategic applications, and update himself on recent developments. Wong confesses that it is sometimes hard to get through to very busy managers—new intelligence has the best chance of hitting home when there is a crisis looming. It is also difficult trying to be proactive, because people need to retune their mental models first in order to understand and relate the incoming information. The annual corporate planning exercise is an opportunity for unlearning old paradigms and creating new frameworks.

One way of shifting paradigms is to use scenario-based planning, a technique first developed at Royal Dutch Shell, which has been enhanced and embellished by a number of consulting organizations in North America and elsewhere. Wong believes that developing a coherent set of shared, common scenarios provides an effective tool that facilitates discussion, organizational learning, and decision making.

Close-Up View of Five Canadian CEOs

So far, we have been describing the scanning systems and procedures of large corporations and multinationals. Thanks to their high profiles in the media, and to publicly available information from their former employees and consultants, we have a fair idea (though not always the most up-to-date picture) of their business intelligence systems. Although we have been discussing mostly scanning systems and structures, it is individuals in the organization who gather in information and use it in consequential ways.

To better appreciate environmental scanning in action, we need to see how individual managers and others have actually obtained and used information. In this section, we move from macroscopic descriptions to a close-up view of how Canadian CEOs scan on a daily basis. Environmental scanning, of course, is not limited to large organizations, and here we will concentrate on the scanning by CEOs of small to medium-size companies which do not have formal scanning systems. We present below five first-person accounts base on personal interviews that were conducted recently with 13 Canadian CEOs in the publishing and telecommunications industries (Auster and Choo 1994a, 1994b; Choo 1993, 1994).

Cable Television/Private Paging

Ben (all names are fictitious) is CEO of one of Canada's largest cable television operators and the largest private paging company. The firm employs 450 people and has annual sales of $65 million. Ben, a certified accountant, is in his early forties; he has been CEO for six years, and has been with the firm for over fifteen years. There are certain types of decisions in which Ben would use environmental information more intensively:

> When it comes to a decision involving new technology, I would scan the horizon much more closely. I would want to answer the question: Has this technology been used anywhere else in any shape or form, not necessarily in the way that we are thinking of? We would tend to look externally much more frequently on a technical issue. On the other hand, when it comes to decisions about the market, I would scan less because I feel confident that our people know our market best. Personally, I do a lot of reading. I look for creative ideas on how new broadcasting technologies are being used to create enhanced services in other countries, be they England, Australia, Asia, or Africa, for example, and then I start thinking about how these applications could or could not be applied in the Canadian context.

In making decisions about the application of paging technology where a few technologies are being combined in new ways, Ben feels that his firm is basically on its own to create ideas and infrastructures. For example, Ben set up an internal Strategic Planning Committee consisting of four people to evaluate and decide upon external opportunities: "The Committee comprises a full-time head, myself, my chief operating officer, and the head of cable operations. We take in information from the functional groups, look for linkages, and ensure that relevant information is disseminated and assessed by the functional specialists."

Ben described how the company came to a recent decision to experiment with the use of Digital Video Compression (DVC) to transmit programs to pay-TV customers. According to Ben, this was the world's first commercial application of DVC technology, and the project partners included four other cable TV operators and a program vendor. Ben identified the main sources of information that eventually led to the project as his own reading of current engineering articles on DVC, his participation in the strategic planning committee of the Canadian Cable TV Association, suppliers, marketing staff, and government regulatory agencies. Ben recalled that

> information from these various sources had to come together for us to decide to go ahead with the project. The technology was first assessed to be ready and stabilized. Suppliers had to be prepared to experiment. Marketing people had to see the possibility of a viable market. Regulators must support the project. All these were integral to the decision making process to go ahead with the experiment.

Telecommunications

Frank is CEO of the second largest long distance telecommunications reseller in Canada. He is in his late thirties and has worked with major Canadian telecommunication companies before joining his present firm. He was appointed CEO about a year ago. When the firm was formed in 1990, sales for that year were $6 million; in 1992, sales for the first quarter exceeded $10 million, and Frank expects annual sales to exceed $40 million. The firm in 1992 employed 47 persons, up from 28 when it started. Frank sees the survival of this firm contingent upon a congenial regulatory climate:

> We operate in a highly regulated environment where the rules are changing with dramatic impact on our long-term survival and business viability. We have to stay totally informed from a legal perspective. At the same time the significance of these regulatory decisions goes beyond the regulatory: we have to take the information as a strategic tool for developing markets and positioning ourselves vis-à-vis the competition. We get a lot of ideas about creating new

products and services in reading how CanPhone [pseudonym for a major Canadian telephone company] files applications and defines [its] positions.

When making decisions about legal and regulatory issues, Frank takes in a lot of advice. He consults the general counsel in the New York head office, while in Canada he has a lawyer who is expert in Canadian law. In describing how he uses environmental information, Frank said that

> sources are very important. Content is clearly important: is the information the regulatory filing itself or somebody's interpretation of the filing? Have we used the source before? It is very important for me to decide who should have the information, to pass on the information to one of my directors. So I become the "focal point" of information coming in. I have a VP who acts as the idea person—I take the idea to him, and he studies it to death to decide if there is indeed an opportunity for [the firm].

Frank recalled how CanPhone responded to the entry of telecommunications resellers in the Canadian market. Frank said that the telecommunications resale market was created in March 1989 when the CRTC (the regulatory body) decided to allow the resale of high-speed digital bandwidth. Resellers could buy digital leased lines, and run them through multiplexing and switching equipment to create their own brand of long-distance services. Shortly after this decision, CanPhone introduced new, significantly lower tariffs for WATS long-distance services. According to Frank, "CanPhone was locking us into long-term leases on high-speed digital leased lines, and then cutting our margins by applying to reduce WATS rates, which we cannot resell but have to compete against."

CanPhone filed the WATS rate reduction in April 1991 with the CRTC, which then made the filing publicly known. Frank's firm proceeded to petition and appeal the filing, and asked CRTC for a public hearing, which it agreed to. Frank's first source of information about CanPhone's rates filing was thus the CRTC. Additional information and analysis came from Frank's contacts at CanaTel [pseudonym], a company at which he once worked. As a result of CanPhone's rates filing, Frank decided to redesign the firm's pricing schedule: to move from a pricing structure based on WATS zones to one that is based on telephone Area Codes.

The new pricing gave greater flexibility in service-price offerings, and customers could compute their savings more clearly. Frank recalled that "we started using this rate structure in the summer of 1991—we were the first to do this, we had some success, and since then, two of our competitors have copied our approach." When the CRTC finally approved CanPhone's new rates in March 1992 (eleven months later), Frank's competitive rate structure was already in place, and he could adjust rates accordingly in less than a week in order to match CanPhone's new prices.

Data Network Services

Harry is CEO of a firm providing packet-switched data network services through fourteen nodes in major cities across Canada, with international access to hundreds of cities worldwide. The firm has annual sales of $8 million and employs 10 persons. Harry has been CEO for two years, and joined the firm six years ago. He has a bachelor's degree in electronics engineering.

Harry said that most of his external information comes from *The Globe and Mail*: "it's something I read every morning almost without exception. Generally, I trust the information appearing in *The Globe and Mail*. . . . *The Globe and Mail* is a very typical source that I use, particularly about government regulation, as well as to get business news about our customer companies." Other sources that Harry mentioned included internal newsletters and press clipping compilations from the U.S. and U.K. parent companies, trade magazines, and telephone calls from business associates. Harry characterizes his way of using environmental information in this way:

> I tend to skim over information, to develop impressions about trends, to develop a feeling for the situation. For example, I read in *The Globe and Mail* today that the Canadian dollar is diving. This is bad news for [us] because our cost is in U.S dollars or U.K. sterling while our revenue is in Canadian dollars. However, reading that one article doesn't make me go out to do something. Instead, it sticks in my mind so that whenever I have to make a decision about currency, that decision would have been different if I hadn't read that article. . . . I tend to use information to build up an image of the trends or a feeling of where things are going. I often cannot use the information I get directly. For example, I may read that the video conferencing market is estimated to be worth $40M next year, that is useful information as it stands, but what I really need to know is the pricing strategy that would get me, say, 25 percent of that market. I get my information "passively," and the chance of getting information that I need right now is small.

Harry related the circumstances that led to the expansion of the firm's data network in Canada. When the firm first started in 1986, it installed equipment in Halifax and Winnipeg, but the provincial telephone companies there had refused to provide interconnection, thus denying its customers dial-up access to the data network. Since dial-up access made up over 90 percent of the business, this meant that the firm's market was limited to Ontario, Quebec, and British Columbia. Harry then explained:

The instance I'm thinking of was a report in *The Globe and Mail* which stated that Manitoba Telephone System was opening its doors, effectively allowing businesses like [ours] to operate. This was quite significant because we've been waiting for two years for this to happen. The report explained the change in regulation and was about 12 column-inches long. I carried the press clipping with me for two months, showing it to people, and mentioning it on e-mail messages. The regulatory change allowed us to install more new equipment in Winnipeg, and to offer new service. Soon after this, the same sort of liberalization happened in Halifax. The combined result was that we could now look at the whole country as our market—we now have the whole country to work from. Once I had information about the new developments in hand, I could now go to headquarters and trigger the process of expanding our business here. I used the information in writing business plans, in writing proposals, and when setting up my business strategy—it was one more important piece in the puzzle.

Book Publishing

Rob is CEO of a publishing firm that is involved with the printing, publication, and wholesaling of books. His firm employs 100 people and has annual sales of about US$40 million. Rob is in his early forties, and joined the firm three years ago as CEO. He describes his daily scanning thus:

The newspaper first thing in the morning. I get the *Wall Street Journal*, *The New York Times*, *The Globe and Mail*, the *Toronto Star*, *The Sun* every day. There are certain things I look for in certain papers. First thing I look for is the exchange rate because we do business with the U.S. and the U.K.—where's the dollar going? What's the one month forward, and three-months forward, and six-months forward? That will affect the decisions that I personally will have to make that day as to whether to buy currency futures or make a purchase or postpone the decision to make a purchase. I look at world events because there are books that we publish that are very much a part of world events. . . . I have a shortwave radio that I keep in my office because there may be events that we hear about but we don't have the full details. The thing that I love about a shortwave is that you can get a far more immediate sense of what is going on somewhere else in the world than you will by the time a piece of news has worked its way through all the bureaucratic filters of the news organizations.

If we have to make a business decision, of course we talk to people who are closest to those factors that will help us make the best decision. If it's a financial decision, we talk to financial consultants. Of course we talk to bankers. If it's something that involves a strategy that may have legal implications, we talk to a number of lawyers. We have lawyers with specific areas of expertise that we talk to. This is ongoing every day, sometimes more than others depending what we're involved in. In terms of the true nature of the business that we're in—books—we get newsletters, magazines. We're renowned as a literary publisher and as a children's book publisher. I happen to like print information because it's portable, I can use it whenever I want to use it and it's eclectic in nature. I can take whatever I need from it.

Rob relates a recent case of using external information to make a strategic decision:

Now, in the past few years a number of economic conditions has radically altered that [retail sales pattern]. We have a terrific recession. We had a war last year. In Canada, specifically, the GST [Goods and Services Tax] was introduced. Those three factors were a triple whammy all at the same time. . . . Price was never so much a determining factor, at least in our business, as it has been for the past couple of years, and certainly with the introduction of the GST. Now what did we do to react to that? We gather our sources from a number of areas: we look at business surveys that are done, we talk to retailers and read their internal and external reports, we talk to people that track consumer trends professionally; poll takers, for example, We look at the cross-border shopping phenomenon which really "blossomed," if that's the right word, with the introduction of the GST.

We looked at all of that and decided that we had to make a very deliberate strategic decision: how do we, in a business that traditionally has very thin margins, compete with the U.S.—and not only U.S. publishers but with entities that were not thought of before as our competitors? . . . All the information we got from external sources as well as our own internal information confirmed that people were primarily concerned about price— not so much about quality but about price. So we had to make a strategic decision about the steps we would take to lower our selling prices to our customers, so they in turn could lower their selling prices to their customers, [and thereby] keep whatever business we could in Canada and to compete on even terms with the U.S., which didn't have the GST and had had lower prices to begin with.

We did that by eliminating duplication of warehousing and shipping in Canada and in effect passing on those savings to our customers. . . . We had a separate distribution set-up in Canada, which had always been the traditional model. The U.S. had their publishing and their warehousing and their distribution for the U.S., and Canada would basically duplicate that operation for the Canadian market. However, now, with electronic ordering and electronic data interchange, with the advent of computer workspaces, an extraordinary variety of workers within any group have immediate access to the information and immediate transferal of the information. We came to the conclusion, after studying this for about six months, that it wasn't necessary for us to duplicate the same warehousing and distribution that existed in the U.S. five hundred miles away.

Journal Publishing

Steve is CEO of a firm publishing and printing a wide range of magazines and periodicals. The firm employs 1,500 people and has annual sales of about US$100 million. Steve is in his early fifties, and joined the firm as CEO four years ago, having worked previously in the marketing area. Here is how Steve describes his scanning style:

I think that since I must ultimately carry the responsibility for the decisions that we make as a company, I feel the need to be informed to some extent, though not in depth, on all the issues that affect the business. [Then] I'm able to know enough about a subject to understand who else will know more about it, where I can get more information, whether it has relevance in fact to what's going on and, as a result, I tend to devour information. I listen to a lot of news programming on radio. I watch a lot of business television. I scan just about every business magazine that exists, industry-specific newsletters, analysts' reports on competitors and suppliers. I read four or five or maybe more newspapers a day. When I say "read," I'm looking for information. Sometimes I will note that I've seen it, or put an "x" on it, ask someone to copy it, because I think I may need it in the next couple of weeks. Or, I may just recall that it's there and do nothing because I know that if in a few months' time I need something on that subject, I can go to the computer and get online with whatever services we're using and recall all that stuff . . . .

I believe that if you go out and listen to everybody, what you'll eventually get is cognitive dissonance—you're going to have your own belief supported by someone and you'll attach yourself to the information that you'll ultimately want to be true. That's useless and deluding so I don't go looking for these kinds of things. You listen to someone you trust and to your own experience and make the decision. Reading another twelve hours on the subject is not going to improve my decision at all. I'd much rather do something I believe in and be proven wrong than do something someone else told me to do that I don't believe in and be proven wrong. . . .

I couldn't live without the *Wall Street Journal*, my acquaintances who are interested in the same business things that I am, [and] daily newspapers. I could probably do without television and the radio, although I feel less knowledgeable if I don't listen to the BBC world news once in a while. I'd have trouble doing without *The Economist* because I think it has good global information. I could easily do without *Time Magazine, Maclean's, Newsweek*. Government officials to me are a total waste of time. I can't imagine that there's anything they can tell me that I didn't learn six months earlier somewhere else.

In a perfect world, I would watch half an hour of business television in the morning between 6 am and 7 am; then I'd listen to the radio for half an hour; I'd be reading *The Globe and Mail*; I'd then read the *Wall Street Journal*. Then during the day I'd read a couple of Montreal newspapers, a couple of other financial newspapers, *The Economist* cover to cover, *Forbes Magazine* and a few other things I find interesting and stimulating. I'll occasionally read *Business Week*; trade publications. Printed and aural sources are important before I then go asking people. I can always find someone who knows more than I've seen or heard in the media because the people writing these stories aren't experts—they often don't ask the right questions. Good reporters get a lot but not as much as someone in the industry. I'd never accept I've learned as much as I need to know from those sources, but it's a starting point.

Steve recalls an interesting incident concerning his re-acquisition of the publishing business that was sold earlier to a large Canadian newspaper publishing and printing conglomerate (CanPub, fictitious):

We had some interviews on the subject of CanPub's sale and our potential interest in buying our business back with several members of the media who, using what they got from us, went to other people and at the end of this whole linkage of meetings and discussions and reports in the press, we gained some insight into the pressures CanPub was under that we had not previously had: specifically, that the purchaser for their printing assets was not going to complete the purchase unless he had the security of our business guaranteed to him. That was a vital piece of information that allowed us to successfully complete the purchase at less than 50 percent of what CanPub was originally asking for that asset because the more important decision they were viewing was the sale of their printing business.

Now how did this happen? It happened by getting outside of the day-to-day [routine], meeting and chatting with people who were in the business. I think that if you work at it, you can learn just about anything you want to know from bankers, accountants, [and] media people who cover the industry . . . if they don't have the answer, [they] go searching for it and sometimes even write it up. If you have a desire to learn something, you can find it out. Most of what's valuable to know, isn't available as a matter of record anywhere; it's the *spin* that people are putting on [that becomes] a matter of record. I'm a big believer that networking and going on a search as a result of normal business contacts that you have yields enormous benefits. People are always trying to sell us something, or do something with us, and if you ask the right five questions, at the end of the meeting you learn a hell of a lot.

There are very few banks in Canada, and they do business with a lot of people. We do business with three banks. Those three do business with most companies in Canada and at this particular meeting I tried something on for size, having learned that the bank with whom we were meeting was also acting as an advisor to one of the parties in the transaction, and I gave them my view of why the transaction from our own end wasn't as interesting as I hoped it would be and one of the bankers let slip, "Oh, we were afraid of that." Once I heard that, I knew that the presumption that I had just made was correct. That was a multi-million dollar bit of information—that slip of someone's lips. It was a perfectly normal reaction to what I had said, but what it served to do was confirm something that I was really speculating about.

You don't get to run a company without having the ability to understand what's being said, and not just what's being said but how it's being said: what the body chemistry usually means that's accompanying it. I was able to use that piece of information together with some other bits and pieces of information— some of which I read on the pages of *The Globe and Mail*, some of which I dug out of other people by asking questions—and put together a set of circumstances that allowed me to complete the transaction at a much more favorable price than I would have otherwise. The route the information took was from their mouths to my ear, and from their gestures to my eye, and that was saved and used directly by me.

Summary

The anecdotal profiles presented above certainly support the general impression that experienced top managers have their own unique skills in making sense of ambiguous developments, detecting weak signals of change, catching the significance of subtly nuanced messages, drawing connections between disparate events, all the while interpreting implications and opportunities for the organizations they lead. These are valuable skills, honed by many years of experience and learning, and their efficacy should not be diluted by unnecessarily increasing the amount of information that these managers have to handle. On the other hand, the top manager is but one person, whose attention resources and cognitive capabilities are limited, and whose information gathering may depend more on circumstance and happenstance than on guidance and selection. What could be helpful is a scanning system to supply top managers with relevant, filtered information that will elevate and intensify their information processing skills.

Much of what the executives revealed of themselves is consistent with our discussion in Chapter 3 of managers as information users, but a couple of important qualifications are raised. There is little doubt that managers, and especially top managers, greatly prefer to obtain their information directly from human sources. At the same time, research data suggests that these face-to-face interactions are taking place in the context of pre-existing knowledge that the manager already has about a particular situation or issue. Sometimes the knowledge comes from experience, but just as important, it also comes from having read widely and carefully about the topic—in other words, from having done the necessary homework so that the right questions might be posed during those personal meetings.

Again, there is little doubt that managers spend most of their time dealing with urgent, operational matters rather than planning for the long term. Nevertheless, the data indicate that the separation between the tactical and the strategic may have been overemphasized, and that both sets of concerns are in practice closely intertwined. The handling of operational crises may cumulatively result in strategic shifts in direction, while the implementation of strategy usually requires a series of operational problems to be solved. The information behavior of managers is complex and dynamic, and we should be mindful of simplifications that render in black and white what in reality has many hues and shades.

Chapter 6

Managing Information Sources

Say from whence
You owe this strange intelligence?

(William Shakespeare, 1623, The Tragedy of Macbeth, Act I, Scene III)

In this chapter, we take a closer look at how the intelligent organization could manage its information sources in order to scan the external environment effectively and gain the high-quality information and feedback necessary to enable organizational learning. One possible misconception should be dispelled right at the outset. Environmental scanning, business intelligence, competitive intelligence, and the other forms of information gathering we have discussed have nothing at all to do with industrial espionage or any other form of illegal or unethical activity. In a world where virtually every organization, person, and artifact is an originator or carrier of information, gathering intelligence is less a matter of procuring well-guarded secrets, and more a matter of separating useful information from the flood of open information that is available legally and cheaply (Steele 1993). The combined economic and political costs of industrial espionage or other clandestine information pilfering cannot be justified when compared with the benefits of gathering intelligence from open sources. Whereas industrial espionage may provide some measure of short-term advantage, establishing a program of systematic scanning for open intelligence endows the organization with a strategic, long-term capability to learn and innovate continuously.

The tremendous proliferation of open sources of information about nations, organizations, personalities, products, technologies, substances, and so on, results from several factors, including statutory requirements, consumer demand, and the spread of information technology. Meyer describes the consequences of living in an age of information glut:

We are living in an era of unprecedented access to information. Today's global telecommunications networks move raw information around the world literally at the speed of light. And as the capacity to move information expands, the volume of available information keeps growing to fill this expanding capacity. . . . In short, raw information from around the world is fairly pouring into government and corporate headquarters, rather like water pouring into the holds of a sinking ship. . . . Today's senior government and business executives are choking on raw information. To their astonishment and growing distress, they are discovering that the only thing as difficult and dangerous as managing a large enterprise with too little information is managing one with too much information. (Meyer 1987, 28-29)

Riding this information tsunami presents a new organizational challenge. Information gathering can no longer be a one-time activity of subscribing to a handful of selected publications or designing call report forms for employees to use. Instead, information collection becomes an organizational function that requires continuous planning, coordination, innovation, evaluation, and fine-tuning. Planning is required to relate information collection to the strategic and tactical goals of the organization. Planning identifies who the information users are and understands how they will be using the information, and matches information needs with the sometimes hidden information resources and specialized expertise within the organization that already exists. The range and variety of sources provides great scope for innovation in the gathering, correlation, and confirmation of information. Creative information acquisition can accelerate understanding—disparate pieces of information may be more swiftly assembled into a coherent view of the external environment, and this in itself is a source of competitive advantage.

The ultimate proof of the information pudding is in its consumption by decision makers. From time to time, key users' evaluations of the information and information sources supporting their data needs must be sought and systematically analyzed. Such evaluations not only show up the weak sources that should be weeded out, but also give insight into users' true information needs. Over time, information needs and organizational goals change, and the information collection plan must be adjusted and revised to ensure a good fit. We discuss these and other related issues in the following sections.

Managing an Information Ecology for Scanning the Environment

As the organization's sensing system, environmental scanning should deploy an array of information sensors with different ranges and resolutions. At one end of the spectrum, organizational radars should sweep the horizon widely, and sound early warning of important trends and forces of change of such potential significance that the organization needs to start preparing its response right away. On the other hand, probes and detectors provide a microscopic view, giving detailed information about specific organizations, products, or activities that could impact short-term performance or viability. Both kinds of information are necessary—individual signals have to be interpreted against an information background provided through continuous scanning; and new information has to be compared with historical data to detect change or deviation. The planning of information gathering therefore begins with designing a balanced portfolio of information sources that adequately balance each other's strengths and weaknesses.

To structure our discussion, we divide sources used in scanning into three broad categories: human sources, textual sources, and electronic sources (Table 6.1). Human sources may be internal (e.g., employees, staff) or external (e.g., customers, suppliers) to the organization. Textual sources supply information that may be in published, written, or broadcast form. They may be subdivided into published sources (e.g., newspapers, periodicals, radio, television), and internal documents (e.g., memos, reports). Finally, electronic sources supply information via computers and telecommunication networks, and may be subdivided into online databases/CD-ROMs and information resources on the Internet.

In practice, the various sources feed on and off one another, forming several intertwining "information food chains," so that information is typically transferred through many intermediate consumers before arriving at the end user. For example, the user who receives news from a colleague may be at the end of a long information chain in which the colleague may have obtained the news by reading an internal memorandum that reported information from a customer who had come across the information when viewing a competitor's product display. Information chains may involve many or few intermediate levels; in some

Table 6.1 Categories of Information Sources

Source Category	Subcategory	Examples
Human Sources	Internal sources	• Sales staff
		• Engineers
	External sources	• Customers
		• Suppliers
Textual Sources	Published sources	• Newspapers
		• Trade journals
		• Radio, television
	Internal documents	• Call reports
		• Memoranda
Online Sources	Online databases and CD-ROMs	• Commercial and government databases
	Internet resources	• Gophers
		• Discussion groups

cases, a user may have obtained the information directly by speaking to the person concerned or reading the original document. Figure 6.1 illustrates the idea of overlapping information chains.

In an *information ecology*, information sources do not exist in isolation, they feed off each other, taking in and processing information before retransmitting it, sometimes adding value and sometimes introducing distortion. Humans tend to be secondary or tertiary information consumers who are high up in the information chain, and this is one reason why most people, including managers, regard human sources as the most important. Sources high up on the information chain may summarize, explain, or interpret data, and so assist users to understand ambiguous situations. Sources low on the chain (or close to the event) may provide immediacy, a richness of detail, or allow users to form their own assessments.

In appraising the many studies that have stressed users' preference for personal sources, one should not underestimate the probability that some form of print, observational, or other information may have been the primary source in the first place. In scanning, extensive information networks that include both

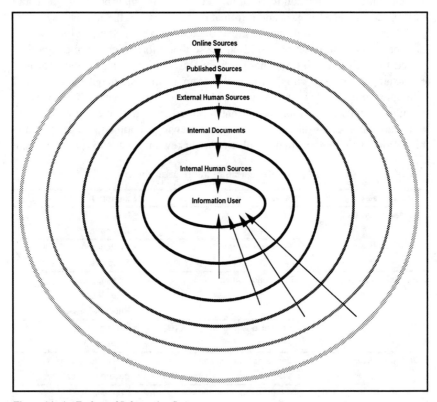

Figure 6.1 An Ecology of Information Sources

short and long information chains are necessary to ensure a sufficiently broad and thorough sweep of the external environment, so that important signals are not missed but are correctly read.

Selection and Use of Information Sources

Information from *human sources* may be preferred when dealing with ambiguous, unstructured problem situations. In these situations, the level of uncertainty is high, information is limited, and the information available is equivocal and subject to multiple interpretations. Tackling the problem depends as much on understanding its context as on knowing the details of the issue. In a variety of judgment call situations, human sources provide the necessary soft, informal, or behind-the-scene information so that the decision maker can exercise depth and intuition in making choices.

When they transfer information, human sources filter and reshape the information in at least two ways—they absorb uncertainty and span informational boundaries. First, information is summarized or selectively highlighted according to what the source feels to be its most salient features. This is similar to the process of *uncertainty absorption* described by March and Simon (1958), in which sources derive inferences from a body of data, and communicate these inferences rather than the raw data. Furthermore, human sources inside an organization have the additional capability to absorb uncertainty in ways that take into account the organization's specific information needs and task situation. Thus, an internal person may summarize voluminous incoming information, filter out irrelevant material, highlight important items, and suggest implications.

Organizations establish boundaries and specialize, and in doing so evolve their own languages and conceptual frameworks. While specialization increases the efficiency of information processing within the organization, it also creates obstacles to the transfer of information between organization and environment. It becomes necessary to recode information messages at the organization's boundaries. These boundaries can be spanned effectively by individuals who understand the coding schemes used on both sides of the boundary, enabling them to search out relevant information on one side and disseminate it on the other side: a process that Tushman and Scanlan (1981) have called *informational boundary spanning*.

Textual sources, including published sources as well as internal documents, are essential elements of any environmental scanning system. Compared with human sources, textual sources generally have a broader information bandwidth and higher transmission accuracy, although they lack the filtering and interpretive qualities of human modulation. Textual sources are especially useful when the information is formal and structured, or when the information has to be communicated accurately, using specialized languages or special formats. There are many kinds of data involving facts, numerical data, or legal definitions that are best presented on paper: organization charts, budgets, financial data, product specifications, market forecasts, economic trends, government rules and policies, technical drawings, location maps, layout diagrams, and so on. In many such cases, the information has to be gone over with a fine tooth comb—scrutinized in detail, compared item-by-item with other information, or analyzed and manipulated further in certain ways. Textual sources, including broadcast sources, are also efficient when doing a general, wide-area scan of the environment.

Ghoshal and Kim (1986) detected a differential use of personal and print sources in their study of managers in sixteen of the largest firms in South Korea. On the one hand, information about the immediate business environment (competitors, markets, existing technologies) is usually obtained from personal sources such as business associates, customers, suppliers, bankers, and so on. On the other hand, information about the broader environment (general social, economic, political, and technological changes) that is used mainly for long-term planning is usually obtained from print sources such as general and trade journals, government publications, and reports from academic institutions, think tanks, and consulting organizations. Auster and Choo's (1994) study of Canadian CEOs appear to support a similar differential usage of personal and print sources: gathering information about the technological, regulatory, and economic sectors of the environment involved the use of print sources to a larger extent than the customer and competition sectors.

Conceptually, *online databases* belong to the larger family of textual or published sources, but the use of online databases in environmental scanning offers a number of distinctive advantages. For the sake of completeness, we preview these advantages briefly here, as they will be discussed in detail in the next chapter.

Online databases can be useful when researching questions on unfamiliar topics or complex issues. The abundance of information in online databases is impressive, but the real power of online databases is in the indexing of multiple fields, and the versatility of search command languages added by service providers. The trained analyst can formulate search strategies that contain many facets or meet several retrieval criteria. Online searching may be controlled to be as broad or as focused as one wishes. Online searching is not limited by the hierarchical indexing of published sources: complex searches that intersect a number of concepts are easy to perform. Online data tend to be more comprehensive and current, and are updated more frequently than published data.

With these capabilities, online databases are well suited to situations when reasonably complete and up-to-date information needs to be gathered swiftly about new companies or products, foreign markets, emerging technologies, developments in other countries, and so on. The versatility of online searching also makes it a useful method to detect patterns, trace linkages, or reveal associations between events, persons, and organizations.

Research on scanning and information needs and uses suggests that three sets of factors are likely to influence the selection and use of information sources in environmental scanning: perceived source characteristics, information traits, and information richness.

Perceived Source Characteristics

What is the effect of perceived source characteristics on source use in scanning? A number of classic studies in information needs and uses, notably those by Rosenberg (1967), Gerstberger and Allen (1968), and Allen (1977), have found that perceived source accessibility was the major source selection criterion; more important, even, than source quality, indicated in terms of the technical reliability or amount of information from the source. More recently, O'Reilly (1982) also concluded that source accessibility was more important than source quality in explaining source use by decision makers in a welfare organization.

Does the pattern suggested by these studies extend to environmental scanning as a special case of information seeking? In a study of environmental scanning by professionals in the corporate headquarters of two large organizations (a bank and a manufacturing firm), Culnan (1983) found that the complexity of the individual's task was a significant factor in influencing source use. The information requirements of performing a complex task may necessitate the use of less accessible sources. For example, in the manufacturing firm, a significant correlation existed between task complexity and the use of less accessible sources such as databases and outsiders.

In a study of scanning behavior by over 200 chief executives of the Canadian publishing and telecommunications industries, Auster and Choo (1993, 1994) found that newspapers and periodicals were the most frequently used scanning sources, followed by subordinate managers, subordinate staff, broadcast media, and internal memoranda and circulars. Figure 6.2 plots the use of sources in relation to their perceived accessibility (measured as time and effort to contact source and ease of getting the desired information), and perceived quality (measured as information relevance and reliability). Each circle represents a source: its size indicates approximately the use frequency, while its position indicates its perceived accessibility and quality. The number following the source name is the mean use frequency of the source (6 = >Once a day, 5 = >Once a week, 4 = >Once a month, 3 = >Few times a year, 2 = <Once a year, and 1 = Never.) The plot suggests that the frequency of source use is related to both perceived source accessibility and quality, with perceived quality appearing to be a stronger factor. Regression analysis revealed that perceived source quality was a much more important factor than perceived source accessibility in explaining source use. The study suggests that the turbulence of the external environment, the strategic use of information acquired by scanning, and the special demands of information needed to deal with ambiguous situations, combine to help

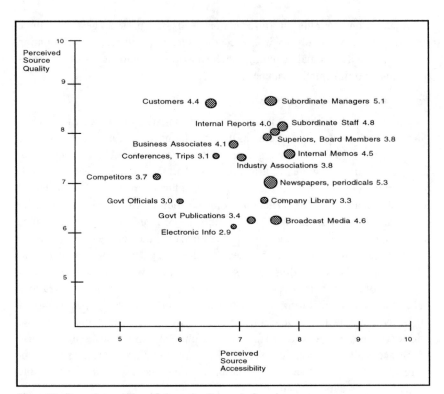

Figure 6.2 Perception and Use of Information Sources in Scanning

explain why source quality may be more important than source accessibility when managers scan the environment.

Information Traits

People select information sources in the anticipation that their needs will be satisfied by the information to be obtained from those sources. This simple statement hides many layers of complexity. As we have discussed in Chapter 2, information needs are neither monolithic nor static, but are created through the interaction of a large number of situational factors that define the information user's specific problem situation. These factors include not only the subject matter of the information required but also the situational variables that represent the information use environment, such as organizational type and style, functional activity, goals, levels of sophistication, connections with other environments, and opportunities and constraints (MacMullin and Taylor 1984).

Consequently, satisfying information needs is not just a content issue of "What do you want to know?" It also has to address situational and process concerns reflected in questions such as "Why do you need to know it?" "What do you know already?" and "How will this information help you?" MacMullin and

Taylor (1984) propose a set of general *information traits* that elaborate the user's need for information—they define the ways that information can be identified and presented so that they can be directly related to the dimensions of a problem situation. To the degree that they represent information needs, they form part of the criteria by which users choose among sources.

The nine information traits are listed in Table 6.2, and defined according to the following continua:

1. *Quantitative*. Information lies on a continuum between quantitative and qualitative data. Quantitative data are specific, but when they are aggregated, they give an overall picture of a situation. Qualitative data on the other hand may give reasons, assumptions, nuances, and details.

2. *Data*. Information lies on a continuum between hard and soft data. Hard data are directly observed or measured, soft data cannot be observed but have to be inferred or assumed.

3. *Temporal*. Information lies on a continuum between historical and forecasting information. There are really three points on this continuum: what has been (historical), what is likely to be (probabilistic), and what should be (prescriptive)

4. *Solution*. Information lies on a continuum between offering a single solution or offering a range of options. Poorly structured problems may seek more options before settling on a course of action.

5. *Focus*. Information lies on a continuum between precision and diffusion. Precise information matches the needs of a well-defined problem situation, whereas diffused information may be more useful for an ill-defined problem.

6. *Specificity of Use*. Information lies on a continuum between the applied and the theoretical. Applied information is immediately useful in an operational sense, whereas theoretical information explains or predicts behavior.

7. *Substantive*. Information lies on a continuum between the applied and the descriptive. Descriptive information is different from theoretical information in that it describes the substance and meaning of a phenomenon without predicting behavior.

8. *Aggregation*. Information lies on a continuum between clinical and census. Clinical or case study information is useful for complex situations where variables are not quantifiable. Census information describes a population or sample in statistical terms.

9. *Causal/Diagnostic*. Information lies on a continuum between causal and diagnostic. Most problem-solving situations require causal information to understand why something happens. Diagnostic information is used to define a problem situation.

Table 6.2 Information Traits

Information Trait	Kinds of Information
1 Quantitative Continuum	• Quantitative • Qualitative
2 Data Continuum	• Hard data • Soft data
3 Temporal Continuum	• Historical • Forecasting
4 Solution Continuum	• Single solution • Option range
5 Focus Continuum	• Precision • Diffusion
6 Specificity of Use Continuum	• Applied • Theoretical
7 Substantive Continuum	• Applied • Descriptive
8 Aggregation Continuum	• Clinical • Census
9 Causal/Diagnostic Continuum	• Causal • Diagnostic

Information Richness

Daft and Lengel (1984, 1986) suggest that organizations have two principal information tasks: interpret the external environment, and coordinate internal activities. Each of these tasks requires the reduction of equivocality and the processing of a sufficient amount of information. People in organizations perform both tasks by using information sources and communication channels of different *information richness*:

> Information richness is defined as the ability of information to change understanding within a time interval. Communication transactions that can overcome different frames of reference or clarify ambiguous issues to change understanding in a timely manner are considered rich. Communications that require a long time to enable understanding or that cannot overcome different perspectives are lower in richness. (Daft and Lengel 1986, 560)

The information media used in organizations determine the richness of information processed. Typical organizational information media may be arranged in order of decreasing information richness as follows: face-to-face meetings, telephone, written personal communications, written formal communications, and numeric formal reports. Face-to-face meetings are the richest information medium because they provide instant feedback, include multiple cues such as voice inflections and body gestures, add a personal touch, and use language variety. Numeric formal reports rank low in the scale because they lack all these qualities. Rich media enable people to interpret and reach agreement about difficult, unanalyzable, emotional and conflict-laden issues. Media of low richness are appropriate for the accurate and efficient transmission of unequivocal messages about the routine activities of the organization.

Rich information media use multiple cues, feedback, and language variety. Managers and others will turn to rich information channels such as face-to-face discussions when they are dealing with ambiguous, complex, ill-defined, or conflict-laden situations. The use of rich information media helps participants to interpret a fuzzy situation and come to an acceptable agreement. On the other hand, media of low richness, such as forms and standard memos, may be efficient means for conveying unequivocal information about routine or well-defined situations. When scanning the environment, managers seem to prefer human or personal sources that utilize rich media to communicate their information. Because managers must confront ambiguous and conflicting cues about the environment, and then create and maintain a shared interpretation among themselves, they use rich media to discuss, analyze, and interpret the environment, and negotiate an understanding of the goals and strategies to pursue. The information richness model implies that people in the organization will choose between rich and less rich information sources depending on the uncertainty and complexity of the task and the external environment.

In summary, our discussion of perceived source characteristics, information traits, and information richness suggests that the choice and use of sources would be made according to the perceived accessibility or quality of the source, the degree of fit between the information's attributes and the requirements of the problem situation, and the need to use rich communication media to resolve equivocality and uncertainty.

Human Sources

Internal human sources consist primarily of the employees of the organization. As part of their normal work, employees, professional staff, and executives receive or are exposed to a daily stream of information about people and events in the outside world: salespeople call on customers, purchasing agents converse with suppliers, engineers attend conferences, executives meet with their counterparts, and so on. Table 6.3 shows some of the internal human sources in a typical business organization and the kinds of competitive information they can develop. As shown in the table, internal human sources act as collectors who derive their information from other, often external sources. They are not, however, passive data transmitters—they add value to the incoming information by doing the first level of filtering and interpretation, based on their work roles and understanding of the organizational context. A large proportion of the external information requirements of the organization can be satisfied by fully tapping into these internal resources.

Unfortunately, most employees are unaware of the potential value of the information they come across and they fail to pass it on to those who can make best use of it. As we discussed in the last chapter, a well-designed scanning system must instill a new information culture by raising information awareness and motivating the sharing of information. Consider the case of a company's sales force. Potentially, they are among the most well-connected sources of information about customers, competitors, and so on. Also, however, they are among the most difficult to motivate to share the intelligence that they have obtained. Salespersons see their goal as meeting sales targets and reporting information as an unnecessary chore, taking up time that could be better spent prospecting sales leads. Companies have tried several ways to motivate information sharing by their sales force, such as setting aside part of the sales commission for information reporting, defining information gathering as part of the job description, and insisting on weekly intelligence reports (see company examples in Chapter 5).

External human sources consist of everyone who could provide relevant information about the external environment; they include customers, suppliers, distributors, competitors, and many others. Information from external human sources, especially those that are trusted or perceived to be in the know, can have a large impact on decision making. Sometimes the information is communicated directly and willingly, as is the case with customers, suppliers, and distributors, who are, to varying degrees, stakeholders in the organization. As stakeholders, it

Table 6.3 Internal Human Sources

Internal Human Sources	Examples of Environmental Information	Examples of Originating Sources
Sales force	Customer needs and preferences; customer perception of competitors and their products; promotion and distribution strategies.	Customers Distributors
Marketing staff	Market share; competitors' media strategies; target markets.	Advertising agencies Trade shows
Public relations staff	Press releases and anouncements; level of public media exposure; media relationships.	Newspapers, publications Radio, television
Purchasing personnel	Supplier relationships; alternative sources; competitors purchasing intentions.	Suppliers
Manufacturing and engineering staff	Production methods; labor-to-capital ratios; labor rates; reverse engineering of competitors' products; production costs.	Professional associations Unions
R&D personnel	Technology directions; R&D investments; competitors' areas of reseach focus.	Journals Conferences
Human resources staff	Executive movements; organizational structures; training and staff development.	Job applicants Job advertisements
Finance personnel	Financial performance; cost of funds; credit relationships with financial community.	Bankers Annual report financial statements
Corporate librarian	Industry news and trends; new information sources; company analyses.	Publications Online databases

is in their own interest to provide feedback and share information with the organization. Sources such as advertising agencies, bankers, consultants, financial analysts, lawyers, and so on, are interested in forging business relationships, and often do their persuading by describing their work or services for other organizations. Other sources are in the business of sharing information, such as journalists, editors of publications, and trade association staff, and would willingly barter news and opinions about industry developments. Competitors themselves are often willing to pool information, especially about common competitors and forces of change that are affecting the industry as a whole. Most competitors know what information is strategic to their own interests, and are willing to share their knowledge in other areas, recognizing that they have as much to gain from the exchange of ideas and insights.

Senior executives, heads of functional and business units, and other managers are in daily contact with many external human sources, and most of them have developed skills and experience in interpreting subtle signals and hidden messages. For them, a casual remark, slip of the tongue, hesitation in replying, or some departure from normal behavior, can be as informative as the verbal content of the information from the external person. (There were a few examples of this in the specific incidents related by Canadian chief executives in Chapter 5.)

Table 6.4 shows the range of external human sources that may be engaged. For the majority of organizations, customers appear to be the most important sources of market intelligence, and their information can come directly or indirectly (via the sales or marketing people). Suppliers and distributors are usually the next most heavily used sources.

Finding and sharing information through other people is a natural, social phenomenon. General and line managers are known particularly as users of human information sources, both internal and external. For them, people sources supply the soft, rich information they need to stay "in touch" with a situation, and to make decisions when necessary. The continued access to and use of soft, personal information allows managers to develop their own kind of tacit knowledge—a form of managerial intuition that is called into play in planning and decision making processes (Mintzberg 1994). Effective general managers have been found adept at building personal networks that can help them to implement their agendas (Kotter 1982).

When it comes to environmental scanning, however, relying only on human sources has its limitations. Although executives have their own circle of friends and contacts, based upon friendship, political alliance, past collaboration, and so on, personal networks fall short in that their scope and coverage is usually fairly narrow. Some executives surround themselves with like-minded colleagues who filter out information that challenge their collective mind set—an extreme consequence of which could be the intelligence and decision-making failure characteristic of "groupthink" (Janis 1982). Close-knit circles may also impede information sharing by refusing to embrace the larger, organization-wide

Table 6.4 External Human Sources

External Human Sources	Examples of Environmental Information
Customers	Competitors' products, pricing, service, personnel changes, etc; customer preferences and complaints.
Suppliers	Competitor procurement needs, priorities; supply and demand pressures; cost, quality, and supply of inputs.
Distributors, agents, dealers	Distribution channels; trade programs; informal news about product lines, pricing and promotion.
Trade or industry associations	Industry statistics; activities of association members.
Bankers, financial analysts	Competitors' financial dealings, financial health and performance; industry trends.
Lawyers	Interpretation of court rulings; government regulatory policies.
Advertising agencies	Competitors' advertising expenditures; product/market positioning.
Government officials	Interpretation of government policies, priorities and long-term directions; international news.
Journalists, editors	Local, detailed information about specific events, firms, persons, etc.
Consultants	Industry, technology, market trends; scanning techniques.

information network, in effect creating their own feudal fiefdoms of private information (Davenport 1993).

The issue is largely one of balance and diversity. Information from human sources often convey a persuasive immediacy and vividness, but they may be directing the spotlight at particular aspects of a problem situation from a particular angle. Information from individual human sources almost always needs to be corroborated and complemented with input from other sources, including other personal as well as formal, textual sources. By offering alternative, possibly contesting perspectives on a situation, the use of diverse sources that balance strengths and weaknesses helps to ensure that information gathering and processing is sufficiently thorough and vigilant.

Textual Sources

Textual sources convey information in the form of streams of texts, delivered over both paper and broadcast media. They are subdivided into *published sources* that include paper-based publications as well as radio and television broadcasts; and *internal documents* generated within the organization. Textual sources are used as a main component of the organization's information sweeping system (the "radar" function), to monitor and provide early warning about issues that could become important in the near future.

When monitoring social and technological issues, it may be helpful to recognize that they tend to emerge and develop gradually over time, moving through different phases of growth (Fig. 6.3). Furthermore, information about an issue appears in different types of media and sources during each phase of its development, so that the level of media coverage and public awareness about a new issue first rises and then falls over its life history, forming a characteristic "issue emergence cycle" (Wygant and Markley 1988). Initially, media coverage and public awareness about the issue is low because the idea is new or its impact is still unclear. Information sources during the *idea creation* phase include specialized journals, the fringe or alternative press, science fiction works, patent filings, and doctoral dissertations. Media coverage and awareness grow as experts write about or discuss the issue during the *elite awareness* phase, using channels such as insider newsletters, research reports, the trade press, and magazines catering to the intellectual or business elites. Once the new issue gathers enough momentum, the popular media, including radio, television, newspapers, and general interest magazines, will then pick it up during the *popular awareness* phase. The growth of public and business interest leads to the *government awareness* phase, where government agencies may be called upon to develop policies, regulatory frameworks, or standards. Based on the legal framework or some other guidelines, institutions and organizations move in the *adoption and routinization* phase to implement their responses and formalize them in procedure manuals, modified codes of practice, new training curricula, and so on. Finally, in the *record keeping* phase, media coverage diminishes substantially, and information is then located primarily in the organization's historical or transactional records.

A large number of *published sources* are available that may be monitored to track specific issues or to follow particular organizations, such as existing or potential competitors. They may be categorized into what the organization says about itself, what others say about the organization, and what the government knows about the organization (Gilad and Gilad 1988). Table 6.5 lists some examples.

In terms of what others say about an organization, probably the most heavily utilized sources are newspapers and the trade periodicals. Local newspapers, published in the cities or states where major competitors are located, can provide detailed information about these organizations, including their future plans, personnel movement, and so on. Newsclipping services are sometimes contracted to collect stories from local newspapers. Basic company and people information may be culled from the growing number of business and trade

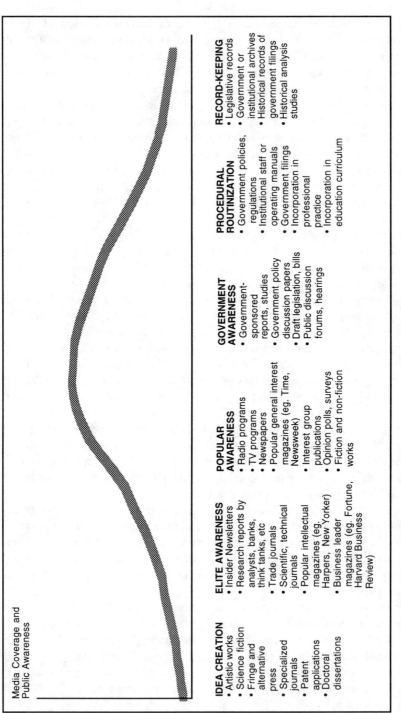

Figure 6.3 Information Life-Cycle of Emerging Issues (Adapted from Wygant and Markley 1988, 122)

directories and indexes, sources which are well-known to any business reference librarian. In the United States, examples of directories and indexes are those published by companies such as Dun and Bradstreet, Moody's, Standard and Poor's, Thomas Publishing, H.W. Wilson, and Information Access Company. Where available, reports prepared by financial analysts can provide in-depth analyses of industries and particular companies.

As shown in Table 6.5, organizations reveal a great deal about themselves through their executives' speeches, company annual or quarterly reports, press releases, advertisements, promotional literature, and so on. When read in isolation, these sources may not seem revealing, but when information from a number of these sources (chairperson's messages in annual reports, financial statements and their footnotes, hiring advertisements, press releases, etc.) are collated and correlated over a period of time, they may presage shifts in strategy and organizational health.

Finally, government requires and collects an enormous amount of data about companies and organizations. Part of the difficulty is finding out what information is publicly available and then negotiating the bureaucratic maze in order to obtain the desired information. Table 6.5 shows only a small sample of government filings that could provide intelligence. In the United States and Canada, for example, the several levels of government (federal, state, munici-

Table 6.5 Published Sources

What others say about the organization	What the organization says about itself	What the government knows about the organization
Business and trade directories, indexes	Annual and quarterly company reports	Antitrust filings
Business, general interest, and technical periodicals	Company newsletters	Environmental filings
Financial analysts' reports	Executives' speeches	Food and drug approval filings
Market research company reports	Interviews	Freedom or access to information filings
Monographs by consultants, executives, researchers, etc	Job advertisements	Government reports
Newspapers (national and local)	Marketing and promotional literature	Government statistical abstracts and bulletins
Radio broadcasts	Press releases	Industry specific information
Television broadcasts	Product advertisements	Patent filings
Trade association newsletters	Trade shows	Regulatory filings
Trade press	Trade union news	Securities commission or stock exchange filings

pal) may each mandate different filing and reporting requirements affecting not just publicly traded companies, but also private companies and nonprofit organizations. The Freedom of Information Act (U.S.) and the Access to Information Act (Canada) allow public access to government-collected data. Applications for such filings, however, should be made through third parties, since a direct filing is subject to a reverse search that will identify your organization as the party seeking the information! Information brokers specializing in obtaining information from government sources may be considered. Governments generally publish considerable collections of statistical and industry information reports, which can give useful background to the current and future state of specific industries.

Faced with a rich embarrassment of published sources, an organization typically subscribes to a host of newspapers, general business periodicals, and trade publications in the hope of adequately covering all the important bases. The information-primed executive endeavors to stay in touch by taking in a daily dosage of these publications, over and above the business biography and latest management bestseller that he or she is determined to finish. At the end of the day, the organization has to evaluate the contribution of its published sources in meeting organizational goals.

The evaluation has to be concerned with the content and coverage of the publications, as well as the procedures by which information is extracted and shared. Stanat (1990) offers a checklist of questions:
— Are the publications too narrow in focus?
— Do they include information on only current competitors,
  rather than potential competitors?
— Do they only cover domestic competitors and markets?
— Who has access to the publications?
— What is the time lag from the receipt of publications to
  your reading the publications?
— What is the procedure if an employee notes a key article?
  Is the article circulated? If so, who is on the circulation list?
— Do information gatekeepers exist within the organization?
  If so, do they accelerate or block the dissemination of information?

Organizations that wish to scan widely by gathering and synthesizing information from numerous external published sources will find this a labor-intensive task. A few organizations have found it more economical and efficient to subcontract the scanning of published sources to an outside service. For example, General Foods Corporation (the desserts division), rather than subscribing to a huge number of journals and publications and hiring a person with the necessary skills to scan, synthesize, and digest information, decided to farm out the work to another firm. Information scanned by the outside service is placed in a database that General Foods' employees can search using a specially customized text-retrieval system. About forty employees are using the system regularly to monitor competitive activity (Stanat 1990).

Internal documents are produced by people within the organization, and may be divided into operational documents, planning documents, and information documents (Table 6.6). The first subcategory of internal documents are those generated from operational activities such as sales reports, production reports, financial reports, memoranda, management information system reports, and so on. We have underscored the importance of sales reports in an earlier section, and highlighted the need to motivate and reward the sales force to prepare call reports that include information of intelligence value. The second subcategory of internal documents are those generated by planning and analysis activities such as strategic planning documents, minutes of meetings, project proposals, special ad hoc studies, consultants' reports, visit reports, and so on. Most of these documents contain assessments of the external environment or discussions of specific issues, and should serve as a moving baseline from which further scanning and analysis may be initiated. The last subcategory of internal documents are the clippings and articles extracted from published sources by the organization's employees, as well as items produced by the corporate library and public relations department.

As may be seen, internal documents constitute another large information reservoir that can feed the organization's scanning efforts. Unfortunately, most internal documentary information is not organized and stored to facilitate search and retrieval. Part of the difficulty is with the provenance—as operational or planning products, they are bundled with the operational or planning activities, and are circulated or held by the people who created them in the first

Table 6.6 Internal Document Sources

Operational Documents	Planning Documents	Information Documents
Sales reports	Strategic plans	News clippings
Production reports	Meeting minutes	Articles from periodicals
Financial reports	Project proposals	Press releases
Human resources reports	Ad hoc studies	Speeches
R&D progress reports	Consultants' reports	Company newsletters
MIS reports	Market research studies	Library newsletters
Operational memoranda	Government filings	Job advertisements

place. Thus, such documents tend to be held locally and scattered all over the organization; no central, coordinated mechanism exists for discovering such information except by asking all potential owners of the desired data.

To mine this latent information resource, organizations need to design an integrated records management and archival policy to enable users to find vital documents, locate specific information that best addresses a query, and learn from history and past experience (see Chapter 2 for a full discussion). Text management and retrieval systems may be implemented to organize, index, and store the more important of the organization's internal documents. This is not a simple task, given the volume of documents that has to be sifted through and the lack of structure of most of these informal documents.

In order to help a large financial institution screen thousands of internal documents and identify those for input into a sophisticated database, Stanat (1990) designed a scoring system based on five attributes of the document: its age; the archival value of its content; estimated number of users over its life-span; its impact or relevance on the business; and the cost of duplication of effort in the absence of the document. Scoring on these five equally-weighted attributes must pass a threshold value for database storage. Scoring is done annually by the line departments. Having identified the significant documents, they have to be represented and indexed in the database to facilitate retrieval. For a Citibank department that needed a standard form for cataloging its internal reports, memoranda, field studies, clippings, advertisements, and planning documents, Stanat (1990) developed a one-page data entry screen with the following headings, all of which would be computer-searchable: document number (used to access the paper copy); title; author; department; subject; key findings; key words. Depending on the requirements of the organization, many refinements and alternatives are possible, such as indexing by company names, product names, project title, key personalities, and geographical location. A balance needs to be struck between the added flexibility from using multiple indexing methods and the need to have a simple, efficient way of capturing and representing each document in the database. The choice of the database management software will also have to reflect the unstructured, free-flowing nature of the data. Most organizations that have implemented such systems have done so by customizing full-text database systems that can efficiently search for words or phrases.

So far we have discussed the use of human sources and textual sources in gathering information for organizational learning. We consider online databases, as well as Internet-based resources and services in the next chapter.

Chapter 7

Weaving a Web of Online Intelligence

"The human mind ... operates by association. With one item in its grasp, it snaps instantly to the next that is suggested by the association of thoughts, in accordance with some intricate web of trails carried by the cells of the brain. It has other characteristics, of course; trails that are not frequently followed are prone to fade, items are not fully permanent, memory is transitory. Yet the speed of action, the intricacy of trails, the detail of mental pictures, is awe-inspiring beyond all else in nature. Man cannot hope fully to duplicate this mental process artificially, but he certainly ought to be able to learn from it."

(Vannevar Bush, "As We May Think," in the July 1945 issue of *The Atlantic Monthly*)

Managing Online Scanning

In the last chapter we discussed how human sources and textual sources are very different categories of information sources that require very different methods of access, approach, interaction, and use. Online information sources have traditionally been regarded as closer to textual sources, since many online databases provide surrogates or representations of documentary information. However, the widespread assimilation of the Internet has created a new form of information space in which person-to-person communications can take place seamlessly with the looking up of textual and non-textual information. As both a communication and publishing medium, we suggest that the Internet is a *social information space*. In this chapter we propose a framework for managing the bewildering range of information sources available online for gathering external information. We will do this by identifying four modes of environmental scanning, and mapping these modes to commercial-online as well as Internet-based information resources, services, and communication capabilities. The more intensive and creative use of online information resources and information sharing capabilities will enable organizations to scan their environments more intelligently, be more knowledgeable, and respond more effectively to environmental forces.

Modes of Environmental Scanning

As was briefly noted in Chapter 4, it is helpful to discern four modes of environmental scanning: undirected viewing, conditioned viewing, informal search, and formal search (Aguilar 1967). In *undirected viewing*, the individual is exposed to information with no specific informational need in mind. The overall purpose is to scan broadly in order to detect signals of change early. Many and varied sources of information are used, and large amounts of information are screened. The granularity of information is high, but large chunks of information are quickly dropped from attention. As a result of undirected viewing, general areas or topics may be identified as being potentially relevant to the organization's goals or tasks, and the individual becomes sensitive to these areas. In *conditioned viewing*, the individual directs viewing to information about selected topics or to certain types of information. The overall purpose is to evaluate the significance of the information encountered in order to assess the general nature of the impact on the organization. If the impact is assessed to be sufficiently significant, the scanning mode changes from scanning to searching. During *informal search*, the individual actively looks for information to deepen the knowledge and understanding of a specific issue. It is informal in that it involves a relatively limited and unstructured effort. The overall purpose is to gather information to elaborate an issue so as to determine the need for action by the organization. If a need for a decision or response is perceived, the individual dedicates more time and resources to the search. During *formal search*, the individual makes a deliberate or planned effort to obtain specific information or information about a specific issue. Search is formal because it is structured according to some pre-established procedure or methodology. The granularity of information is low, as search is relatively focused to find detailed information. The overall purpose is to systematically retrieve information relevant to an issue in order to provide a basis for developing a decision or course of action.

The individuals in an organization are simultaneously engaged in all four modes of scanning. They view the environment broadly in order to see the big picture as well as to identify areas that require closer attention. At the same time, they are searching for information on particular issues in order to assess their significance and to develop appropriate responses. Etzioni (1967, 1986) compares this "mixed scanning" to a satellite scanning the earth by using both a wide-angle and a zoom lens: "Mixed scanning ... is akin to scanning by satellites with two lenses: wide and zoom. Instead of taking a close look at all formations, a prohibitive task, or only at the spots of previous trouble, the wide lenses provide clues as to places to zoom in, looking for details." (Etzioni 1986, p. 8) Effective environmental scanning requires both general viewing that sweeps the horizon broadly and purposeful searching that probes issues in sufficient detail to provide the kinds of information needed for decision making.

A Framework for Managing Online Information Gathering

Our analysis of scanning modes suggests a framework for managing the complementary use of different categories of online sources to gather information during the various scanning modes. During **undirected viewing**, the goal of broad scanning implies the use of a large number of different sources and different types of sources. These sources should supply up-to-date news and provide a variety of points of views. The World Wide Web appears to match these requirements well. The Web is a laissez faire information marketplace offering a huge diversity of sources presenting information through a wide range of perspectives. Information often becomes available on the Web more quickly than through print channels. The immediacy, variety and eclecticism of the Web makes it a useful medium for detecting early, weak signals about trends and phenomena that could become significant over time.

During **conditioned viewing**, the individual has isolated a number of areas of potential concern from undirected viewing, and is now sensitized to assess the significance of developments in those areas. The individual wishes to do this assessment in a cost-effective manner, without having to dedicate substantial time and effort in a formal search. The Web can provide a number of ways of obtaining information to make initial sense of emergent phenomena. Many market research companies, financial institutions, industry associations, and government organizations make available on Web pages their reports, bulletins, and newsletters that analyze ongoing developments in their areas of watch. Some academics, authors, consultants, industry observers, and knowledgable experts have used the Web to share their insights and predictions, and to stimulate further discussion.

During **informal search**, the individual has determined the potential importance of specific developments, and embarks on a search that would build up knowledge about those developments, and deepen understanding of their implications and consequences. In conducting an informal search, both the Web and online databases can address the requirement for information that is directed at specific issues, but that still does not cost a great deal of time or money to acquire. On the Web, search engines can be used to locate information on Web pages, newsgroups and mailing list discussions. Librarians and specialists have compiled Web-based directories and lists of potentially useful Web resources. Using commercial database search services, the individual can retrieve even more complete and focused information. Many commercial services also provide a selective dissemination of information capability to automatically retrieve and deliver information about a particular organization, technology or issue.

During **formal search**, the individual or organization undertakes a systematic, structured effort to gather information about an issue in order to make a decision and develop a course of action. The search is formal because it follows some pre-established procedure or methodology. Formal searches could be a part of for example, competitor intelligence gathering, patents searching, market demographics analysis, and issues management. Formal searches prefer information from sources that are perceived to be knowledgable, or from information systems and services that make efforts to ensure data quality and accuracy. Online databases meet these requirements better than Web sources, and offer the important additional advantage of allowing the individual to formulate search queries that can deal with complex, cross-disciplinary questions, or that can home in on specific information to answer a particular question. Primary sources may be used in a formal search, and here the Web provides a means of identifying and contacting human experts from around the world.

Figure 7.1 shows how the four modes of scanning are supported by a continuum of online information gathering and communication methods that range from:

- The chaotic, informal World Wide Web to the structured, formal online databases
- Secondary sources to primary sources
- Many-to-many communications (newsgroups, mailing lists) to one-to-one communications (e-mail, telephone)

As we move from undirected viewing to formal search, the need increases for specific, actionable information whose reliability may be assessed. In viewing modes, breadth of scan takes precedence over depth, in order to avoid missing important signals of change. The Web can provide an efficient, economical way of achieving this broad sweep. In search modes, information depth, speci-

UNDIRECTED VIEWING	CONDITIONED VIEWING	INFORMAL SEARCH	FORMAL SEARCH
Detect Signals	Assess Significance	Elaborate Issue	Probe Issue
World Wide Web/Internet Services ⟶		Online Databases Search Services	
Secondary Sources ⟶		Primary Sources	
Many-to-many Communications ⟶		One-to-one Communications	
Coarse-grained, fuzzy focus ⟶		Fine-grained, sharp focus	

Figure 7.1 A Framework for Managing Online Information Gathering

ficity and accuracy are the criteria, and here online databases can better satisfy these needs. Cost perceptions may also vary across the scanning modes. In viewing modes, when organizations are still developing a focus for their information search, they may be less willing to spend money in buying data. (To be sure, viewing the Web is hardly a cost-free activity — employees take a longer time to find information on the Web, and they are often distracted by other 'interesting' sites of information.) In search modes, organizations can justify expenditures to meet the requirement for fine-grained, sharply focused, and dependable information.

The Internet: A Social Information Space

The Internet began as a scientific research network that linked the host computers of government organizations, research institutes, and universities. The Internet is a global matrix of thousands of large and small computer networks that exchange data through a suite of common communications protocols, based primarily on the Transmission Control Protocol and the Internet Protocol (TCP/IP). As at the beginning of 1997, an estimated 16 million hosts are connected to the Internet, and as many as 57 million people may be using the net (Matrix Information and Directory Services 1997). A total of 194 countries are now on the Internet, and it has become easier to count countries that do not have at least one Internet connection – there are only 46 countries which are not yet connected. Of the 19.5 million host computers on the Internet in mid-1997, about 4.5 million hosts are in the commercial domain (.com), 2.9 million are educational (.edu), 2.2 million are network resource related (.net), 0.5 million are military (.mil), and 0.4 million are government (.gov) (Lottor 1997). Internet resources and services are quickly becoming strategic information tools for a growing number of commercial, government, and non-profit organizations.

Each day, hundreds of thousands of people on the Internet exchange electronic mail, participate in online discussion groups, and explore new sites and resources. The Internet is many things to many people. For some, it is the world's largest electronic mail network, for others, it is a global bulletin board, a huge public library, a sprawling software storehouse, and for many business managers, the Internet represents a once-in-a-lifetime marketing and distribution opportunity. According to MIDS, Internet users may be categorized into three levels: Core Internet, Consumer Internet, and the Matrix. As of early 1997, there are 36 million Core Internet users of computers that can *distribute* information through interactive TCP/IP services such as the WWW or FTP (File Transfer Protocol). There are 57 million Consumer Internet users of computers that can *access* information through the WWW or FTP. Finally, there are 71 million users of electronic mail worldwide. (MIDS 1997).

Yet the most striking feature of the Internet, rising above the universality and robustness of its technical connections, is that net users have evolved their own information culture based on the norms of open access, information sharing, and lending a helping hand. Howard Rheingold (1993) describes the experience as belonging to a virtual community that operates like a

> gift economy in which people do things for one another out of a spirit of building something between them, rather than a spread-sheet-calculated quid pro quo. When that spirit exists, everybody gets a little extra something, a little sparkle, from their more practical transactions; different kinds of things become possible when this mind-set pervades. ... The same strategy of nurturing and making use of loose information-sharing affiliations across the Net can be applied to an infinite domain of problem areas, from literary criticism to software evaluation. It's a good way for a sufficiently large, sufficiently diverse group of people to multiply their individual degree of expertise, and I think it could be done even if the people aren't involved in a community other than their place of employment or their area of specialization. (Rheingold 1993, p.59)

Organizations connected to the Internet can break out from the traditional model of managing information as a form of exercising control over access to information. In the Internet-enabled paradigm, information management may be based simultaneously on widespread access to an expanded range of information resources, and on the capability to implement far-reaching communication and information sharing strategies that bestow competitive advantage. Mary Cronin elaborates,

> The Internet delivers what Peter Drucker calls the most important information resource, awareness of the world around them, directly to the desktops of all the employees connected to the network. ... Employees directly connected to the global network can provide their company with important competitive information. Each staff member using the Internet may be in contact with hundreds of outside people in the course of a day — including potential and existing customers, competitors, suppliers, and international partners. Well-informed employees can spot marketing opportunities, the emergence of new competition, unmet customer needs, and a host of vital information — but only if the company has organized its internal information-sharing structure to incorporate their insights. ... Businesses operating within the traditional model are slower to recognize these opportunities because of their preoccupation with information control. On the other hand, companies ready to move away from a hierarchical information access model and develop an information management strategy based on distributed information access can reap the benefits of a better motivated, more flexible, better-informed workforce. (Cronin 1994, p.16-18)

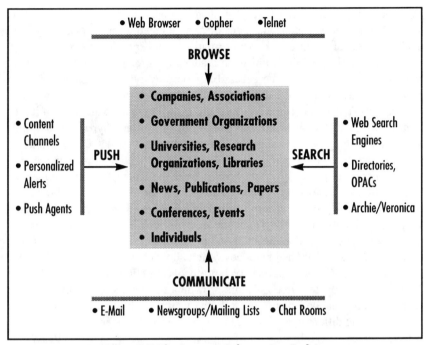

Figure 7.1 The Internet Information Ecology

The Internet has evolved to be the world's largest network of open sources of information. The challenge before organizations is learning to manage a balanced use of its various tools for knowledge sharing and knowledge retrieval in order to effectively prospect this vast but unruly information lode. Figure 7.1 presents a typology of the four principal categories of services available on the Web and Internet for information sharing and retrieval: (1) browsing, (2) "pushing," (3) searching, and (4) communicating.

Browsing

The Internet provides three main ways for browsing its vast information space: the World Wide Web, Gopher, and Telnet. Each of them provides a single interface to view and retrieve information of different media types. By hiding the complexity of disparate data types and alternative access methods, these browsing mechanisms help users to navigate resource sites smoothly and to scan for interesting information quickly. Browsing the Internet is therefore an information seeking activity that could be important during the viewing modes of environmental scanning.

The most popular and flexible way to browse the Internet is to do so in the **World Wide Web**. As Tim Berners-Lee, the inventor of the Web, conceived it, the World Wide Web is a connected information domain in which all information, from any source, can be accessed in a consistent and simple way. The World Wide Web is a concept, a set of communication protocols, a body of available software, and a web of information. *Conceptually*, the Web follows the fundamental principle of universal readership — once an item of information is available, it should be accessible from any type of computer, in any country, by any authorized individual who only need to use one simple program to access it. To help the user navigate and cope with the huge amounts of information involved, the Web provides two basic operations: hypertext jumping, and text searching. Web documents are hypertext pages which contain links or pointers that the reader can click on to jump directly to other related documents or information objects. Hypertext linking frees the reader from the sequential organization of pages, and allows her to pursue her own thread of browsing. Some Web sites provide access to computer-generated indexes that the user may search by entering text. The result of the search is a hypertext document containing links to the documents found by the search engine. The Web is also a *set of protocols* or defined practices which allow client and server computers to communicate. Three important Web protocols are URLs, HTTP, and HTML. URLs or Uniform Resource Locators provide a unique address to every document and information object on the Web, even though these objects may be accessed using different protocols. HTTP (Hypertext Transfer Protocol) defines a fast, efficient, flexible method of communication between Web clients and servers that allows clients to send requests and servers to send documents and objects of any data type. HTML (Hypertext Markup Language) is a document markup language that every Web client can read and interpret to format a document for display on the client. HTML uses tags to indicate how a document is structured and laid out, and how to create links to other documents. The Web is a *body of available software* for viewing and serving Web documents and information objects. Individuals use a HTML browser to view Web documents, and a HTML editor to create their own pages. Server software implement the HTTP protocol in order to efficiently and reliably deliver requested documents and objects. The Web constantly experiments with and evaluates new software recommendations, programming interfaces, and software code through Internet standards bodies and organizations like the World Wide Web Consortium. Finally, the WWW is a *web of information* that contains a bewildering variety of information and data types. As a universal medium, the Web is open and inclusive, and provides a single point of access to information presented from a variety of protocols, including those protocols that predate the HTTP standard. Thus, information on a FTP (File Transfer Protocol) server, a Gopher server, or a Telnet host can all be accessed via a Web browser.

Browsing the Web offers a number of advantages when scanning the environment in the modes of undirected or directed viewing. Because it is widely available and used, the Web has become a publishing medium of enormous reach, so that if an organization wants to disseminate information broadly the

Web would be considered a conduit of choice. At the same time, putting out information on the Web is a relatively simple task that has fewer complex technical requirements and that takes much less time than conventional publishing. The combination of its ability to reach out and to publish quickly often imply that information on the Web is more current and frequently updated than comparable print sources. Just as significantly, on the Web one can more readily encounter information that represents a broad range of positions and interests. Although some of this information can be prejudiced or unreliable, many experienced users enjoy the unfiltered, spontaneous nature of information on the Web, and have found the diversity of sources and perspectives to be stimulating and enriching (Basch 1996). Using a browser application to navigate the Web also offers a number of technical efficiencies. Retrieving document pages and multimedia information objects is as easy as clicking on the hyperlinks found on a given Web page. Pages and Websites can be searched easily by supplying simple keywords and the returned results consist of more hyperlinks that lead directly to information objects that answer the query. Useful pages and sites can be "bookmarked" for future visits — bookmarks can be organized into levels of folders representing hierarchies of subject topics or areas of scanning interest. Collections of bookmarks accumulated over time can become personalized knowledge resources. Bookmark collections themselves are databases in which owners can search for site names and Web addresses. Some Websites provide a notification capability, so that users can be automatically alerted when specified pages or content has been modified. In summary, the World Wide Web is rich in both content and tools: its information is eclectic, current, and constantly refreshed, and it also provides tools that simplify navigation, search, and retrieval. Its comprehensiveness, timeliness, and ease-of-use renders the Web a useful information lens through which to catch early glimpses of trends and signals of change in the external environment.

Before the World Wide Web, one of the most popular tools for locating information on the Internet is the **Gopher**, navigational software developed at the University of Minnesota which provides a menu-based searching system to discover, access, and retrieve Internet resources. The primary difference between Gopher and the Web is that there is no hypertext in Gopher: everything is either a document or a hierarchical menu. Information at Gopher sites are typically organized into complex hierarchies that may be many levels deep. Gopher makes it easy for the user to burrow through several levels of directories and subdirectories in order to find the needed information. A Gopher user is presented with a menu of items, each representing a document, file, or a link to another menu or subdirectory that may be at the same site or at some other location. To access an item, the user simply selects it on the menu. Conceptually, Gopher represents resource space as hierarchical trees, with the individual documents or resources at the leaves. Gopher menus at different sites may be interconnected at certain points, but access is always based upon moving up or down hierarchical menus. Gopher is an invitation to travel and explore the Internet, discovering and bookmarking interesting sites en route. If the user encounters an interesting item, Gopher can download and save the file or document, or send it to the user or another person by electronic mail.

Telnet is a common method for Internet users to log in to a remote host computer in order to access library catalogs, databases, and other public services that have been made available on that host. Telnet is both a protocol and a software application. As a communication protocol, Telnet defines a set of rules and procedures for a client computer to establish a temporary connection with a remote host and to emulate the behavior of a computer terminal that the host will recognize. As an application, the Telnet software consists of two parts: the client running on the user's computer and the server running on the host. The client software sets up a network connection with the host, takes input from the user, transmits it to the host in a standard format, receives output from the host in a standard format, and displays that output on the user's computer screen. The server software waits for a request in standard format, services a received request, sends the results to the client in standard format, and then waits again. To facilitate browsing, a Telnet session could present the user with lists or menus of services and information resources which the user then selects and navigates.

Pushing

On the Internet, push technology refers to the software and protocol technologies that deliver information to the users' desktops without the users having the need to search for the information. Push technology offers important benefits for both end users and publishers. With push technology, users can specify what information they are interested in receiving; have new information alerts automatically delivered and presented on the screens of their workstations; and access the Web pages containing desired information by clicking on links. For publishers, push solutions offer new ways of establishing and maintaining relationships with customers; new channels of marketing and advertising; and new modes of distributing information, software applications, and services.

Most push systems today are really conventional "pull" systems in disguise — push software periodically polls information sources and pulls down new data onto the users' desktops. Observers have noted that push technology has been around for a long time, since the first push application on the Internet would have been electronic mail. (One company which has been doing "true push" since the 1980s is Palo Alto-based Tibco Software: its publish-subscribe model uses a software information pathway called The Information Bus (TIB) to distribute information as soon as it is published, and to subject-tag the information so that users receive only information they have subscribed to.) Today's push technology can deliver content through dedicated push client and server software, or as HTML e-mail, or as part of the functionality of the Web browser, or as an embedded feature of the desktop interface. It is possible to discern four modes of push-enabled delivery: self-service delivery, aggregated delivery, mediated delivery, and direct delivery (Resnick 1997). In self-service delivery systems (eg. Freeloader from Individual Inc), users select Web pages to download for later, offline viewing. In aggregated delivery systems (eg. Pointcast Network from Pointcast Inc), content and advertising from a variety of sources are packaged together into a single offering. Their mode of operation is similar to that of television and broadcasting networks. In mediated delivery systems (eg. Communicator from Intermind Corp), users control what content they want to receive from publishers and marketers, typically by selecting from a menu of choices on the mediator's Web site. Finally, in direct delivery systems (eg. Microsoft's Active Desktop or Netscape's Home Port), the personal computer's desktop interface itself pulls information off the Internet.

One variation of the push theme is to employ a software agent to forage for and bring to the desktop information about topics that the user has selected. Of some interest to environmental scanning is a service called NewBot from Wired magazine's online division. NewBot users enter keywords that define the subjects they are interested in monitoring. NewBot then crawls a comprehensive set of news sources on the Web continuously and automatically, and returns with an organized digest of found items which include dates and times, their sources, Web page addresses, headlines and brief abstracts. Users can then scan the digest quickly and click on selected items to go to the pages containing the full story. NewBot claims to be able to find, filter, and deliver breaking news on the Web within a few hours of their being made available.

Apart from different modes of delivering information to the desktop, it is also useful to distinguish three levels of push: pushed HTML pages received as e-mail; pushed Web sites; and pushed content channels (Karpinski and Santales 1997). In pushed HTML, publishers can send Web pages as e-mail that retain the page layout, graphics, and active links. Users receive the Web pages they have subscribed to automatically, and can click on links to view additional pages or visit sites, all from within their electronic mailboxes. Over and above individual pages, entire Web sites can also be monitored, subscribed to, or even downloaded. These sites can be updated automatically, or users can choose to be notified of changes and modifications. Perhaps the most versatile form of push is the creation of content channels on the users' desktops which automatically download updated content from specified servers and services. Content can be anything that can be digitized and transferred over the Internet: application software, documents, files, images, news, updates, and so on. For push channels to become widespread, standards need to be agreed upon about delivery protocols and document formats. Thus, Microsoft is proposing a Channel Definition Format which lets users define the content on Web sites which are to be pushed, tagging items like headlines, text, and graphics, as well as how often content is changed. Web site administrators create and place CDF files on their servers, and users download these files to their push clients in order to establish the channel connection. (Instead of defining a new channel format, Netscape has added elements to its JavaScript scripting language so that it enables push channels.)

The application and commercial market for push technology is still very fluid at the time of writing (fall 1997). Although an early innovator like Pointcast Inc has claimed over one million users, many of the recent commercial startups have found it difficult to win over corporate customers or to develop viable business models. The acceptance of push channels depends on the resolution of a number of issues in the areas of distribution, design, and content (Veen 1997). In terms of distribution, channels (and push technology in general) can consume inordinate amounts of bandwidth, soaking up significant proportions of the available capacity in any organization. In terms of design, some content providers have tended to overemphasize eye-catching visual effects, often at the expense of fast performance and navigational simplicity. In terms of content, much of the information being distributed is mainstream, generic and limited to a small number of sources, thus negating one of the original rationale for having channels — the capability to deliver highly customized, relevant information culled from a variety of sources. Newer push technology vendors have begun to address these concerns. For example, a push product called Headliner from Toronto-based Lanacom Inc uses its "content agent" technology to deliver filtered and summarized information from a virtually unlimited selection of sources through an unobtrusive, uncluttered interface, thereby conserving both network bandwidth and users' attention spans. In summary, push media will succeed only if they can build new information-based relationships with content consumers that do not make undue demands on communication and cognitive resources.

Searching

While browsing the Web and Internet may be appropriate for the undirected and conditioned viewing of the environment, during the informal search mode, which involves looking for specific information to increase knowledge and understanding of some issue, it becomes necessary to search rather than just browse the Internet. A number of indexing and search services are accessible on the World Wide Web that allow individuals to easily and quickly find and retrieve information according to words and conditions that they specify. In essence, there are two broad categories of Web indexes: search engines that scan indexes of Web pages for keywords and other attributes, and manually constructed tables of contents that list Web sites by subject categories (Hearst 1997).

Web **search engines** construct and update their indexes by periodically dispatching programs (Web crawlers, spiders, or indexing robots) to every Web site. These crawler programs download pages from the sites and extract indexing information that are used to describe the content of those pages. Different search engines have different ways of doing this — some apply sophisticated algorithms to identify important words and phrases, others simply include words and phrases that occur (or that occur most frequently) on the page. The resultant data together with the URL or address of the page are then stored in the search engine's database. An individual searches this database using a Web browser to submit queries. The search engine returns with a ranked list of Web pages and their URLs which the individual can click on to access the actual pages.

Popular Web-based search services such as Alta Vista, Excite, InfoSeek, Lycos, Open Text, and WebCrawler vary considerably in their search capabilities. At the time of writing, most services, but not all (one exception being InfoSeek), allow users to include simple Boolean operators in their search statements. Proximity searching is only supported in a few services (Alta Vista, WebCrawler). Again, few services support explicitly the use of wildcards (Alta Vista does), although services like InfoSeek and Lycos automatically truncate or include word spelling variations. Phrase searching is more generally available. Field searching, when supported, is limited to attributes such as the page title; URL; link; or media title (image, audio, etc) — author names, dates, and institutional affiliations are generally not searchable. Few services recognize the use of metatags that might be used to specify keywords or content descriptions (Alta Vista and InfoSeek do).

Although Web search services vary greatly in their approaches to indexing, searching, and displaying results, they do share a number of common features (Ding and Marchionini 1996, p. 136):

> 1. An easy-to-use interface. They either provide a search form for users to do keyword searching or present a hierarchical menu for browsing, and some provide both search form and subject menu. Most search forms have reasonable default parameters for truncation, logical operators, and search results limits.

> 2. An automatically constructed database of Web resources. The system (service) collects and updates indexed webpages by using a robot program running throughout the WWW. Queries are matched against this database, which is updated based on both the robot's continuous hunting and user's requests.

> 3. Output with relevance ranking, based on term frequencies, term locations and other criteria. The output format varies from one search service to another, but all of the result pages have links to the primary sources.

> 4. No numbered sets. None of the search services provides reusable output data sets as are available in Dialog and other biblio-

graphic retrieval systems. The entire query formulation must be entered in one statement.

5. Online documentation. This is usually provided in forms of FAQ pages, searching tips and "what's new" page.

In their evaluation of three popular Web-based services, Ding and Marchionini (1996) found that the precision ratio for all the three search services was low: less than 55% for the the three search services, even when only the first 20 retrieved items were taken into account. Furthermore, search services are mainly limited to topic specification so that the user could not constrain the search to, for example, certain types of information (government reports, newspaper articles, press releases) or certain time periods. Ding and Marchionini argued that search services should "enable users to take more control over the search process and results by offering such functions as reviewing search history, adjusting search strategies, editing and sorting search results, and choosing preferable delivery formats." (p. 139)

Search services are constantly enhancing their capabilities and adding new functionalities thus making the selection of search engine a complex decision. Many useful comparisons of Web search services may be found on the Web itself, and one example would be that maintained by Westera at the Curtin University of Technology library (http://www.curtin.edu.au/curtin/library/staffpages/gwperonal/senginestudy/compare.htm). It is also worth noting that an increasing number of organizations and sites now offer search engines of their own that are customized to retrieving information from the local sites or databases.

Although automated indexing relying on computer processing power seems an attractive option — search engines can service millions of queries and index millions of pages in a day — there are several weaknesses of automated indexing when compared with human indexing (Lynch 1997). Web crawlers cannot identify important characteristics of a document such as its overall theme or genre. They do not index sites that require passwords for entry (and a growing number of sites with valuable databases are requiring registration and passwords), and they do not index graphics or images, so that for example, a home page consisting of an imagemap might not be indexed properly. Web documents are not structured with standard fields so it is not possible to extract automatically such basic data as the author's name, the publication date, and the institutional affiliation. One solution being researched is to define a set of metadata elements (such as title, author, document type) that are attached to the Web pages and may be retrieved by crawler software for indexing (Lynch 1997).

Another approach to finding information on the Web is to use human indexers to classify Websites according to broad subject areas. One of the best known of these is Yahoo! which employs human editors to create a hierarchical subject-oriented guide for the World Wide Web and Internet. Yahoo! is a database of links to other sites and does not try to add much original content. Starting from the 14 top-level categories on its front-page, users can drill-down into progressively narrower subject categories. Websites are submitted by users themselves, and because of its popularity on the Web, Yahoo! has good coverage of business organizations and resources. As a directory service, Yahoo! concentrates on its indexing and arrangement of sites, so most entries contain little or no description, and only a small number of sites are reviewed or rated.

The distinction between subject directories and search engines is blurring. Yahoo! for example provides a keyword search of its subject categories, and when the search fails, Yahoo! offers direct links to several search engine services. Conversely, search engines are putting up subject-oriented guides. InfoSeek includes a directory service on the same page as its search engine service. The directory service is created through a combined use of human and artificial intelligence: InfoSeek's team of librarians uses neural network-based software to dynamically build and maintain its directories, which the company claims to offer "the most current and comprehensive ontology of Web sites in the world." Instead of trying to be comprehensive, Lycos' Top 5% Sites offers a selective directory of web sites that its reviewers rate to be among the top 5 percent. Sites are rated according to their information content, design and presentation, and overall attributes such as amusement and charm.

The choice of a search engine becomes the critical first step in initiating an Internet search. Whereas an online search begins with a selection of a database to search in, an Internet search begins with the selection of a search engine or service. One might look to evaluation studies to help determine which search engine to use. Unfortunately, the number of rigorous evaluation studies on Web search services is small (a list is maintained by Koch at Lund University and is available at http://www.ub2.lu.se/desire/radar/lit-about-search-services.html). Moreover, the reported findings do not appear to agree with one another (Chu and Rosenthal 1996). Part of the divergence is due to the differences in methodologies and evaluation criteria applied by different studies. Chu and Rosenthal (1996) propose an evaluation methodology for Web search engines based on the following five dimensions: composition of the Web indexes; search capabilities; retrieval performance; output options; and user effort.

No matter which search engines is used, there remains the dilemma that each search engine is likely to locate some highly relevant sites that none of the others have found: "Every search engine will give you good search results some of the time. Every search engine will give you surprisingly bad search results some of the time. No search engine will give you good results all of the time." (Feldman 1997). When a search has to be thorough, it becomes necessary to use several search services at the same time.

We may summarize the advantages of Web-based search services as follows. The services are free, being mostly supported by advertising. They provide access to up-to-date, current information, since publishing on the Web can be accomplished much more quickly than conventional methods. Search results contain links to the actual Web documents, as well as additional links to related resources for further exploration and elaboration. Many services can also retrieve images, graphics and audio information. Generally, Web-based search services can perform well with simple queries that consist of specific names, a few keywords, or unambiguous subject terms. These advantages can turn into limitations in practice. Although the services carry no charges, users can spend a great deal more time and effort in locating information on the Web than when searching through better-organized fee-based services. Information on the Web may be fresh and current, but it is also hard to judge the veracity or quality of the information presented. Many page links are not updated so that they become dead links. Not all kinds of search queries are well suited to searching on the Web. Generally, Web search engines perform less well with complex queries that involve multiple search facets, or that specify multiple retrieval conditions. Most search engines offer limited control of the search process: they do not allow users to focus the search by limiting the search to non-subject related attributes (for example, document type, time period, genre); and they do not allow users to modify the search strategy in incremental steps (by for example, creating intermediate search sets).

Although many Web-based search engines also retrieve information on Gophers and FTP servers, there are specialized tools for searching these information spaces that were popular before the advent of the Web. **Veronica**, which stands for Very Easy Rodent-Oriented Network Index to Computer Archives, is a tool that searches words in directory and file names at one or many Gopher sites, and includes the use of Boolean operations and search term delimiters to increase search precision. **Jughead** is a similar tool that limits searches to items in the local Gopher server. Besides these dedicated search aids, a Gopher menu item may also represent a searchable directory, and users may then enter search words to look for within that directory. **Archie** is a system for searching indexes of files that are available on public servers on the Internet. Archie allows users to search the filenames or descriptions of the files and returns with the names of servers containing those files. Users may then use anonymous FTP to transfer the desired files or documents.

Communicating

More than a browsing medium, the Internet is also a communications medium where individuals and groups interact with each other through electronic mail and its enhanced services such as mailing lists and newsgroups. Stefik (1996) observes that electronic mail has at least three unique advantages: fan-out, electronic distribution, and asynchronous communication. Fan-out enables an individual to poll a large number of people simultaneously. It is also not uncommon for information requests to be re-directed to knowledgable persons who are not in the initial distribution. Electronic distribution delivers the message to the recipients regardless of where they may be. Asynchronous communication means that individuals could read and reply to electronic mail when they are ready or want to, and avoid playing telephone tag. Electronic mail can be an alternative way of finding information: instead of looking through databases or publications, a question may be posted to a mailing list or newsgroup. Electronic mail also makes it possible to contact the individual who created the information in the first place, and seek clarification, clarify the context, or ask for more data. A study based on interviews with 35 expert Internet searchers found that: "Ultimately, the Net offers something unparalleled in any other research environment: global access to people who know. Just about everybody I spoke with about Net resources drew a distinction between people and publications between the knowledge-base of expertise offered by the Internet population, and the database of formal collections ..." (Basch 1996, p. xx)

As an **electronic mail** network, the Internet now spans the globe, with over 70 million people using electronic mail worldwide. Mail gateways have been established to nearly all the major commercial networks, consumer online services, government or academic networks, and bulletin board systems that are in operation today. Via these mail gateways the Internet is acting as the matrix through which messages from these disparate networks are routed to each other. For most business users, the most attractive service provided by the Internet is its global electronic mail service that can reach colleagues and customers as well as organizations and markets almost anywhere in the world. Electronic mail on the Internet is reliable, cheap, and flexible. Development of the Internet began in the late 1960s at the height of the Cold War, under the aegis of the US Department of Defense. The Internet was designed from the outset to be a robust, reliable network that will connect defense-related computer centers, and to be able to withstand the onslaught of a nuclear attack. Today, the dependability of the Internet is almost taken for granted — should particular systems or networks go down, messages are moved along alternative routes to their destinations. For users in schools, universities, public libraries, freenets, and government organizations, access to the Internet is often free of charge. For business organizations, access to the Internet may be obtained inexpensively, at rates significantly lower than any of the commercial services. At the present time, providing Internet access is a burgeoning industry, and is still very much a buyers' market. Finally, electronic mail via the Internet is flexible, allowing users to attach graphics, photographs, maps, video clips, sound files, as well as word-processed documents to their messages. These attachments are transmitted efficiently as text files that have been encoded and compressed from their original binary forms. Offsetting these advantages are a few limitations: Internet electronic mail is not necessarily secure; messages may be forged; and the delivery of Internet mail is not always assured, as receiving systems may be down or closed. Considering that hundreds of millions of messages travel on the Internet every month, the Internet has become the de facto standard for the exchange of e-mail between people and organizations around the world.

While basic electronic mail is communication in a one-to-one mode, electronic discussion groups supported by mailing lists and newsgroups provide communication in a one-to-many or many-to-many mode. A **mailing list** is typically a group of people who exchange electronic mail about a subject that interests them. Many Internet mailing lists are maintained by list manager software (such as LISTSERV or MAJORDOMO) that reduces the need for human intervention: members can subscribe and unsubscribe to groups, choose the way they wish to receive messages, search previous messages, and so on, all by sending commands as mail messages to the list manager software, which has its own email address. A member of the mailing list can create a message, which may be as short as a question, or as long as a newsletter or journal, and mail it to a single Internet address of the mailing list which contains the addresses of everyone in the discussion group. The list manager software then sends a copy of the message to every member, each of whom receives the message as regular electronic mail. Such discussion groups may be moderated, in which case a human moderator looks at each new message to check its relevance and approve its distribution to the group. Other discussion groups may be unmoderated (every message is sent out to the group), or closed (membership is restricted to certain people). Members can also send commands to the list manager software to search and retrieve discussion group archive files using a sophisticated set of search capabilities that includes Boolean combinations, nested parentheses, soundex matching, and so on. There are tens of thousands of mailing list-based discussion groups on the Internet, bringing together people and experts around a wide range of topics, subject areas, professional specializations, social interests, and so on.

Newsgroups are the most popular form of discussion groups on the Net, and historically predates the Internet. While mailing list discussion groups of the last paragraph are essentially one-to-many electronic mail communications, newsgroups are more like many-to-many bulletin board systems. Members of a newsgroup read news articles that are posted on a common bulletin board that is seen by everyone in the group. Members can scan the titles of articles, select the ones to read, and reply to them if they wish. News articles are not sent as electronic mail, instead, members use news reader software to access and view articles. News reader software organizes the articles into threads of related postings that reply to a particular question or issue, so that members can read a thread of connected articles in sequence. Most newsgroups maintain a list of answers to Frequently Asked Questions (FAQ) that anyone may consult. Some newsgroups also keep their discussions in archives which may then be searched or retrieved. Newsgroup articles come from several sources, such as Usenet, local news sources, mail reflectors, and Clarinet. By far the most important source is Usenet, which is a set of computers that exchange newsgroup articles, as well as a set of voluntary rules for passing and maintaining newsgroups. Usenet newsgroups show boundless variety, encompassing businesses of all shapes and sizes, community groups, government agencies, universities, and on and on. There are seven major Usenet newsgroup categories, identified by the following newsgroup name prefixes:

comp Newsgroups discussing computer science related topics.

news Newsgroups concerned with managing and maintaining the news network.

rec Newsgroups discussing recreational activities, hobbies, arts.

sci Newsgroups discussing research in science and engineering.

soc Newsgroups addressing social, political, and cultural issues.

talk Newsgroup forums for debate on controversial topics.

misc Any newsgroup whose discussion does not fit the above categories or crosses over several categories.

Each major Usenet newsgroup category may contain hundreds or thousands of discussion groups. In addition, there are several alternative newsgroup categories:

alt A very large and open-ended category of newsgroups discussing "alternative ways of looking at things." Almost anything and everything can and does appear.

biz Newsgroups related to business, including the posting of advertisements, product announcements, etc, which is not acceptable practice in other groups.

Usenet newsgroups are arranged hierarchically. For example, a newsgroup with the name biz.comp.software.demos would discuss computer software demonstration products. Newsgroup names five or more levels deep are not uncommon. The sprawling hierarchy of Usenet newsgroups, subdivided into many sublevels of discussion groups with narrowly defined interests, provides a fine-grained stratification that no conventional business mailing list or directory can hope to match. Selecting which newsgroup to join becomes an important decision that could mean the difference between being part of a community sharing useful information and having to work through a confusing haze of noisy information to find the occasional gem. Whereas searching for information in a database is more like tracking and hunting (desired articles and reports), joining newsgroups is more like fishing, so that selecting what newsgroups to join is analogous to deciding where to put fishing nets (Stefik 1996). For business users, newsgroups may be useful for finding answers to specific questions, tracking particular technologies or products, and gauging a group's opinions or sentiments about some issue.

Summary

To summarize our discussion so far, we suggest some plausible generalizations about how the four main types of information seeking services available on the Internet can support the various modes of environmental scanning. **Browsing** on the Internet, whether using a HTML viewer, or a Gopher or Telnet client, could be a useful way of providing the scope and coverage that is required in the *undirected viewing* mode of scanning. Thus, browsing on the Web allows a number of different sources to be looked over quickly by simply entering addresses, selecting bookmarks, and following hyperlinks. Selecting links on related topics can amplify and elaborate existing knowledge about the topic. Viewing links on topics not previously thought to be relevant can suggest new associations and provide additional insight. **Push** services on the Web extend the range of sources covered, helping to ensure for example, that information from important sources are not missed. Push technology also matches well the requirements of *conditioned viewing* since it is an efficient way of automating and customizing the delivery of information about a particular topic without the user having to search for new information time and again. **Search** services on the Internet and the Web would be utilized in all modes of environmental scanning, but may be expected to play an especially important role during the *informal search* mode of scanning. The objective of informal search is to gather information about specific issues and with specific attributes in order to elaborate on the issue sufficiently so as to be able to determine the need for action by the organization or group. **Communication** services on the Internet could likewise take on increased urgency during the *formal search* mode of scanning, when one is tracking down a knowledgeable individual or group for action- or decision-oriented information and advice. Generally, the information gathering capabilities available on the Internet and the Web can support all the scanning modes we have discussed, and are particularly well suited to address the needs of undirected viewing, conditioned viewing, and informal searching.

Embarrassment of Riches

Table 7.1 shows the spectrum of Web-based and online resources that could support the various modes of viewing and searching the environment. For broad, undirected viewing, there is a huge number of news Websites that provide international, national, and local news, many of them providing news that is updated every few hours. For conditioned viewing, value-added information and analysis are being offered by market research companies, trade and industry associations, financial institutions, and government agencies. For informal searching, free services may be selected from a competitive array of Web-based search engines and directory listings, some of which include source evaluations. Finally, for formal searching, search engines that specialize in indexing newsgroups and mailing lists can be used in conjunction with electronic mail to make contact with knowledgable experts or organizations. During formal searching, commercial online services provide a much more structured and interactive environment in which to retrieve focused, pertinent information that addresses complex, multi-faceted queries. It is worth noting that commercial online search service vendors are moving to the Web, adopting it as a conduit for providing search services to professional as well as casual users. For example, Dialog has implemented Dialog Web for information specialists who can use Dialog's sophisticated command language to finesse their searches, as well as easy-to-use Dialog Select for novice users.

Web-based Business Resources

Table 7.2 shows a selection of Web-based information resources and services that can provide the range of information needed to develop business intelligence. The list is obviously only a small sample of the vast resources on the Web, and is intended to be indicative of the scope, variety, as well as quality of the information that is available, often for free or at low cost. The resources are organized according to the modes of environmental scanning we have discussed: undirected viewing, conditioned viewing, informal search, and formal search. Good places to start would be the Website maintained by Sheila Webber, a lecturer at the University of Strathcylde, and the directory of competitive intelligence resources maintained by Helene Kassler of Fuld & Company (addresses of both sites are in Table 7.2). The latter has also written a paper that highlights several creative techniques that may be used to mine for competitive intelligence on the Internet (Kassler 1997).

Table 7.1   Web-based and Online Sources for Viewing and Search

UNDIRECTED VIEWING	CONDITIONED VIEWING	INFORMAL SEARCH	FORMAL SEARCH
Detect Signals	Assess Significance	Elaborate Issues	Probe Issue
World Wide Web/Internet Services ———————➤		Online Databases Search Services	
• **News Websites** (International, national, regional newspapers; major publishers; newswire services; conferences)	• **Market Research Websites** (Reports from market research, consulting firms; trade and industry associations)	• **Web Search Engines** (Search web pages, newsgroups, mailing lists, FAQs)	• **E-mail, Newsgroups, Mailing Lists** (Identify and contact individuals)
• **Personalized News Services** (Customized newspapers; individualized alert services; search agents)	• **Financial Institution Websites** (Reports, newsletters from investment banks, financial analysts)	• **Web Directories and Lists** (Search directories of sources evaluated by specialists)	• **Online Database Search Services** (Retrieve focused information on complex, multifaceted issues; purchase in-depth "insider" information)
• **Pushed Information**	• **Government Websites**	• **Online Database Search Services** (Search databases for more detailed, complete, reliable information)	

Table 7.2a   A Selection of WWW Business Information Resources (1)

1. Resources for Broad, Undirected Viewing	Uniform Resource Locator	Description
1.1 News Websites		
Reuters	http://www.yahoo.com/ headlines/news	*Direct access to current Reuters news reports in sections such as Top Stories, World, Business, Politics, and Entertainment. Includes news in audio formats.*
Business Wire	http://www.businesswire.com	*Hour by hour listing of headlines from press releases of private, public, and other organizations. Search past two days news releases by keyword or state.*
American City Business Journals	http://www.amcity.com	*American City is largest publisher of metropolitan business newspapers in the US. Site provides links to each newspaper's home page. Searchable.*
Trade Show Central	http://www.tscentral.com	*Access to over 30,000 trade shows. Search directory by industry category, location, date, etc. Automatically request information about show, registration.*
1.2 Personalized News and Channels		
Personal Journal from Dow Jones	http://interactive.wsj.com/ archive/personal.cgi	*Personalize up to five folders of news from Wall Street Journal, Dow Jones Newswires, and Interactive Journal newsroom. Specify by keywords, companies, or industries.*
NewsTracker from Excite	http://nt.excite.com	*Customize news channel by naming topics, and entering search terms that describe each topic.*
In-Box Direct from Netscape	http://form.netscape.com	*Subscribe to IBD newsletters which are sent to Netscape Mail in-boxes as Web pages (HTML mail).*

Table 7.2b   A Selection of WWW Business Information Resources (2)

2. Resources for Conditioned Viewing	Uniform Resource Locator	Description
2.1 Market Research Websites		
The Market Research Center from ASI	http://www.asiresearch.com	*Comprehensive directory of market research companies and organizations, including their e-mail, phone, and postal addresses.*
The Investext Group	http://www.investext.com	*Investext is a major provider of company, industry and market analysis. Access to over 1 million investment reports, market research reports, and trade association research studies.*
Find/SVP	http://www.findsvp.com	*Searchable online catalog of market intelligence reports organized by broad industry categories. Also provides quick, cost-effective research over the phone as well as more in-depth research.*
Profound for the Internet from M.A.I.D plc	http://www.profound.com	*Access to structured business information: after identifying a report in a search, Profound provides a detailed table of contents that shows the location of the exact information sought. User pays for only the information selected.*
2.2 Financial Institutions		
Hoover's Online	http://hoovers.com	*Search and access to Hoover's Company Profiles (detailed financial and competitive analysis), and to Company Capsules (free, covers over 10,000 firms).*
Corporate Finance Network	http://www.corpfinet.com	*Access to news, resources, and best practices from finance and technology companies on the Web.*

Van Kasper & Company	http://www.vkco.com	*Van Kasper is a California-based private brokerage and investment banking firm. Its site provides original investment analysis of eight major industry groups.*
Bankers Trust Global Research Group	http://www.bankerstrust. com/global/global.html	*Access to Bankers Trust's investment opinions and risk valuations on countries, markets, industries and companies. Sections on market economics, market commentary, and product-specific.*

2.3   Associations

American Society of Association Executives	http://asaenet.org	*ASAE's 23,000 members manage trade associations, individual membership societies, voluntary organizations, and nonprofit associations. Access to directories of its member and affiliated associations.*
Society of Competitive Intelligence Professionals	http://www.scip.org	*SCIP has over 5,000 individual members (mostly professionals) in many countries. Publications section has useful links to its Competitive Intelligence Review and other resources.*

2.4   Government Sites

U.S. Fedworld Information Network	http://www.fedworld.gov	*Gateway to the hundreds of U.S. Government Web sites: searchable by keyword or by categories. U.S. Govt Information Locator Service searches abstracts that describe information products available from Federal Govt.*
U.S. Securities and Exchange Commission EDGAR Database	http://www.sec.gov/ edgarhp.htm	*Documents filed with SEC are available online 24 hours later. Searchable by company name, form type, and date range. Analysis of forms filed in the previous week are in the Current Events Analysis section.*

U.K. CCTA Government Information Service	http://www.open.gov.uk	*Access to many U.K. government departments and local authority sites. Includes press releases. Link to the U.K. Office for National Statistics.*
Japan Information Network	http://www.jinjapan.org/stat/	*Access to a variety of economic, social, demographic, and trade statistics; directory of Japanese government and business organizations. Link to Trends in Japan section with business analysis.*

Table 7.2c   A Selection of WWW Business Information Resources (3)

3. Resources for Informal and Formal Search	Uniform Resource Locator	Description
3.1 Search Engines		
DejaNews	http://www.dejanews.com	*Comprehensive newsgroup search engine, providing 22 months of searchable Usenet postings in over 20,000 newsgroups. 86 million articles (2/1997). Author Profile feature provides newsgroup summary of articles from a specified person.*
Liszt	http://www.liszt.com	*Searchable directory of mailing lists. Liszt automatically catalogs of public lists on thousands of list servers worldwide. Includes information about how to join and know more about a list.*
Reference.com	http://www.reference.com	*Searchable directory of Usenet newsgroups, publicly accessible mailing lists, and Webforums. Altogether over 120,000 Internet forums are searchable.*

3.2   Web Directories and Lists

Business Information Sources on the Net	http://www.dis.strath.ac.uk/business/general.html	*Maintained by Sheila Webber, lecturer at the Dept of Information Science, University of Strathclyde. Current and well organized, with sections on News Sources; Statistical, Economic and Market Information; Company Directories; Company Profiles; and Country Information.*
Argus Clearinghouse	http://www.clearinghouse.com	*A central gateway to "value-added topical guides which identify, describe and evaluate Internet-based information resources." Guides are rated by staff, many with library science Masters degrees from the University of Michigan.*
Competitive Intelligence Guide from Fuld & Co.	http://www.fuld.com/i3/	*Directory of links of over 300 Internet resources with information related to competitive intelligence. Sections on Industry-Specific Resources and International Resources.*

3.3   Online Services
(Fee-based services)

Dialog Select from Knight-Ridder Information, Inc.	http://dialogselect.krinfo.com	*Search over 250 Dialog databases covering more than 200 topics such as News & Media, Business & Finance, Technology, Energy & Environment. Intended for end users, with "built-in search intelligence" to simplify search.*
DowVision from Dow Jones Business Information Services	http://bis.dowjones.com/dowvision	*Access to headlines and full texts of major newspapers such as The Wall Street Journal, The New York Times, LA Times, The Washington Post, and Financial Times. Folders can be set up to track news on specified topics.*
Insite Pro from Information Access Company	http://www.insitepro.com	*Flat-fee access to IAC's databases including PROMT, Trade & Industry Database, Newsletter Database, Computer Database, and Magazine Database. Search by keywords, free text, and topic list. Retrieves graphs, charts.*

Companies Using the Internet for Environmental Scanning

More and more organizations are using the Internet to support the gathering and sharing of business intelligence. Not surprisingly, many of the early adopters were the larger companies in the technology-oriented industries. The rapid diffusion of the Web as a platform for constructing internal, corporate-wide Internets often means that information about industry and market developments of special relevance to the organization is being selectively disseminated through these so-called Intranets. Case studies of organizations using the Internet/Intranet are growing in number, and we sketch a few examples below.

Digital Equipment Corporation has been a long-time user and supporter of the Internet. Among its many Internet successes may be counted the use of the Web to provide marketing information to customers throughout the world, a pioneering program that allows Internet users to test drive its new server computers, bundling of Web client software with every Digital computer sold, and a heavy internal use of the Web and the Internet as a strategic information and communication resource (Jarvenpaa and Ives 1994). Digital claims that some fifty of its employees regularly monitor Digital product-related newsgroups, where over 84,000 users every month share their problems and solutions, and exchange opinions about Digital products, customer service, competing products, and so on (Thorell 1994).

At Oracle Corporation, a leading vendor of relational database systems, monitoring newsgroups and discussion groups on the Internet is an important method of ensuring current awareness about the competitive position of its products in the database software market, and about how well its existing systems are functioning in the real world (Cronin 1993). For example, an Oracle users' discussion group has more than 700 participants from many different kinds of organizations located all over the world. They use the discussion group to exchange information, ask for help, as well as evaluate products from Oracle and competing vendors. The discussions are frank and knowledgeable, and provide invaluable feedback and market insight.

Internet business users are not limited to computer technology vendors. Consider J.P. Morgan, the fifth-largest bank in the US. Although often seen as a conservative and cautious money-center bank, it has embraced the Internet with a pioneering boldness (Wilder 1995). Professionals at the bank use the Net to access the most current economic research being done at universities. J.P. Morgan's strategists need to keep up with the latest theories and predictions by economists from around the world, a growing number of whom are publishing their research electronically on the Net. Today, thousands of J.P. Morgan employees at their worldwide branches are able to scour the Internet for whatever data they need and are discovering new uses every day — for example, mortgage-backed securities analysts would retrieve government census data to analyze trends in property values, while junior research analysts would search for corporate financial reports. An associate at J.P. Morgan's New York headquarters observes: "Walk the floors and you'll see Mosaic browsers everywhere. It's really become ingrained in the way people operate here."

Ford Motor Company's Intranet, called the Ford Hub, contains a directory of information categories including News, People, Processes, Products, and Competition (Stuart 1997). The menu for the Competition category provides access to information on benchmarking, automobile shows, global market information, competitor news, product-cycle plans, and patent information. Ford's in-house standards call for pages to be dated and linked to the author's name and other contact information, so that users can send content managers questions, as well as referrals and reminders about keeping content current. Since its inception in 1986, the Ford Hub is being accessed by over 80,000 Ford employees worldwide.

Cadence Design Systems is a San Jose-based supplier of electronic design automation software, services, and solutions to electronics companies around the world. Its business strategy requires in-depth knowledge of its customers' needs and the environments they compete in. Cadence maintains a Web site that keeps its staff well informed about industry news: instead of the typical list of 14 different trade journals that a sales staff would need to keep up with the technology and the market, the Web site provides access to direct daily news feeds about Cadence, its industry, customers, competitors, as well as focused topics such as automative electronics. The Cadence site also links to the Websites of its customers so that the sales and consulting staff can keep up-to-date with press releases, news articles, financial performance, and other important information about their customers' businesses. (Netscape, 1997)

Hise (1996) relates several creative instances of small and medium-sized companies gathering useful intelligence from the Internet. Art Anderson Associates is a $4 million engineering and architecture business designing ferry vessels and port facilities for overseas locations. The firm is counting on the Web and newsgroups run by overseas tourism boards to help provide early leads about new markets. For example, to get the latest news on development and tourism in Singapore, executives would use the Singapore Website to determine which industries are most active and who are the major players. Another firm, Mobius Computer, is a $7.5 million manufacturer of computer systems used by Fortune 1000 companies. Mobius keeps a close watch on these companies' financial reports that are available online, in order to develop a sense of who might be in the market for new or upgraded systems. Mobius' CEO also uses the Internet to collect product information and lists of references from competitors and potential customers. Each day, the executive samples five or six newsgroups from a larger list of two hundred discussion groups on topics pertinent to his business.

An informal survey on the use of the Internet in business intelligence conducted by the Montague Institute, a training and consultancy firm based in Massachusetts, found that the majority of the respondents were affiliated with the market research function, with the others being from departments such as the library or information center, competitive intelligence department, and strategic planning department. Respondents reported that "secondary research," that is, finding published information, was their most important use of the Internet, followed by "monitoring government information," "internal collaboration," and "primary information (on new products)." Improving the quality of information and increasing the cost-effectiveness of acquiring information were the leading reasons that their companies deployed the Internet in the intelligence function (Montague Institute, 1997).

An exploratory study surveyed the business use of the Internet for competitive intelligence purposes, and found that "there is extensive, sophisticated and creative use of the Internet in support of the competitive intelligence function in organizations. Respondents feel that they are monitoring the competitive environment with greater ease than before thanks to Internet access. It is obvious that the Internet massively extends access to open source information ..." (Cronin, et al., 1994, p. 222). The responses from the survey participants seem to suggest two modes of information foraging on the net: the Internet is being used both as a traditional *business intelligence tool*, and as an *organizational learning tool*. In the traditional mode, organizations are monitoring various Internet discussion groups in order to keep themselves informed about competitors' products, technologies, and strategies, directly from customers, reviewers, and other knowledgable experts who populate these discussion groups. Internet discussion groups are also being used to maintain a high level of current awareness about issues that are occupying an industry, a market, or even a competitor. Beyond business intelligence applications, some businesses appear to be using the Internet as an *organizational learning tool*. The Net carries more than just raw information, it is also an outpost for scouting skills and expertise, and a fertile breeding ground for the germination and nurturing of ideas. In discussion groups, the diversity of knowledge, experience and points of view broadens the outlook of everyone in the discussion group. There is a heightened awareness of what is possible, and one's closely held assumptions, once exposed to the scrutiny of others in a group, are subject to challenge or ratification. Double-loop learning takes place as new mental models gradually replace existing frames of reference. By affirming an information culture that upholds open mindedness and intellectual curiosity, the Internet can act as a catalyst to learning and adaptation. Based on the findings of their survey, the authors look ahead at the prospect of Internet use for competitive intelligence:

> The Internet has the potential to become a major strategic information tool for commercial enterprises. Many companies, large and small, are already using the Internet to gain an edge in an increasingly competitive business environment, both domestically and internationally. It may well be that the Internet is the next major phase in the evolution of the competitive intelligence function in

advanced organizations, especially as commercialization of the network intensifies. (Cronin, et al., 1994, p. 204)

The Value of Online Databases

The number of online databases has been expanding rapidly, from about 770 in 1982 to well over 9,000 in 1996 (Williams 1997). One-third of the databases are in the Business subject category, that is, there are more than 3,000 online databases providing business information. For at least the past decade, business databases have formed the most numerous subject category, and the usage of business databases has also been one of the fastest growing categories. The number of online searches has been growing exponentially every year since the early 1980s (when PCs were first mass-marketed), and the recent spread of the Internet appears not to have dampened the use of online databases. In 1995 alone, more than 72 million online searches were conducted on databases from the five major US vendors of word-oriented databases (Williams 1997).

Using online databases to learn about the external environment offers a number of distinctive advantages. To begin with, online information is generally more current and comprehensive than print sources, and online searching is more speedy and flexible, especially when dealing with complex questions. Compared with their print counterparts, online databases are likely to contain information that is more recent and up-to-date. A growing number of government and business documents are available online hours or days before they appear in print. Online records also tend to be updated more frequently. Many business and news databases are updated daily or even every few minutes. Most major online service vendors provide a capability to search multiple databases simultaneously, and as many as hundreds of databases may be looked up at the same time.

For many kinds of information needs, looking for the information online can save substantial amounts of time. For example, when gathering detailed information on a particular company, an experienced searcher can retrieve the data from online databases in a few minutes compared with what might otherwise require days of rummaging through company annual reports or telephoning other companies to find out. A unique, strategic advantage of online searching is that it can find information that would otherwise be impossible or laborious to locate from print sources. Print sources provide information access through indexing or classification systems that are primarily hierarchical in structure. For example, to find a company in a directory, one might start with a broad business or industrial category, select a country or region, move down to specific states or cities, and then look up the company name in alphabetical order. Although the print directory may contain detailed product, financial, and organizational data about the company in question, such data fields are not searchable. Questions such as "find me health care companies that have been involved in merger and acquisition activity over the past three years" could take a long time to answer.

Online databases on the other hand are well suited to multi-faceted queries because many more fields in an online data record are indexed and searchable, and because intermediate search results may be combined in various ways to answer questions that require the logical intersection of two or more concepts. This ability to finesse a search can enable the organization to home in on the precise information it needs, or to explore possible associations and linkages between events, trends, and other developments. Online databases also allow searching on non-subject related attributes such as document type, institutional affiliation, country, publication date, and so on. Using these attributes to limit the search results can significantly enhance the value and usability of the information to end users. In summary, the versatility of online searching, coupled with the breadth and currency of online information, provides a competitive edge to the learning organization. Although online databases are available to all subscribers, the full potential of online databases can best be realized by the creative, skillful searcher who can mine online resources more deeply. The innovative search analyst takes full advantage of the indexing systems of bibliographic databases to find precise, relevant information; she designs search strategies that will extract nuggets of intelligence from huge full-text databases; she knows how to retrieve and interpret strategic information from secondary sources (for instance, patent databases can supply information for technology assessment and intelligence on a company's product development strategy); and she links disparate data from different databases to develop a fuller profile of an issue or organization.

Business Online Databases

Table 7.3 shows a sampling of about 30 online databases that may be used in an environmental scanning program. Although only a tiny fraction of the available databases, they nevertheless illustrate the range and depth of information that may be obtained from online sources. For discussion purposes, the databases are grouped into six information use categories which in practice overlap considerably: online databases for general business and management news; demographic data analysis; technology assessment; industry-specific analysis; marketing and market research; and company-specific analysis.

For keeping up with *general business and management news*, **ABI/Inform** is a widely used database: its inclusion of abstracts as well as indexing descriptors facilitate both broad and precise retrieval of information on general trends as well as specific topics. A significant proportion of its sources are international journals that provide foreign business news and analysis. Articles from many journals in ABI/Inform are available via facsimile.

Introducing World Reporter-Product of a Unique Initiative! Three leading information companies —Dialog, Dow Jones Interactive, and Financial Times

Table 7.3   Online Databases for Environmental Scanning

Online Database/(Provider)	Information Use	Content and Coverage
ABI/Inform (UMI)	*General news and management*	Indexes, abstracts, and full texts from over 1,000 international business journals.
Business Dateline (UMI)		Full texts from over 350 local and regional newspapers in the US and Canada.
Business Wire (Business Wire)		Continuously updated texts of news releases from over 10,000 sources in business, government, etc.
Japan Economic Newswire Plus (Kyodo News International)		Complete texts of all English newswires reported by Kyodo News Service, Japan's largest news agency.
Trade and Industry Index (Information Access Company)		Indexes and abstracts of over 300 trade and industry journals, plus 1,200 other publications.
CENDATA (US Bureau of the Census)	*Demographic data analysis (US)*	Numeric and full-text demographic data from 1990 census (age, income, occupation, education, etc).
Ei Compendex Plus (Engineering Information, Inc.)	*Technology assessment*	Abstracts from the world's significant literature of engineering and literature.
INSPEC (Institution of Electrical Engineers)		Online Physics Abstracts, Electrical & Electronics Abstracts, and Computer & Control Abstracts.
JAPIO (Japan Patent Information Organization)		Comprehensive source for patent applications in all technologies from 1976 to the present. Online version of Patent Abstracts of Japan.
NTIS (National Technical Information Service, US Dept. of Commerce)		Reports of US government-sponsored research, development, and engineering Government-aided research in Japan, Germany and France.
US Patents Fulltext (US Patents & Trademark Office)		Full texts of patents issued from 1974 to present, including details on purpose, structure, and function of device or substance.

Biobusiness (BIOSIS)	*Industry-specific analysis*	Abstracts from 600 technical, business sources on business applications of biomedical research.
Chemical Business Newsbase (Royal Society of Chemistry)		Abstracts of scientific, business, and government information on the chemical and allied industries.
Computer Database (Information Access Company)		Indexes, abstracts and full texts from journals on every aspect of computers and telecommunications.
FINIS: Financial Industry Information Service (American Bankers Association)		Abstracts from 200 journals, books, press releases, brochures, reports, etc., on banks, brokers, credit unions, insurance firms, investment houses, and so on.
Pharmaprojects (PJB Publications)		Reports on progress of new pharmaceutical products at all stages of development.
Company Intelligence (Information Access Company)	*Marketing and market research*	Directory data and recent news stories on 150,000 private and public US companies, and 30,000 non-US companies.
FINDEX (Cambridge Scientific Abstracts)		Indexes and abstracts of most industry and market research reports commercially available.
Industry Trends and Analysis (Decision Resources, Inc.)		Summaries and full reports on industry forecasts, technology assessments, market overviews, etc.
Investext (Thompson Financial Networks)		World's largest database of company and industry analysis, with over 320,000 reports by analysts at 180 investment banks and research firms worldwide.
PTS Marketing & Advertising Reference Service (PTS MARS) (Information Access Company)		Abstracts and full texts of advertising and marketing data on a wide variety of consumer products and services.
PTS PROMT (Information Access Company)		Abstracts and full texts of 1,000 of the world's important business journals, newspapers, etc.

Disclosure Database (Disclosure, Inc.)	*Company-specific analysis*	Detailed financial data on over 12,500 publicly owned companies from US SEC filings.

Dun's Electronic Business Directory
(Dun & Bradstreet)

Online directory of over 8.9 million public and private businesses, and professionals in the US, data based on interviews by D&B.

FBR Asian Company Profiles
(FBR Data Base, Inc.)

Directory of companies with an English name in manufacturing, international trade, and investment.

ICC International Business Research
(ICC Stockbroker Research Ltd.)

Full texts of over 13,000 stockbroker UK and European companies by leading British and international analysts.

M&A Filings
(Prentice-Hall Legal & Financial)

Detailed abstracts of merger and acquisition documents released by US SEC since 1985.

Media General Plus
(Media General Financial Services, Inc.)

Detailed financial data on 5,100 public companies: stock prices and volumes, 5-yr. balance sheets, financial ratios, industry comparisons.

Moody's Corporate Profiles
(Moody's Investor Services)

Descriptive and financial data of all companies on New York and American Stock Exchanges.

SEC Online
(SEC Online, Inc.)

Actual, unedited full texts of reports filed by public companies with the US SEC.

S&P's Corporate Descriptions plus News
(Standard & Poor's Corporation)

In-depth strategic and financial information on over 11,000 public companies, including recent financial news, interim earnings, subsidiaries, bond ratings.

TRW Business Credit Profiles
(TRW Business Credit Services)

Financial reports of 2.5 million public and private US companies: payment history, bankruptcy, tax & legal history, UCC filings, banking relationships.

Information jointly introduced **World Reporter**, a new online database that combines the timeliness of newswire services and the added value of full text, indexes and abstracts. World Reporter is updated hourly and carries both full text, indexes and abstracts of local-language news. Each record is indexed by business descriptors, country and region, product and company names. World Reporter provides access to local, regional and international news (including Africa, Asia, the Gulf States, Latin America, the Pacific Rim, and countries of the former Soviet Union).

To monitor regional and city newspapers that cover local companies and employers in greater detail, **Business Dateline** provides the full texts of over 350 local newspapers in the US and Canada, with 2,000 articles being added each week. The **Canadian Business and Current Affairs** database contains abstracts, full texts, and indexes to over 500 Canadian business and general journals and newspapers published. It contains abstracts for about 20,000 business articles per year from 1991 through 1994 and provides the full text for articles from over 100 of the periodicals and news sources covered in the bibliographic database, starting from 1993 to the present. For a continuous feed of business news, **Business Wire** transmits the full, unedited text of press releases from over 10,000 business, government, and research sources. Business Wire produces hourly recaps of all stories sent throughout the day, providing a useful way of scanning the latest news headlines.

In databases for US *demographic analysis*, the underlying data are from the 1980 and 1990 population census conducted by the Bureau of the Census in the US Department of Commerce. **CENDATA**, the Bureau's own database, gives prompt access to many of the Bureau's reports — time-series data are often available online within one hour of media release, while statistical briefs come online long before they appear in print.

There is a large number of databases that may be used for *technology assessment*. Two of the largest engineering databases are INSPEC and Ei Compendex Plus. **INSPEC** (the Database for Physics, Electronics and Computing) contains summaries from the Science Abstracts family of journals that began publication in 1868. A single classification scheme indexes all records from 1969 onwards, and a well designed thesaurus helps users to find appropriate subject terms. **Ei Compendex Plus**, the online version of The Engineering Index, provides worldwide coverage of about 4,500 published sources in all branches of engineering. The US government is a major sponsor of research and development activities, and the **NTIS** database from the National Technical Information Service provides access to the results of these research programs. Through NTIS, users may purchase research reports from over 600 agencies including NASA, Department of Energy, Department of Transportation, and Department of Commerce. NTIS also provides access to the results of government-sponsored research and development from countries outside the U.S. including the Japan Ministry of International Trade and Industry; laboratories administered by the United Kingdom Department of Industry; the German Federal Ministry of Research and Technology; the French National Center for Scientific Research; and many others. **Federal Research In Progress** database provides access to information about ongoing US government funded research projects in the fields of physical sciences, engineering, and life sciences. All records include title, principal investigator, performing organization, and sponsoring organization, and most records provide a description of the research.

A growing number of databases cater to the analysis of specific industries or industry groups. For example, the **BioBusiness** database contains current and recent information on the biotechnology industry for business executives, financial analysts, marketing professionals and so on. **Chemical Business Newsbase** from the Royal Society of Chemistry in the U.K., is an important business database containing information affecting chemical markets or products, with a particular emphasis on European news. **FINIS** provides marketing information for companies in the financial services industry, including banks, brokers, credit unions, insurance companies, investment houses, real estate firms, and related government agencies. The **Pharmaprojects** database contains reports on the progress of new pharmaceutical products at all stages of development — in 1995, it has data on 6,500 products in active development, and 11,500 products whose development has been terminated. Pharmaprojects is compiled from both published and unpublished sources. Information is obtained directly from the companies involved in product development, and from research scientists' presentations at conferences. each year, manufacturers are contacted to comment on their entries in the file. Other examples of industry-specific databases are Coffeeline, DMS/FI Market Intelligence Reports (defense and aerospace), Health Planning and Administration, Materials Business File, and PIRA (pulp and paper industries).

For *marketing and market research*, **FINDEX** points to well over 10,000 market and industry reports that are commercially available from US and international publishers. Each record contains a report summary and information about how to obtain the full report. **Investext** contains the full text of over 700,000 company and industry reports written by investment analysts at more than 300 major investment banks and research firms in Wall Street and worldwide. Investext provides in-depth analysis and data on 50,000 publicly traded companies, including sales and earnings forecasts, market share projections and research and development expenditures. Other reports analyze specific industries/products and businesses in geographic regions. **PROMT** (Overview of Markets & Technology) provides detailed abstracts from over 1,000 of the world's business publications and reports, and is a good source for information on industry trends, new products, and corporate plans. MARS (Marketing and Advertising Reference Service) focuses on the advertising and marketing of consumer goods and services, and is widely used to do research on market size and share, market evaluation, and competitors' market positioning strategies.

Numerous databases provide high-quality, in-depth financial and business information for *company-specific analysis*. **Disclosure** contains detailed balance sheets and earnings information on over 12,500 publicly traded companies, with data extracted directly from filings made to the US SEC (Securities and Exchange Commission). **Dun's Electronic Business Directory** is a directory of over 9.4 million public and private businesses and professionals in the US, with data collected through interviews. **Media General Plus** is another widely used database for information on stock prices and volumes, balance sheets for the past five years, financial ratios, and industry comparisons. **Moody's Corporate Profiles** combine financial data and narrative descriptions of all companies on the New York and American Stock Exchanges, with the financial data obtained from the companies themselves. Moody's provides detailed debt issue descriptions and histories, its own credit ratings, as well as company background information. **Standard & Poor's Corporate Descriptions plus News** offers strategic and financial information, and also gives individually rated issue-by-issue debt descriptions together with detailed stock data. Examples of databases with directory and research information on foreign companies are FBR Asian Company Profiles, ICC International Business Research (U.K. and European companies), and the Kompass database family.

Companies Using Online Databases for Environmental Scanning

Given their range and versatility, online databases would appear to be tools that are indispensable for any environmental scanning effort. Some studies suggest that the larger corporations have indeed embraced the use of online databases for business intelligence. For example, in Lester and Water's (1989) study of environmental scanning in six large U.K. corporations, online database services were used in several departments in all six companies. In five firms, the planning department made more use of online services than any other department. The sixth firm accessed online services through a corporate library. One planning department supplied business information to the rest of the company by relying entirely on online databases. Two other planning departments also adopted a similar approach, but not to the same extent. In fact, online use varied widely. The least frequent user reported an average use of only two to three hours a month. The most heavy user searched at least one of eight online services every day (this was the department that depended on online data to supply information to the rest of the firm). A planning department that consisted of a single planner accesses his one online service on his desktop workstation daily, often spending a whole afternoon on it.

In a study of the use of external information sources by managers of Norwegian banks and insurance companies (Olaisen 1990), 500 managers from over 80 companies were surveyed. Forty five percent had experience with using an external database while 28 percent were using at least one external database frequently. Follow-up interviews showed clearly that the more familiar a person was with electronic information sources, the more that he or she would be using them. For more experienced users, electronic sources tended to be more important than print sources. The trend among managers younger than forty was towards a greater use of electronic information sources — 41 percent of managers younger than 40 were using an external database frequently. A person who used many print sources was also likely to use many electronic sources, and vice versa. In the opinion of the 45 percent of managers who had used electronic information systems, electronic information and newspapers and journals were nearly equal in importance. However, the two sources were used differently. An online database was used for a specific task or concrete problem, while a newspaper or journal was scanned for general information and to find items that were sent on to another person. The main problem with online databases was that "They are not user-friendly enough. The knowledge in the databases is not organized for the daily use of busy business managers. The bad organization of information prevents many managers from using the databases." (Olaisen 1990, p.204)

Hart and Rice (1991) analyzed the use of online databases in four U.S. organizations which regularly used online information but differed in their problem-solving activity: a medical center, law firm, aerospace company, and trading floor of a large bank. Respondents indicated that the usage of online information is associated with perceived improvements in work performance. On average, respondents indicated that perceived effectiveness had increased, while the time spent in finding information had decreased. For improvements in work effectiveness, the correlations are twice as high for tasks that are more routine. For decreases in time spent in finding information, the correlations are considerably higher for tasks that involve greater amounts of information. The authors conclude that "while the expanding information economy increases information processing requirements for organizations, and the convergence of computers and telecommunications offers opportunities for improved performance and strategic advantage, the potential of online databases will be better realized when their relationships to organizational problem-solving requirements, database types, task characteristics, information processing requirements, and access methods are better understood and managed." (Hart and Rice 1991, p.477)

The rise of the Internet is providing fresh impetus for change and innovation in the online information industry. Thus, Dialog is providing multiple levels of services via the Web to professional users and end users: a command searching mode for researchers on Dialog Web, and a guided search mode (using Web-based forms) on Dialog Select. LEXIS-NEXIS offers a number of Web-based search tools aimed at legal researchers, accounting professionals, sales professionals, and executive users, as well as current awareness products that push news to company e-mail or Intranet (Tracker), or deliver personalized news via the Web (Info Tailor). The Internet is seen as presenting both new markets and new threats. On the one hand, the rapid assimilation of the Internet has raised awareness and spurred new interest in commercial online services. At the same time, the free availability of a vast range of information on the Net and the means to easily search it, bring into question the relative value of commercial services that are sometimes thought to be costly and hard to use. In a series of articles evaluating the future of online databases, Fuld (1996) has urged commercial online services to perceive their products not just as databases that are repositories of data, but more as "decision bases" that can bring salient information into focus in a timely manner so as to enable decision making. To transform into decision-bases, online databases will have to be enhanced at three levels: "At the ground floor, databases must have the value-added coding needed both to identify the most important information and to cut out useless information. The next level of the decision base must offer visual summaries of the data. Such summaries will help the reader grasp general trends or spot relevant information. At the third and final level, a decision base must offer analytical assistance to the decision maker." (Fuld 1996, p.1) In terms of coding, the indexing in some of today's business databases can be relatively one-dimensional, primarily identifying an industry group or a type of event. Decision-bases would need to include codes that indicate for example, the importance of the information and how the information could be used in strategic analysis. In terms of summarizing, online data could be summarized in various ways to reveal trends and patterns. Fuld cites the example of databases such as Derwent's patent files or Chemical Abstracts which group their data into clusters using regression analysis, and use these categories to analyze a company's R&D position. Besides clustering, geographical maps may be used to display the location and record counts of retrieved articles. Histograms or bar charts may be used to show trends and suggest extrapolations. Content analysis may be used to track the emergence of new words and concepts. In terms of analytical assistance, Fuld suggests that online data could be classified according to categories in established planning tools and frameworks such as those used in SWOT (strengths, weaknesses, opportunities, threats) analysis. Fuld also identifies five decision areas that online data could target initially: forecasting new opportunities, tactical decisions, investment insights, leadership profiles, and early warning.

Merging Information Spaces: The Internet and Commercial Databases

Basch (1996) interviewed 35 experienced Internet searchers, and one of the questions explored was the differential use of the Internet and commercial database services. One respondent highlighted the differences in stark terms:

> As a traditional online searcher, I've found the whole Internet experience, from the beginning, to be almost the reverse of traditional online — slow versus fast, chaotic versus precise, communication versus data, and now, with the Web, graphics versus text. (John Marcus, quoted in Basch 1996, p. 200)

A common theme emerged when several of the respondents emphasized the social nature of information seeking on the Net. For example:

> On the Net, your search for information is a social process. Information is not a thing to be sought, found, obtained, and taken home with you; information is a process that leads to a sharing of knowledge between yourself and others. You use commercial databases, on the other hand, when you need concrete, quasi-physical information: facts, data, numbers, lists. That's when you turn to a database. (Bob Bethune, quoted in Basch 1996, p. 5)

Overall, Basch concluded that the real strength of the Internet lies in its "gray matter": "not just the elusive, ephemeral literature that the standard bibliographic machinery tends to overlook, but the whole range of unofficial and quasi-official publication — as that word is understood on the Net — including conversations in newsgroups and listservs and elsewhere. Ultimately, the Net offers something unparalleled in any other research environment: global access to people who know."

Kassler (1997) stressed that the uniqueness of the Internet is that it is simultaneously a database and an advertising medium. Companies and organizations are enthused about the new medium, and willingly provide an abundance of information on the Web in the hope of stirring up interest and enthusiasm about their products, services, and causes. The medium is further enriched by the extensive use of hyperlinks. Hyperlinks connect partners, affiliated companies, and related information sites, making it easy to assemble a composite picture of the focal organization.

Although we have emphasized the distinct but complementary strengths of Web-based information and commercial databases, there is growing momentum for these two resource spaces to merge into a larger network of online information. Thus, commercial database vendors are rushing to make available their services on the Web. In many cases, their goal is to persuade both professional and casual users to adopt the Web browser as their main gateway to information products and services, possibly enhanced with "intelligent" features (such as contextual help and automatic query expansion) that take advantage of the Web's capabilities. The new ecology of online information readily available to most organizations is altering the dynamics through which they compete and cooperate. With widespread information and expertise sharing, industries as a whole become more knowledgeable, more responsive to customer needs, and more innovative in applying emerging technologies. The logic of competition is now based upon a shrewd and early interpretation of the business environment and the agile exploitation of niches and opportunities. The logic of cooperation is derived from being well informed about the needs and capabilities of potential partners and seeing how synergy may be derived from matching skills and positions. The winning organizations are those that have learned to be more expert at harvesting information and converting it into knowledge, strategies, and actions.

Chapter 8

Learning to Be Intelligent

In living systems, a dynamics of information has gained control over the dynamics of energy, which determines the behavior of most non-living systems. How does this domestication of the brawn of energy to the will of information come to pass?

(Christopher Langton 1991, Artificial Life II)

The knowledge of knowledge compels. It compels us to adopt an attitude of permanent vigilance against the temptation of certainty. It compels us to recognize that certainty is not a proof of truth. It compels us to realize that the world everyone sees is not the *world but a world which we bring forth with others. It compels us to see that the world will be different only if we live differently. It compels us because, when we know what we know, we cannot deny (to ourselves or to others) that we know.*

(Humberto Maturana and Francisco Varela 1992, The Tree of Knowledge, page 245)

The Intelligent Organization

This book began with the premise that an organization is an open system that exchanges energy, resources, goods, and services with its environment. The most valuable resource of the organization is its information, or more accurately, information that has been processed and distilled into knowledge that can guide action. There are three kinds of knowledge in an organization. *Tacit knowledge* is practical know-how that is embedded in an employee's ability to make judgement and exercise intuition. *Rule-based knowledge* is formal knowledge that has been encoded as procedures and programs in order to maximize operational efficiency. *Cultural knowledge* provides the assumptions and beliefs that are used to describe and explain reality, as well as the conventions and expectations that are used to assign value and significance to new information and knowledge. All three forms of knowledge are critical to the organization — tacit knowledge ensures that organizational tasks are performed effectively so that the organization's goals are attained; rule-based knowledge enables a sufficient level of efficiency, control, and coordination; while cultural knowledge engenders the purposeful focus that holds an organization together.

The intelligent organization is skilled in managing and mobilizing all three forms of organizational knowledge. It pursues its goals in a changing environment by adapting its behavior according to knowledge about itself and the world it operates in. The intelligent organization is, therefore, a learning organization that is proficient at creating, acquiring, organizing, and sharing knowledge, and at *applying* this knowledge to develop its behavior, position, or objectives. For the intelligent organization, learning and adaptation must paradoxically embrace their own opposites. A crucial part of organizational learning is to *unlearn* those assumptions and norms inherited from the past that are no longer valid. A powerful way of adapting to the environment is to know when to *enact* the environment so that it will develop in ways that are advantageous to the organization. These are the dual challenges facing the learning organization.

Organizational learning is a continuous cycle of activities that include sensing the external environment, perceiving the external changes taking place, interpreting the meaning and significance of these changes, and developing appropriate adaptive behaviors based on the interpretation. Organizational actions and decisions alter the external environment, generating new messages and signals that, in turn, drive the cycle of learning. How an organization perceives a situation and interprets its meaning depends on the frames of reference and rules of interpretation that it has learned from past experience and represented in its organizational memory. Practitioners and researchers have stressed that effective organizational learning requires mastery of this cycle of learning activities at the personal, group, and organizational levels. Building the learning organization requires establishing a new organizational climate that promotes the accumulation and sharing of knowledge, an open-mindedness to deal with the unfamiliar and the unfavorable, and the boldness to experiment and innovate. Knowledge creation is everyone's concern, and not the responsibility of a specialized few.

Information Management

The basic goal of information management is to harness the organization's information resources and information capabilities to enable it to learn and adapt to its changing environment. Information creation, acquisition, storage, analysis, and use therefore provide the intellectual latticework that supports the growth and development of the intelligent organization.

The central actors in information management must be the information users themselves, working in partnership with a cast that includes information specialists and information technologists. Information management must address the social and situational contexts of information use—information is given meaning and purpose through the sharing of mental and affective energies among a group of participants engaged in solving problems or making sense of unclear situations. Conceptually, information management may be thought of as a set of processes that support and are symmetrical with the organization's learning activities. Six distinct but related information management processes may be discerned: identifying information needs, acquiring information, organizing and storing information, developing information products and services, distributing information, and using information.

The identification of information needs should be sufficiently rich and complete in representing and elaborating users' true needs. Since information use usually takes place in the context of a task or problem situation, it is helpful to recognize that information needs consist of two inseparable parts: that pertaining to the subject matter of the need (what information is needed), and that arising from the situational requirements of utilizing the information (why is the information needed and how it will be used). Asking questions such as whether the problem is well or poorly structured, are the goals specific or amorphous, are the assumptions explicit and agreed upon, and is the situation new or familiar, will indicate the kinds of information that could be of greatest value to the user. Depending on the information use requirements, information could emphasize hard or soft data, elaborate existing goals or suggest new directions, help define problems or make assumptions explicit, locate historical precedents or provide future forecasts, and so on. Identifying information needs therefore not only involves determining the topics of interest to the user, but also the attributes of the information to be provided that will enhance its value and usefulness.

Information acquisition has become a critical but increasingly complex function in information management. Information acquisition seeks to balance two opposing demands. On the one hand, the organization's information needs range widely, reflecting the breadth and diversity of its concerns about changes and events in the external environment. On the other hand, human attention and cognitive capacity is limited so that the organization is necessarily selective about the messages it examines.

Thus, the first corollary says that the range of sources used to monitor the environment should be sufficiently numerous and varied as to reflect the span and sweep of the organization's interests. While this suggests that the organization would activate the available human, textual, and online sources; in order to avoid information saturation, this variety must be controlled and managed. The selection and use of information sources has to be planned for, and continuously monitored and evaluated just like any other vital resource of the organization. Furthermore, incoming information will have to be sampled and filtered according to its potential significance. Such sampling and filtering is an intellectual activity best performed by humans—it requires human judgment based on knowledge of the organization's business as well as the strengths and limitations of information resources.

Organizing and storing information may be facilitated with the application of information technology. Traditional data processing technologies were first used to raise work efficiency, whether in the office or on the shop floor. The operational use of computers generated an abundance of detailed information about transactions, customers, service calls, resource utilization, and so on.

While such systems are tuned to provide high throughput performance, they are inefficient at and sometimes incapable of retrieving the information that decision makers need to have for planning and problem solving. Organizations with significant volumes of transactional information could need to reorganize and unify operational data from several sources, and provide friendly but powerful analysis tools that allow decision makers to trawl the raw data for strategic insight, so that, for example, they can discover patterns and opportunities buried in the lodes of data about customer behavior. The information assets of an organization are not confined to the transactional; they vary from the highly ordered to the ephemeral, and some of the most valuable information may be hiding in sales reports, office memos, study reports, project documents, photographs, audio recordings, and so on. The classification, storage, and retrieval of textual and unstructured information will become a critical component of information management. The learning organization needs to be able to find the specific information that best answer a query, and to collate information that describes the current state and recent history of the organization. Well integrated archival policies and records management systems will enable the organization to create and preserve its corporate memory and learn from its history.

In developing information products and services, the objective is not only to provide information that is relevant to the users' areas of interest, but also to provide information in a form that increases their usability. In other words, information products and services should deliver and present information so that their content, format, orientation, and other attributes address the situational requirements that affect the resolution of the problem or class of problems. This represents a value-added approach to the design of information products and services. The potential usefulness of messages is enhanced by increasing their ease of use, reducing noise, improving data quality, adapting the information to increase its pertinence, and saving the user time and money. Information services need to be constantly innovating, in a continual effort to move closer to satisfying the many facets of the users' information needs.

The purpose of distributing information is to encourage its sharing. A wider distribution of information promotes more widespread and more frequent learning, makes the retrieval of relevant information more likely, and allows new insights to be created by relating disparate items. The delivery of information should be done through vehicles and in formats that dovetail well with users' work habits and preferences. The separation between information provider and information user should be dissolved: both ought to collaborate in the dissemination and value-adding of information to help ensure that the best information is seen by the right persons. To encourage users to be active participants, it should be made easy for them to comment on, evaluate, and re-direct the information they have received.

Information use is a dynamic, interactive social process of inquiry that may result in the making of meaning or the making of decisions. The inquiry cycles between consideration of parts and the whole, and between practical details and general assumptions. Participants clarify and challenge each other's representations and beliefs.

Choices may be made by personal intuition or political advocacy, as well as by rational analysis. Managers as information users, for example, work in an environment that has been described as informationally overloaded, socially constrained, and politically laden. As new information is received and as the manager reflects and acts on the problem situation, the perception of the situation changes, giving rise to new uncertainties. The problem situation is redefined, the manager seeks new information, and the cycle iterates until the problem is considered resolved in the manager's mind.

The organization's information structures and processes will have to be as open, flexible, and vigorous as the processes of inquiry and decision making they support. Information managers and specialists should be participants in decision processes so that they gain both a first-hand understanding of the information needs that emerge as the process unfolds and the extent that these needs are satisfied.

Understanding Environmental Scanning

Environmental scanning is the acquisition and use of information about events, trends, and relationships in an organization's external environment, the knowledge of which would assist management in planning the organization's future course of action. To the extent that an organization's ability to adapt effectively to its environment depends on knowing and interpreting external change, environmental scanning constitutes a strategic mode of organizational learning. The significant body of research on scanning shows broad agreement on a number of issues.

Environmental scanning improves organizational performance. Several studies show that scanning is associated with higher levels of organizational achievement—for large companies as well as small businesses across a wide range of industries, and for nonprofit organizations such as educational institutions and hospitals. The general result is that scanning organizations outperformed organizations that did not scan or scanned inadequately. For commercial organizations, the improved performance was measurable in financial terms; for example, the firm's return on assets and stock price-earning ratios over a period of time. For nonprofit organizations, improved performance was revealed by quantitative measures related to better resource utilization, and by qualitative indicators such as increased communication and greater participation in planning and decision making.

Nonetheless, the practice of scanning alone is insufficient to ensure performance. Studies have found that the crucial element is the ability to integrate scanning with organizational learning. Scanning should be well-aligned with strategy—the scope, depth, and sophistication of environmental scanning should match the information processing requirements for implementing the organization's growth strategy. The information obtained from scanning should have the relevance and quality to serve as vital input to the organizational learning processes. Perhaps most important, the organization's information culture should embrace the values that promote learning at all levels, including a diligent inquisitiveness about external changes, a willingness to share information and understand new points of view, and a boldness to innovate and experiment. The sophisticated scanners are those organizations who excel in their capability to obtain information—and to use the scanning information to develop strategic advantage.

The amount of environmental scanning varies with the level of perceived environmental uncertainty. Managers and others who perceive the environment as more unclear tend to scan with greater frequency and intensity. The environment is perceived as more uncertain when the rate of change is high, and cause and effect relationships difficult to discern. Studies that have investigated the effect of uncertainty have consistently found that the degree of doubt about the perceived environment is a good predictor of the amount of scanning.

Business enterprises tend to concentrate their scanning more on market-related sectors. They are most interested in information about customers, suppliers, competitors, distributors, and so on—those who have a direct impact on the conduct of business. Industries where developments in specific environmental sectors are considered strategic, however, would monitor those sectors intensively. For example, companies in an industry undergoing regulatory changes will scrutinize relevant government activities closely.

Many studies have identified the sources that managers use when scanning the environment. The general pattern emerges that managers scan with a wide range of human, textual, internal, and external sources. At the same time, managers clearly prefer personal sources (customers, distributors, suppliers, colleagues, etc.) and regard them as the most important. Researchers have found that, in explaining managerial source use in scanning, the perceived quality of the source may be just as or more important than perceived source accessibility. Because environmental scanning involves making sense of fuzzy, ambiguous situations, managers try to find the most dependable and relevant information they can, even though more time and effort may be required.

Each organization needs to develop its own customized scanning system that addresses its aspirations, position in the environment, and internal strengths and assets. Because scanning itself is a learning activity, it takes time for organizations to grow effective scanning systems. Staff members at all levels need to be reoriented, contacts have to be established, internal expertise identified, files built up, and systems rolled out. Practitioners and consultants have observed that some of the best scanning systems have been used for five years or more. Researchers have hypothesized that scanning systems evolve over time through four stages, from an initial *primitive* state, through *ad hoc* and *reactive* states, to the most advanced *proactive* mode.

Designing an Effective Environmental Scanning System

As our survey of scanning practices in Chapter 5 has revealed, no universal model, no textbook solution exists for the problem of gathering and using business intelligence. Perhaps the most important consideration in the planning and design of scanning practices is to take into account the organization's existing culture, particularly the employees' attitudes and beliefs about information creation, access, and sharing. In some cases, it may be necessary to change information culture and politics before organizational scanning can become effective.

Although there exists no single recipe for success, our survey of scanning practices and the opinions of many experienced practitioners and consultants in the field seem to converge on four general principles, which in a sense represent the summation of the insights of the experts and professionals (Bernhardt 1993; Dedijer and Jéquier 1987; Fuld 1988, 1985; Gilad and Gilad 1988; Gilad 1994; Gordon 1989; Herring 1988, 1991; Meyer 1987; Prescott 1989; Stanat 1990; Sutton 1988; Tyson 1990). Thus, the state of our knowledge suggests that environmental scanning should be:

- planned and managed as a strategic activity
- implemented as a formal system;

and that

- users should participate actively throughout the scanning process
- information management should provide a firm foundation for the scanning system.

Environmental Scanning Should Be Planned and Managed as a Strategic Activity

Scanning is not a support task to be relegated to the back office. A common misperception is that scanning and business intelligence activities are a luxury available only to organizations that enjoy high sales and profits, but anathema to others in the current climate of budget restraint and cost cutting. In fact, it is precisely because competition for resources and markets has become so ferocious that organizations now and in the future will have to depend more than ever on being well informed about their environment. Environmental scanning makes a direct contribution to an organization's strategic purpose.

Over any five-year period, approximately thirty percent of the firms on the Fortune 500 list disappear or are restructured. Many have failed to respond adequately to the signals of a business environment that is being reshaped by economic, political, social, and technological forces. In Chapter 4 we presented several studies that showed a link between scanning and organizational performance. Scanning the external environment is a powerful source of competitive advantage and is central to the development of an intelligent organization that continuously learns and innovates.

As a strategic function, top management must champion the scanning program. In the case of both Motorola and Eastman Kodak, two companies that have highly regarded scanning programs, the role of the chief executive officer in initiating and sustaining the effort was the critical success factor (Herring 1991).

The scanning function is not like a production line operation to be started by the turn of a key, it is much more like a research and development effort, where the investment is for the longer term, but the payoff may be spectacular. Like any R&D department, the scanning program must be given a critical mass in order for it to take off. There must be a significant investment of high-quality people resources and information management resources. The program must be given time to mature, to develop its network of contacts, establish files and databases, and build up its foundation of knowledge and expertise. From his experience and research, Fuld (1991) believes that successful programs take three to five years to mature. A study he conducted found that the most effective scanning departments were at least five years old or were run by executives who had been with the firm for five or more years.

Scanning as an organizational function is often poorly understood, and yet it requires the cooperation of nearly every department. As a result, the leadership of the scanning program becomes another crucial element. The program manager should be someone with the drive and authority to make it work—perhaps a rising star—and given the necessary clout to coordinate and integrate information from across many functional areas. The manager should combine intelligence gathering know-how with business knowledge, and analytical ability with creative vision. She or he should be politically astute, occupying a seat on the major executive decision making committees.

The litmus test of any scanning program is that its output, its intelligence, is actually used to make plans and decisions. It is one thing to declare the scanning function to be strategic, and quite another to ensure that it produces actionable information that is really used to improve the organization's position. For this to happen, it must be clearly understood who will use the scanning information and how they will apply it in practice. Scanning information must address as well as anticipate the needs of the organization's strategic and tactical planning activities. Management must again show the example, engender cultural acceptance, and promote the widespread use of scanning information in decision making.

Scanning Should Be Implemented as a Formal System

Many practitioners believe that the scanning program should be organized and implemented as a formal, structured, continuous system, although the most common form of scanning is still ad hoc and informal. When scanning is done informally, it is dependent on the interest and available time of particular individuals, effort is duplicated, information falls between the cracks, while large gaps appear in the information gathering and analysis. Diffused, localized scanning also means that there is no integrated perspective of how the competitive environment is changing. Instead of being a powerful source of competitive advantage, it degenerates into a low-priority activity whose benefits are unclear. Herring warns that "the continued operation of a company's intelligence activities in an informal and unstructured fashion is a danger in itself. Such intelligence operations tend to diffuse both information and responsibility. This was exactly the position that the U.S. intelligence found itself in prior to Pearl Harbor." (Herring 1988, 9)

Another misperception is that small organizations cannot afford formal scanning systems. In fact, small and medium-sized organizations need to know about their environment as much as, if not more, than their larger counterparts. Their resources may be limited, but an effective scanning system can be based on simple measures such as raising every employee's information awareness; reading, clipping, and circulating significant news from newspapers and the trade press; asking managers to maintain and share spreadsheets and directories about customers, competitors, suppliers, and so on; and forming focus groups to discuss important external developments. Some consultants have observed that owners of small firms are natural intelligence collectors, being always on the alert for competitive information. What they need is to start a formal but modest system to organize the information that they collect.

A formal scanning system should be planned, continuous, and coordinated. Planning ensures that information gathering is based on the organization's goals and critical information needs. Continuous monitoring enables the organization to detect deviations from the norm and so sense early warning signals. Sustained monitoring also allows the scanning system to grow its information networks and build up its knowledge base. Information gathering should be decentralized, so that everyone in the organization is on the lookout for valuable information. Some of the best information comes from line managers and employees who interact regularly with customers, suppliers, competitors, bankers, officials, and others.

Information gathering and analysis should be decentralized to the business units, where there is specialized or local "tacit" knowledge to evaluate the information close to source. At the same time, the distributed information gathering must be managed at a central locus. The central unit performs three functions: integrates incoming information and analyses into an organizationwide perspective; coordinates scanning efforts to reduce duplication and maximize efficiency; and acts as a clearing house where, for example, all available information on a topic may be traced. Bridging the work of the central and business units are project or study teams that are formed to analyze special issues in depth. These teams bring together the detailed knowledge of the line employees and the analytical expertise of the staff professionals.

According to Gilad and Gilad (1988), The business intelligence system consists of five functional components: collection, evaluation, storage, analysis, and dissemination (see Figure 8.1). Based on the strategic and tactical objectives of the organization, a set of critical information needs may be defined—this is the information that management requires to plan and decide about organizational strategies, projects, and programs. These critical information needs drive the intelligence system.

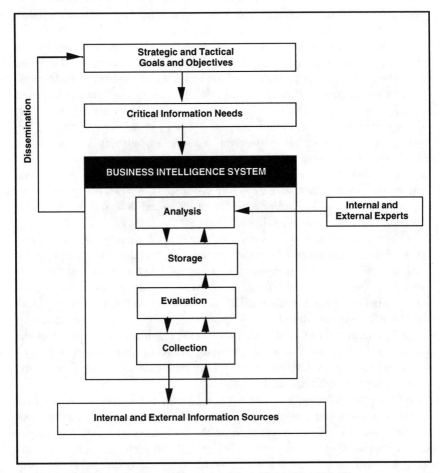

Figure 8.1   The Business Intelligence System (adapted from Gilad & Gilad 1988, 18)

— The system's *collection* component gathers information from a wide range of internal and external sources. Every employee, business unit, and functional department is a potential collector and source of information.

— The *evaluation component* examines the incoming data for reliability, usefulness, urgency, and so on. Urgent information is routed directly to the right users. Much of the inflow is discarded for lack of relevancy or accuracy.

— After filtering, information is organized for storage. The *storage* component ensures that information is filed and indexed to facilitate retrieval and dissemination.

— In the *analysis* stage, data elements are compared and collated, interpretations are made, implications are studied, and alternative responses are considered. Analysis is done with the help of internal and external experts, sometimes using formal techniques.

— Finally, the *dissemination* component packages the analyzed data into information products that are distributed to management and others. The new information may change strategies and plans, resulting in a continual cycle of setting information needs, collecting, and analyzing information.

Users Should Participate Actively Throughout the Scanning Process

Users are usually perceived only as consumers of the end products created during the last step of the scanning and analysis process. In reality, users can contribute substantially to nearly every stage of the process, beginning with the articulation of information needs and the context in which the information is to be used. The performance of any scanning system is measured by the extent to which the intelligence and insight it produces have been acted on advantageously by the organization's decision makers.

Therefore, users are at the center of the scanning process, and their information needs initiate new cycles of information gathering and analysis. Every person and department in the organization is a potentially valuable collector of information and source of knowledge. The organization is awash with data about its customers, competitors, suppliers, and trends and events in the external environment. Unfortunately, much of this information is invisible, hidden, and untapped. People in the organization need to become aware of the value and significance of the information that they encounter every day and for which they often do not give a second thought.

Above all, workers need to be motivated to gather and share information. As Fuld (1988) observed, there are, unfortunately, organizational disincentives that tend to discourage participation. There is a general lack of awareness of the role and importance of scanning and gathering information. The size, structure, and specialized compartmentalization of an organization often deter the exchange of information. The net result is that the lack of cooperation is the single most difficult problem for organizations trying to build their own intelligence scanning systems.

A 1985 SRI International report on managing competitive intelligence found that although employees in the sales and marketing departments are privy to some of the best information about the external environment, they are among the hardest to motivate to share their information. In one company, a new reward structure was attempted: sales commissions would be cut 30 percent, and sales representatives could make up that 30 percent by submitting timely, informative sales reports that include competitive intelligence. Firms such as Abbott Laboratories, Anheuser-Busch, and Faber Castell require their sales forces to fill out competitor-activity reports at the end of each week.

The scanning or intelligence unit can help promote awareness and cooperation. It could produce newsletters and conduct briefings that heighten employees' awareness and appreciation of competitive information. Employees volunteering useful information should be given recognition; for example, Kodak's intelligence unit pulls together information that has been contributed and presents them to the chairman and vice-chairman with the names of the contributors. By producing timely, useful information for the other departments, the scanning unit can convince the other departments of the benefit of cooperation and information sharing.

In the analysis and interpretation of the collected information, the participation of user managers and experts can make a huge difference in the quality and relevance of the output intelligence. Experienced managers of line departments often make ideal analysts who can integrate isolated pieces of information into a whole perspective, because they combine understanding of organizationwide goals with detailed knowledge of the field and an intuitive sense of what is probable and possible. Internal experts with in-depth knowledge about a wide range of subject areas can be found in every department and at all levels of the organization.

An internal network of experts is one of the most strategic resources of the scanning and intelligence function. Identifying and cultivating experts within the organization is not only an effective way of building a serious in-house information capability, it also helps to create an information culture that will enhance the organization's intelligence and learning capacity over the long run. Many organizations already recognize the value of in-house expertise and are mobilizing this resource. We have seen how AT&T has set up its AAA network to provide access to internal experts. Several other firms have developed similar electronic yellow pages to point to sources of information and expertise. Many organizations regularly form study teams and focus groups that pull together the talents of technical experts, experienced line personnel, librarians, and intelligence analysts to analyze the implications of major external developments.

Prescott and Smith (1987) suggest that a project-based approach to information gathering and analysis would produce custom-made intelligence that better addresses the needs of particular projects such as new product development, changes in distribution channels, and introduction of new technology. In this approach, a project team would be struck based on the project's technical and information requirements. Team members could include experienced functional managers as well as individuals with specialized expertise who work together to identify relevant competitors, critical success factors, and information sources; and arrive at an assessment of the potential for project success.

Information Management Is at the Core of the Scanning Function

A substantial proportion of the information that an organization needs for scanning and intelligence analysis already exists within the organization. Unfortunately, the information is scattered in bits and pieces, and the people who have the information are often unaware of its value to the organization and the need to share it with others. Information skills and resources exist in the organization's library or information center, planning office, research and development department, and other units. To bring these assets together into a viable scanning system requires a unifying set of information management strategies that enables the organization to collect, coordinate, store, analyze, and disseminate information systematically.

Thus, Gilad recommends that the design of a business intelligence system be based on just three principles, all of which in fact relate to the management of information resources and capabilities:

— One central location for convergence of bits and pieces of data from all over the organization

— A distributed force of collectors and analysts (decipherers)

— A system capable of storing information so as to enable easy retrieval and communication. (Gilad 1994, 170)

A central locus is needed to coordinate, interrelate, and integrate the disparate streams of information and analysis produced in the organization. The danger of an uncoordinated scanning system is a confusing proliferation of messages and studies, and a wasteful duplication of effort. The role of the central coordinator is like that of a network manager, ensuring the smooth flow of information, reducing noise in the network, and optimizing the use of shared resources. The central coordinator works with departmental coordinators to make certain that all the available pieces of the puzzle are fitted into a coherent picture for planning and decision making. Both data collection and information analysis are distributed throughout the organization. At the collection level, everyone in the organization is on the lookout for signs and cues. For analysis, the organization nurtures a network of local experts who can decipher incoming signals into relevant messages.

News clippings, memoranda, reports, files, and so on generated from decentralized collection and analysis may have to be organized, structured, and stored in a database. The database should serve two objectives: facilitate information retrieval and information sharing. The database becomes part of the organization's shared information network, which acts as a central repository of intelligence and as a system for interconnecting cooperating individuals who gather, analyze, and disseminate information (Stanat 1990).

At one end of the spectrum an intelligence database may be no more than a collection of manual files organized by subject areas (such as competitor, technology, regulatory action, etc.). At the other end of the spectrum it could be a computerized full-text database where virtually all the information is captured digitally. For example, Motorola's MIRIS (Motorola Intelligence Research Information System), developed at an estimated annual cost approaching a million dollars, is used to monitor the business, political, and economic environment of the firm's worldwide interests. Instead of a traditional corporate library, nearly all business intelligence is entered directly into the MIRIS database. According to Fuld (1988), over 80 percent of the records in MIRIS come from online database searches, with the remaining 20 percent from in-house reports, newsletters, and market studies. MIRIS has been used to evaluate plant-site alternatives, assess the political risk of countries, and analyze acquisition candidates and potential business partners.

There are many intermediate options that organizations have used successfully to support scanning and analysis, including directories and microcomputer-based databases and spreadsheets. Whichever the route taken, the information in the storage system must be indexed using schemes that reflect the real needs of the organization and its decision makers. Even the most rudimentary manual files should be properly categorized and cross-indexed. Apart from facilitating retrieval, indexes can also act as communication tools. William Sammon, a strategic planner for Pfizer, related how by distributing the intelligence file index to managers, the use of and interest shown in the files increased. Furthermore, once they started looking through a file's contents, managers were able to say exactly what was missing and needed to be added for the future (Sammon, et al., 1984).

The dissemination of scanning information and processed intelligence can take a surprisingly large number of formats. Newsletters are the most common medium for distributing scanning information, but sufficient care should be given to their design and layout so as to enable readers to quickly browse and assimilate the news they are interested in. Reference binders, or "databooks," which contain competitor profiles, market forecasts, and technology trends, as well as pointers to other resources, may be kept in the central library or distributed to departments. Notice boards and displays are sometimes used to exhibit information about competitors, their products and strategies, and can be an effective way of raising the competitive awareness of employees. A few firms have also created demonstration rooms where employees could personally try out competitors' products (Volvo, for example, has a center where competitors' cars may be test driven). Electronic mail systems and electronic bulletin boards are increasingly becoming the communication mode of choice for many organizations with far-flung business units or large numbers of field staff members.

For executive decision makers, the scanning system may produce a hierarchy of intelligence reports that vary in their planning horizons and amount of detail (Bernhardt 1994). Periodic information briefings keep executives abreast of current developments in the outside environment. Special intelligence reports provide critical information to help executives make decisions about specific strategic issues.

Summary

The main points of our discussion on information management in support of environmental scanning are summarized in Figure 8.2. The figure elaborates upon the process model of information management that we developed in Chapter 2.

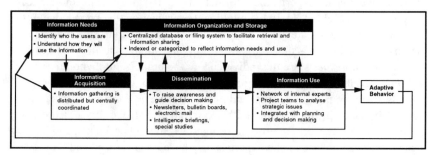

Figure 8.2 **Information Management in Environmental Scanning**

Looking Ahead

Learning requires organizations to try to decipher the forces and dynamics in the external environment that shape the future and to read their impact on the organization. Although difficult, the task is not impossible. Recent applications of planning approaches that emphasize envisioning and learning, and system models that represent the complex, dynamic interactions between system parts and the environment, seem to hold promise as new tools for organizational learning. In the following sections, we discuss how the intelligent organization could marshal its knowledge and skills through information partnerships; how new ways of thinking about the future could vitalize organizational learning; and how information management, with its integrating focus on the user and information processes, will increasingly become the basis for competition and organizational growth.

Information Partnerships for the Intelligent Organization

Information and information skills have a tendency to become fragmented in an organization that specializes in its functions. Traditionally, librarians look after the organization's collection of printed information and records managers maintain internal files and documents, while information technologists design and build computer-based systems to process operational data. The information users, the raison d'être for this flurry of information activity, are often only episodically or peripherally involved, and a gap results between their real information needs for decision making and the information captured and delivered through the organization's information systems and services.

The intelligent organization breaks away from functional fragmentation. It forges new partnerships that bring together the organization's capabilities to create, organize, and use knowledge, and to build infrastructures that enable the effective management of knowledge. At the heart of the intelligent organization are three groups of experts who need to work together as teams of knowledge partners: the domain experts; the information experts; and the information technology experts (Table 8.1). In the intelligent organization, the knowledge of the three groups of domain experts, information experts, and information technology experts meld into a superstructure for organizational learning and growth.

The *domain experts* are the individuals in the organization who are personally engaged in the act of creating and using knowledge: the operators, professionals, technologists, managers, and many others. The domain experts possess and apply the tacit, rule-based, and background knowledge (discussed earlier) in their day-to-day work, interpreting situations, solving problems, and making decisions. The knowledge and expertise they have is specialized and focused on the organization's domain of activity. Through their coordinated efforts, the organization as a whole performs its role and attains its goals. Through their knowledge creation and use, the organization learns, makes discoveries, creates innovations, and undergoes adaptation.

The *information experts* are the individuals who have the skills, training, and know-how to organize knowledge into systems and structures that facilitate the productive use of information and knowledge resources. They include librarians, records managers, archivists, and other information specialists. In organizing knowledge, their tasks encompass the representation of the various kinds of organizational information; developing methods and systems of

Table 8.1 Knowledge Experts in the Intelligent Organization

Groups of Experts	Goal	Primary Activity	Focus
Domain Experts	Knowledge Creation and Use	To engage in organizational learning, innovation, and adaptation.	Organizational Effectiveness
Information Experts	Knowledge Organization	To facilitate the productive use of information and knowledge resources.	Enlightenment
IT Experts	Knowledge Infrastructure Building	To facilitate the accurate, reliable, efficient processing of data and communication of information.	Process Efficiency

structuring and accessing information; information distribution and delivery; amplifying the usefulness and value of information; and information storage and retrieval. Their general focus is to enhance the accessibility and quality of information so that the organization will have an enlightened view of itself and its environment. The information experts design and develop information products and services that promote learning and awareness; they preserve the organization's memory to provide the continuity and context for action and interpretation.

The *information technology experts* are the individuals who have the specialized expertise to fashion the organization's information infrastructure. They consist of the system analysts, system designers, software engineers, programmers, data administrators, network managers, and other specialists who develop computer-based information systems and networks. Their general focus is to establish and maintain an information infrastructure that models the flow and transaction of information, and accelerates the processing of data and communication of messages. The information technology experts build applications, databases, and communication networks that allow the organization to do its work with accuracy, reliability, and speed.

In the intelligent organization, the knowledge of the three groups of domain experts, information experts, and IT experts form a pyramidical structure that supports learning and growth (Figure 8.3). In order to work together in teams consisting of domain experts, information experts, and information technology experts, each group will need to re-orientate its traditional mindset. *Users as domain experts* will need to separate the management of information from the management of information technology. Information technology, in most cases,

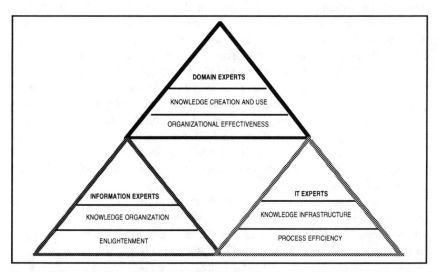

Figure 8.3 Knowledge Pyramid of the Intelligent Organization

has been heavily managed, whereas the management of information processes—identifying needs, acquiring information, organizing and storing information, developing information products and services, distributing information, and using information—has been largely neglected.

Users need to understand that the goals and principles of information management are quite different from the objectives and methods of information technology management. Users could participate fully in these information processes, not just as end-consumers of information products or services, but as active agents in every activity of the information management cycle, especially in clarifying information needs, collecting information, sharing information, and transforming raw data into usable information. As Drucker (1993) emphasizes, users should share the responsibility of identifying and communicating their information needs, and not abdicate this work completely to the information or information technology experts. The most valuable information sources in the organization are the people themselves, and they should participate actively in an organization-wide information collection and information sharing network.

Information technology experts are the most prominent group in today's technology-dominated environment. The management of information technology has remained in the media's spotlight for many years, with no signs of diminishing interest. Academics, businesses, consultants, and government all continue to extol the strategic application of information technology. IT experts have indeed become proficient at fashioning computer-based information systems that dramatically increase operational efficiency and task productivity.

At the same time, the very same systems that are so remarkable for their speed and throughput are equally well known for their incapability of satisfying the information needs of the decision makers. By representing and manipulating information at the data-element level, many systems do not provide more holistic information about processes, subject areas, or even documents. Thus, an information system that processes vast numbers of transactions per minute may be incapable of answering key questions such as: How long does the company take to develop new products? What is the firm's current market share? What is the turnaround time for a customer order? Computer-based information systems concentrate on formal, structured, internal data, leaving out the informal, unstructured, external information that most decision makers require. Their operating criterion is efficiency over flexibility, and they are designed to optimize resource utilization rather than to simplify knowledge discovery or problem solving.

IT experts need to move the user to the center of their focus—developing a behavior-based, process-oriented understanding of information users in terms of their needs and information use dispositions. People in organizations are not content with structured transactional data, they also want information technology to simplify the use of the informal, unstructured information that forms the bulk of the organization's information resources. They also want external data:

information to help them understand how the external environment is changing, what other organizations are doing, and how the organization is doing vis-à-vis its peers. In other words, users want a seamless web of formal and informal data, and internal and external data, represented in structures and models that are meaningful to them for cultivating insight and developing choices.

Information experts—the librarians and specialists who work in corporate libraries or information centers, the records managers, the archivists, and so on—have long been regarded as part of the organization's support staff, working quietly in the background, often uninvolved in any of the critical functions. Yet because these individuals have the skills that are most needed to effectively acquire, organize, and distribute information, the intelligent organization cannot afford to do without their contribution and participation in its strategic activities.

Information experts have to break away from their restraints and recast their function. Their roles are not limited to custodians or gatekeepers of information. They could provide training, advice, and consultation to users about the selection of information sources, the design of information search strategies, and the evaluation of information. They could participate in planning and decision making activities, where they can help ensure vigilant information gathering and processing, and develop an intimate understanding of how information is actually used. This feedback will in turn suggest ways of improving the acquisition, organization, and distribution of relevant information.

Information experts need to understand how information bestows meaning and purpose to people interacting at the cognitive, affective, and social levels. They can then add value to the information they provide so that the information addresses both the content-related and contextual requirements of the information use situation. Information experts also need a firm grasp of the business and agenda of the organization, and they should be early adopters and sophisticated users of new information technologies.

Paradoxically, in the so-called "information age," the information experts and the functions they perform (corporate libraries, information centers, records centers, archives) are in danger of being left behind. Davenport and Prusak (1993) believe that librarians often operate under an obsolete conceptual model of what makes an information service today. In the 1920s and 1930s, the earliest model of operation of the corporate library was as a "warehouse," whose main objective was to build up a collection of printed information and establish formal systems to control and store the acquired material. Information distribution was limited, for it was the librarian's duty to ensure that resources do not leave the library illegally. Later the operational model became one of an "expertise center," a place where one could find human subject matter experts to answer questions and direct them to library resources. While this model was an improvement over the warehouse concept, it failed to recognize that many more subject matter experts in an organization are not information professionals working in the library. For Davenport and Prusak, the warehouse model must be "blown up": librarians must not see themselves as warehouse custodians, or even as centralized providers of expertise, but rather as overseers of an organization wide multimedia network that connects information providers and resources with the users of information:

> They must be concerned with the structure and quality of the content that goes out over the network (programming), in what format it is distributed (media selection), to what audience it is directed (broadcasting vs. narrowcasting), and how the receiver's behavior changes in response to the content (advertising response). However, just as television networks do not produce all of the programs they broadcast, the role of the information network executive in firms should be to encourage wide participation in information creation and dissemination. Broadly speaking, the role of the information professional becomes the establishment of connections between those who have information, and those who want it. (Davenport and Prusak 1993, 408)

An alternative frame of reference for the role of the information experts is sketched by a recent study of corporate libraries and information centers at eight large Japanese companies engaged in banking, electronics, insurance, manufacturing, research services, and telecommunications (Prusak and Matarazzo 1992). The study's principal findings highlight the differences in approach towards information management between these successful Japanese firms and the conventional view of corporate libraries in western companies:

> 1. Japanese firms place a tremendous value on information and do not feel the need to justify information management expenditures. Information management is considered an essential cost of doing business, and there is little concern about how to justify the investment or measure the payback of an information center.
> 2. Business information, events, and situations are perceived and presented in their contextual settings. All the information centers visited had large and well-used collections of corporate histories and biographies. Incoming information is almost always discussed in its contextual settings, which may be historical, political, technical, or cultural/sociological.
> 3. The mission of the information function is closely aligned with the strategic thrust of the organization. The information centers understood clearly the company's direction and their role in moving the organization towards its goals.
> 4. Information technology is seen as an enabler of information management, not the primary component. Information management is not viewed as a subset of a technological function.
> 5. The management of the information function is alternated among all company managers. The manager of the information function rotates every

three to five years, allowing many managers to learn how information is used and valued in the organization, and to appreciate the need for a consolidated information management strategy. The information management function is seen as being as important as the other managerial functions.

6. Japanese managers read. The researchers saw senior executives actually reading in their corporate information centers and libraries. Japanese executives regard reading as a necessary component of managerial work, and are not embarrassed to be seen reading during the business day.

The intelligent organization understands that the discovery and use of knowledge can best be achieved through *strategic information partnerships* that combine the skills and expertise of its domain experts, information experts, and IT experts. This collective synergy is necessary to weave a seamless web that draws together structured and unstructured, internal and external, as well as historical, current, and future-oriented information; to create the tools and methods to access information and select the best available information sources; to design information architectures based on a rich understanding of users' information and communication requirements; and to integrate the organization's information processes into a springboard for organizational learning and development.

Collaborative vigor is needed to plow the organization's information homelands in order to transfigure data into knowledge. Through strategic information partnerships, the intelligent organization can significantly enhance each of the information processes that make up the information management cycle. Already organizations are reaping the benefits of synergistic information partnerships.

The Toshiba Business Information Center has successfully integrated the use of computer, networking, and electronic media technologies to enlarge its role from simply storing information to gathering, value-adding, and distributing information (Mori 1994). The Center provides an electronic information tool on end users' desktops that allows them to access the latest news, journal articles, government reports, and many other sources. All the information in this database is customized by the Center staff who know which information should be directed to which group of users. The Center staff members read articles and reports as soon as they are available to select relevant items, assign key words, and add them to the database—with a turnaround time that is much shorter than any commercial database service.

Press releases, overseas news, and government announcements and reports are faxed to the center immediately after release. Their headlines are captured by an optical character reader, and original images and charts are kept in an optical file system. Users scan the headlines and request needed images, which are then transmitted by fax, allowing them to obtain information even before it appears in newspapers.

Mori concludes that the Center could not have been successful without its "professional expertise and technology. The Center staff's intensive knowledge and ability enables them to establish a 'filter' to select and organize information on behalf of the Center's users. The Center staff consistently strives to identify information needs within the Toshiba Group or even in respective divisions. . . . Secondly, the [Center] would not function without today's technologies such as OCRs, optical filing systems, LANs, and e-mail systems." (Mori 1994, 279-280)

The current crop of workgroup computing platforms provides functions to simplify the tracking, sharing, and accessing of information across many internal and external sources by several groups of users in the organization. Companies such as Price Waterhouse (Dilno and Whitmire 1992), Lotus Development Corporation (Liberman and Rich 1993), and MCI Communications (Bates and Allen 1994) have all combined the talents of information experts and information technology experts to implement successful workgroup applications.

Consider the experience of MCI Communications' Corporate Information Resources Center in Washington, DC (Bates and Allen 1994). Using Lotus Notes as the platform, the Center has developed a database that serves as the institutional memory holding information that staff members have learned and other staff should know about; a discussion database to post questions on policy, the status of ongoing projects and so on; databases of press releases, speeches, and related materials; a customized news-filtering service from selected external news sources and online database sources; a central database on journal subscribers, experienced searchers, market research reports, and so on; and a capability to access newsgroup discussions on the Internet, including the functionality to scan for items of interest or to search back items using keywords.

In designing these databases, the Center needed to work with technical experts with detailed knowledge of Notes. As for the information experts, their role was summarized thus:

> Information professionals are ideal "internal information consultants"—we understand how to organize information, we know how to take advantage of Notes' features, and we recognize the information needs of each work group. . . . A trained information professional can review a department's information needs and help the system administrator develop databases to best organize that information. The skill set of a librarian experienced in database design and information management is an excellent fit for the needs of Notes information content administration. . . . In some organizations, librarians have become "information trustees," overseeing the establishment and maintenance of databases on Notes. They set standards for database construction and documentation, ensure consistency among databases, and identify the person responsible for regularly updating the databases. They review all databases before they are made available to users, ensuring that the information is up-to-date

and will be adequately managed by the originating organization. (Bates and Allen 1994, 34-35, 38)

Another powerful form of information alliance levers the domain knowledge of the users with the information experts' knowledge of information sources and content. As an example, take the case of Bell-Northern Research (BNR), a company jointly owned by Northern Telecom and Bell Canada that is a global leader in the design and development of advanced telecommunications systems. In 1993, the BNR Information Resource Center in Ottawa launched its Strategic Program Support Service, an information partnership program to support new product development (Birks 1995). When a product development project is initiated, the IRC dedicates professional and clerical resources to the project. The assigned information specialist joins the development team and works with senior management and team members to define an information profile for the project: "This profile builds a complete information context for the emerging product design, covering technical, competitive and market information from internal and external sources. Typically, the information specialist scans incoming electronic and print information, filters it according to the project requirements and issues a weekly report to the entire development team. Critical technical or marketplace events are announced to the team immediately and there may be a need for focused information research in specific areas such as competitor analysis." (Birks 1995, 24) The information specialist is thus collaborating with the domain experts during the most critical phases of the product development, in the building up of the business case, and in defining the features and functionality of the new product.

Leading companies in the United States likewise are breaking away from traditional practices to meet the requirements of today's competitive arena:

— At Upjohn, staff from clinical pharmacology and two internal libraries formed a Products and Markets Information Research Team (Dommer 1991). The team synthesized information from commercial databases and internal sources to provide timely and accurate information to assist management decision making about resource allocation in response to competitors' actions.

— At McDonnell Douglas, corporate librarians and competitor intelligence analysts teamed successfully to analyze the advanced manufacturing capability of a competitor in order to present to management an assessment of the competitor's probability of launching a certain product within a time frame and attaining a set of design and technology objectives (Gib and Walraven 1992). The participants concluded that the multidisciplinary approach multiplied the respective strengths of both the information specialists and the intelligence analysts and provided the firm with a competitive advantage.

— At 3M, the Business Library decided that, instead of trying to track all of the company's thousands of competitors on its own, it would package its knowledge about intelligence gathering as a training workshop on "Gathering

Competitor Intelligence" (Anderson 1992). The workshop proved to be extremely successful, playing to sellout crowds for four years, over which time more than five hundred 3M employees attended the seminar. The workshop, prepared with input from 3M's competitive intelligence practitioners, covered sources of competitive information, methods of collecting information and doing research, and the principles of creating an intelligence system.

— At Digital Equipment Corporation, one corporate library evolved into a Marketing Information Services Group consisting of a team of librarians, other information professionals, and marketing consultants who develop corporate intelligence, conduct their own market research, and provide insight on strategic marketing issues (Linder 1992). The group also established a videotext information system that linked more than 10,000 sales and marketing staff throughout the United States.

Given the widespread recognition that people, not printed materials and online databases, are the organization's most precious information sources, it is surprising that so little has been done to help users find people who have the desired expertise or knowledge. To fill this gap, corporate librarians are well-placed to act as human switching exchanges, helping users connect with human sources:

> The modern librarian will catalogue not only printed materials or even knowledgeable information professionals, but also that Jane Smith is working on a sales force compensation project, and that Joe Bloggs knows a lot about the metallurgical properties of wheel bearings. When another division or customer calls to find out this sort of information, they will finally have a place to go. Several of the firms we have worked with already feel that this is a valid role for librarians; at one telecommunications firm, for example, librarians were referred to as 'human PBXs' because of their ability to make connections between people requiring information and people possessing it. (Davenport and Prusak 1993, 411)

In summary, the intelligent organization cross-pollinates the knowledge of its domain experts, information content experts, and information technology experts. Probably the least developed of these resources are the information content experts, who have hitherto largely confined themselves to a reactive, supporting role. We believe that the knowledge and skills of these information experts are an indispensable cornerstone of the intelligent organization's knowledge pyramid. Information experts, however, will have to move from the background to the center of the organizational stage, holding the reins of information management jointly with users and the technology experts so as to help steer and shape the information policies, structures, processes, and systems that will nurture organizational learning.

We have seen how several successful organizations have learned to draw upon the skills of the information content experts to extract, filter, and disseminate vital external information; design and develop workgroup application suites that are effective platforms for information sharing and information management; work side by side with domain experts in collecting and analyzing strategic intelligence; and act as trainers and consultants who transfer information gathering and research skills throughout the organization. Much more can be done, and the creation of effective information partnerships is a vital step towards the intelligent organization.

New Ways of Organizational Learning and Understanding the Future

Organizational learning requires "knowing" enough about the future to plan and respond to a changing environment. Future learning does not seek a detailed forecast of coming events, but is aimed at understanding what forces, relationships, and dynamics will influence the form and direction of change. Although some organizations may think that even this is an intractable task, a few organizations (such as Royal Dutch/Shell, Canon, and Motorola) have been able to repeatedly unlearn and relearn their mental frames of reference as they successfully anticipate and manage the future. Recent years have seen the diffusion of planning approaches that emphasize learning and envisioning rather than forecasting, and the intensification of cross-disciplinary research by biologists, computer scientists, economists, physicists, and many others that offer the promise of new ways of analyzing and modeling complex social systems.

Scenario Planning

As a method of planning and learning about the future, the use of scenario-based planning has been spreading over the past few years. The Royal Dutch/Shell company began developing the scenario planning technique in the 1960s and 1970s (Wack 1985a, 1985b). In the early 1970s, scenario planning helped Shell discern differences between Iran and Saudi Arabia (while everyone else continued to regard the Arab nations as a homogeneous cartel) and to anticipate the events that led to the 1973 oil crisis. In 1981, Shell was able to sell off its excess reserves (while other oil companies were stockpiling following the Iran-Iraq war) before the glut caused the price collapse. More recently, by recognizing the demographic and economic pressures on the Soviet Union (while Western politicians saw only an "evil empire"), Shell's scenario planners were able to anticipate glasnost (Kleiner 1994).

What is scenario planning? Because today's organizations thrive in a highly volatile and uncertain environment, anticipating, understanding, and learning about the future requires not just systematic analysis but also creativity, insight and intuition (Schwartz 1991). Scenarios, or stories about the future, combine these elements and so provide a rich cognitive framework for designing robust strategies. Peter Schwartz, founder of Global Business Network, a group of con-

sultants that includes several Shell planning alumni, explains the value of scenario planning:

> The test of a good scenario is not whether it portrays the future
> accurately but whether it enables an organization to learn and
> adapt. . . . Unlike traditional forecasting or market research, sce-
> narios present alternative images instead of extrapolating current
> trends from the present. Scenarios also embrace qualitative per-
> spectives and the potential for sharp discontinuities that econo-
> metric models exclude. Consequently, creating scenarios requires
> decision-makers to question their broadest assumptions about the
> way the world works so they can foresee decisions that might be
> missed or denied. Within the organization scenarios provide a
> common vocabulary and an effective basis for communicating
> complex—sometimes paradoxical—conditions and options.
> (Schwartz 1991)

Creating scenarios involves four steps: refining the sense of purpose; understanding the driving forces; plotting the scenarios; and rehearsing, conversing,
and designing strategy (Kleiner 1994, Schwartz 1991). In refining the sense of
purpose, scenarios provoke learning by addressing genuine concerns and by
challenging existing mental models. In identifying the driving forces, a differentiation is made between predetermined elements that are reasonably predictable (using for example, demographic data) and key uncertainties that are
unpredictable or uncontrollable. Predetermined elements set the boundaries of
the scenarios, while key uncertainties point out the most serious consequences
of the decisions taken. In plotting the scenarios, two or three examples are created as learning tools, illuminating the issues most critical to the success of the
decision. Finally, in rehearsing and designing strategy, the scenarios are fleshed
out through conversation, and their implications are thoroughly thought through.

Systems Thinking

Systems thinking is another important intellectual tool that a learning organization can exercise to analyze its interactions with the environment. With
ideas from cybernetics and general systems theory, systems thinking approaches the study of social systems as groups of related elements that are organized
for a purpose. The system grows and maintains stability under a range of possible futures through control and communication or information-flow mechanisms that include feedback loops, time-delays, and the attenuation of information entropy. In recent years, systems thinking has been experiencing a second
renaissance, as many organizations became interested in or introduced the ideas
of management gurus such as Stafford Beer and Peter Senge.

Beer was invited by President Allende of Chile in 1971 to apply managerial
cybernetics to the management and control of the Chilean economy (Beer 1981).

Beer was to design and build an electronic operations room linked by computer programs and communication networks to government and industry. The brain of Project Cybersysn was to be a cybernetic model of the Chilean economy, a model that could be manipulated for simulation purposes. Unfortunately the project came abruptly to an end in 1973 with Allende's assassination. By that time, according to Beer, the telecommunications network linking the socio-industrial economy of Chile had been functioning for months, all computer program suites were working as expected, and about 60 percent of all the enterprises in the economy were already included in the system. Beer's book, *Brain of the Firm*, which served as the project "bible," has been reissued in 1994.

Peter Senge is Director of the Center for Organizational Learning at the Sloan School of Management, Massachusetts Institute of Technology. The center has eighteen corporate sponsors, including AT&T, Ford, Motorola, and Federal Express, each of whom ponies up $80,000 annually to set up pilot learning programs (Dumaine 1994). Senge's ideas draw richly from system dynamics, a field created by Jay Forrester (another MIT professor and Senge's mentor) some forty years ago. As part of systems thinking, Senge has developed a number of "systems archetypes" that may be used as templates to perceive the underlying structures in complex situations. These archetypes are causal loop maps that elucidate how complex systems interact through, for example, delay, feedback, side effects, and external constraints. In the archetype named "Tragedy of the Commons," for instance, "individuals use a commonly available but limited resource solely on the basis of individual need. At first they are rewarded for using it; eventually, they get diminishing returns, which causes them to intensify their efforts. Eventually, the resource is either significantly depleted, eroded, or entirely used up." (Senge 1990, 387) As we have discussed elsewhere in this book, Senge's prescription for a learning organization is not limited to systems thinking (there are four other "disciplines"), but it is certainly the prescription's most unique ingredient.

The Science of Complexity

All social and economic systems (human societies, global markets, trading blocs, and so on) can be characterized as large-scale, complex, and adaptive. They are complex in that a huge number of independent actors are continuously interacting in a great many ways. Yet the system as a whole spontaneously organizes itself so that certain collective group properties emerge that do not exist in the individual actors. Furthermore, these systems are adaptive, so that they seem able to learn from experience and evolve as the environment changes. Seen in this light, social systems are not much different from living systems such as the billions of neurons collaborating in the human brain, or the millions of species of life forms evolving for survival on the African savanna.

The new science of "complexity" is concerned with the study of such complex, adaptive systems. As a cross-disciplinary endeavor, it embraces the work of

Nobel laureates as well as rising stars in biology, chemistry, computer science, economics, evolutionary ecology, information theory, particle physics, philosophy, mathematics, and many others. Their common purpose is to discover the rules and processes that explain how structure, coherence, and cohesiveness become the emergent properties of complex, adaptive systems (Waldrop 1992).

Researchers have found that complex systems remain coherent and viable because they can simultaneously maintain enough stability for sustenance and enough creativity for growth—the system components do not calcify into immutable forms nor break out into anarchic turbulence. Instead, complex systems are able to balance order and chaos through their capabilities to process information. A complex system fails both in an information-poor environment where information movement and retention is limited, and in an information-laden environment when information moves so freely that no structure can be maintained. A complex system is viable only at the transition between these two phases, where sufficient information is retained to provide a framework for interpretation, and where sufficient new information is constantly prodding new structures and innovations (Langton 1991, Levy 1992).

The global economy is an example of a complex, adaptive system: its overall direction is determined by the interaction of many dispersed units acting in parallel. These units serve as building blocks for constructing units at the next higher level. The building blocks are recombined and revised continually as the system accumulates experience so that the system as a whole adapts (Holland 1988, 1992). Niches in the global economy are constantly being created by new technologies, while the very act of filling a niche provides new opportunities (through parasitism, symbiosis, competitive exclusion, etc.) so that *perpetual novelty* results. Because niches are numerous and continually created, the economy operates far from an optimum. Instead, the global economy operates like an *adaptive nonlinear network* similar to the central nervous system, immune systems, and ecologies.

Examples of the adaptive, nonlinear interactions in the economy are the activities of speculators in a stock market, the anticipation of shortages and surpluses, learning effects in technology-use, and the niche expansion that occurs when a successful innovation spawns numerous related activities. Like all complex, adaptive systems, the global economy is constantly anticipating the future, making predictions based on internal models or assumptions about the world, and using these predictions to prescribe behavior. Thus, the anticipation of an oil shortage can have profound effects regardless of whether the shortage actually comes to pass.

The analysis of adaptive, nonlinear networks requires new methods to discover and represent building blocks, and to simulate the emergence of structure through the interaction of these blocks (Holland 1988). Holland's approach is to use parallel, message-passing, rule-based systems (called "classifier systems") in which rules activate in parallel, and are in constant competition so that new rules (representing better knowledge) are generated by combining old rules. By analyzing the dynamics of multi-agent interaction, internal models, and the emergence of new building blocks, Holland is working towards a new understanding of the forces driving change in the global economy.

The assumption of *diminishing returns* is a canon of classical economics—it acts as negative feedback that stabilizes prices and markets to a predictable equilibrium representing efficient resource allocation. Unfortunately, many economic phenomena seem immune to any stabilizing forces, and they do not settle down to any predictable equilibrium state. Brian Arthur, an economist at Stanford University, suggests that in these cases a mechanism of increasing returns takes effect, creating positive feedback in the economy so that small chance events early in the history of a market, industry, or technology can tilt the competitive balance in favor of a participant, selected not according to some rational criteria, but according to some combination of initial conditions (Arthur 1990).

Consider a situation where several companies of about the same size enter a new market at the same time. Small, random events early in the game, such as unexpected orders, chance meetings with buyers, and managerial whims, may allow one of the companies to enjoy a small lead that accumulates and becomes magnified by positive feedback or increasing returns so that the company eventually becomes market leader. Recall the domination of the VCR market by the VHS format. The market started out with two competing formats (Beta and VHS), both backed by large corporations and costing about the same. Market shares fluctuated between the two formats, and it was initially impossible to say which system would win. Increasing returns on early gains eventually tilted the balance towards VHS—growing numbers of VHS players encouraged video tape retailers to stock more VHS titles, thereby increasing the attractiveness of owning a VHS player and persuading more people to buy one. Through this positive feedback loop, VHS accumulated enough of an advantage to become the industry standard.

Arthur believes that increasing returns operates most strongly in the knowledge-based sectors of the economy (computers, pharmaceuticals, telecommunications). Increasing returns may be modeled as dynamic processes based on random events and natural positive feedbacks, or nonlinearities (Arthur 1990). Such models could record the particular set of random events leading to each solution, and so allow us to study the probability that a particular solution would emerge under a certain set of initial conditions. Maneuvering a company through an industry with positive feedbacks requires luck as well as timing: a feel for when a change from one pattern to another is most possible. Arthur's theoretical work can help identify these states and times, and can guide decision makers in applying the right amount of effort to effect the change.

Two Chilean biologists have suggested that the identifying characteristic of all living systems is that they are continually self-producing. This process of self renewal is defined by the system's organization of relations that exist among its components in order that it belong to a specific class of living organisms (Maturana and Varela 1992).

The biological cell is a fine example of an autopoietic system (*autopoiesis*, from the Greek for self-production). A cell's molecular components are dynamically related in a network of ongoing interactions, known collectively as "cell metabolism." Cell metabolism produces components that form a boundary, the cell membrane, between the cell's interior and its environment. Interestingly, this membrane not only limits the network of transformations, but also participates in that network. Without this spatial segregation, cell metabolism would disintegrate and the cell would cease to exist.

Thus, a network of dynamic transformations produces its own components essential for a boundary, while the boundary is essential for the operation of the network of transformations which produced it as a unity. "The most striking feature of an autopoietic system is that it pulls itself up by its own bootstraps and becomes distinct from its environment through its own dynamics, in such a way that both things are inseparable. Living beings are characterized by their autopoietic organization." (Maturana and Varela 1992, 46-47) A number of researchers have used the theory of autopoiesis in biological systems as a metaphor for conceptualizing organizations as self-producing systems (Morgan 1986, Wheatley 1992, Kickert 1993, Braman 1994, and others). For example, Morgan develops useful insights by interpreting the autopoiesis theory:

> First, a creative application of the theory helps us to see that organizations are always attempting to achieve a form of self-referential closure in relation to their environments, enacting their environments as projections of their own identity or self-image. Second, it helps us to see that many of the problems that organizations encounter in dealing with their environments are intimately connected with the kind of identity they try to maintain. And third, it helps us to see that explanations of the evolution, change, and development of organizations must give primary attention to the factors that shape an organization's self-identity, and hence its relations with the wider world. (Morgan 1986, 240)

Braman (1994) interprets organizational autopoiesis in informational terms. Because autopoietic transformations are more successful when systems are self-conscious and self-reflexive about these processes, there are implications for records management, management training, and organizational communications. Information systems should be designed to bring together information about the past as well as the present, and combine the knowledge of local conditions with more general knowledge. For an autopoietic organization to develop healthy relations with its environment, three characteristics are necessary: "adequate modes of information collection and processing; internal processes for incorporating and responding to what has been acquired from the environment; and a sufficient level of complexity [adequately matching the amount of external variety]." (Braman 1994, 364)

The New Dynamics of Competition

The dynamics of competition and organizational growth will become increasingly based on the effective management of information and knowledge. Information is not just another factor of production (such as land, labor, and capital), but the *enabling factor* that determines how the other factors of production ought to be combined and utilized in order to maximize organization performance. Competition and entrepreneurship is the necessary result of the unequal distribution of information and the differential ability of organizations to create and apply knowledge. Competition between organizations becomes a process of discovery and learning that opens up new fields of knowledge, promotes emulation of successful strategies, and hastens the diffusion of useful innovations (Picot 1989).

Peter Drucker (1993, 1994) describes today's world as a post-capitalist society in which the basic economic resource or means of production is no longer capital, nor natural resources, nor even labor. The central wealth-creating activities no more depend on the allocation of capital or labor. Instead, value is now generated by the application of knowledge to work, by boosting productivity, and inducing innovation. The basic economic resource is, and will continue to be, knowledge: the post-capitalist society is the knowledge society. In the knowledge society, the leading social groups are the knowledge workers—knowledge managers, knowledge professionals, and knowledge employees who understand how to put information to productive use.

> In fact, knowledge is the only meaningful resource today. The traditional "factors of production"—land (i.e., natural resources), labor, and capital—have not disappeared, but they have become secondary. They can be obtained, and obtained easily, provided there is knowledge. And knowledge in this new sense means knowledge as a utility, knowledge as the means to obtain social and economic results. These developments, whether desirable or not, are responses to an irreversible change: *knowledge is now being applied to knowledge.* Supplying knowledge to find out how existing knowledge can best be applied to produce results is, in effect, what we mean by management. But knowledge is now also being applied systematically and purposefully to define what new knowledge is needed, whether it is feasible, and what has to be done to make knowledge effective. It is being applied, in other words, to systematic innovation.

> The right definition of a manager is one who "is responsible for the application and performance of knowledge." This change means

that we now see knowledge as the essential resource. Land, labor, and capital are important chiefly as restraints. Without them, even knowledge cannot produce; without them, even management cannot perform. But where there is effective management, that is, application of knowledge to knowledge, we can always obtain the other resources.

That knowledge has become *the* resource, rather than *a* resource, is what makes our society "post-capitalist." This fact changes—fundamentally—the structure of society. It creates new social and economic dynamics. (Drucker 1993, 42, 44-45)

Thus, we identify the fundamental factor that determines success or failure in the post-capitalist society: the capacity of organizations and their knowledge workers to develop higher-order comprehension about how to create, find, and apply information so as to raise organizational performance. This higher-order knowledge defines the know-how to manage information in the organization effectively. Information management, designed and implemented as a coherent set of policies, processes, procedures, systems, and structures, creates an information use environment that promotes learning, collaboration, information sharing, and knowledge generation.

Because information is recognized as the key resource, it is keenly sought—the intelligent organization is more proactive and intrusive in interpreting and enacting its external environment; it gathers information more intensively, and takes full measure of the abundance of open-source information. The intelligent organization is skilled at kindling the expertise and experience of its own members to transmute information into knowledge and insight. Information is used to learn from the past as well as to unlearn the past; to anticipate the future as well as to enact the future.

In the intelligent, knowledge-based organization, information management aligns well with the organizational mission and goals. Just as organizational strategy and objectives must not remain static but regenerate from time to time, the information management function itself must respond to change and new demands, and seek constant innovation and adaptation. Designing the information management architecture becomes a critical component of an organization's strategic envisioning or planning process.

Consider the case of Nippon Steel Corporation, the world's largest steel manufacturer. Beginning in 1986, the company sought to reinvent itself, to move from a resource-based to a knowledge-based company (Bowonder and Miyake 1992). It decided to branch out into electronics by diversifying aggressively into computing and electronic equipment. On its own and in joint ventures with other companies, Nippon Steel in 1988 spawned four new information and communication systems businesses in remote computing services, hardware and software system services, office and factory automation systems, and systems integration services. Hitherto, Nippon Steel's information strategy had concentrated on learning by doing and learning by using, applying information and information technology to improve the efficiency of its manufacturing operations, optimize real time processes, and provide information for quick decision making and managerial control. While its experience in working with advanced computing and communications technologies laid the foundation for its diversification, the change-over required a major shift in the information management approach. The new information management strategies to support the organizational transformation were driven by four imperatives:

- need to have a rigorous organizational learning system that can scan, assess, and utilize information on new technologies with a view to seek new business opportunities
- commitment to develop and use full potential of IT and IS
- horizontal information flow systems for quick assimilation of new information as well as organizational information accumulation
- ability to innovate rapidly through concurrent engineering. (Bowonder and Miyake 1992, 55-56)

According to the researchers, "the most critical aspect of information management is continuous environmental monitoring or scanning to reduce environmental uncertainty." (Bowonder and Miyake 1992, 48) Scanning provides the input to an organization wide intelligence system that encompasses business, commercial, financial, and technological intelligence. Intensive environmental scanning, organizational learning, information sharing, and rapid innovation have helped Nippon Steel to initiate strategic action for the development of whole new businesses.

The other major challenge to effective information management is the instilling of an information and learning culture in the organization. Despite much admonishment about constructing information systems as technical artifacts, the situation remains that the most systems in place today are motivated and measured by technological and efficiency benchmarks. How many systems and information managers would know the answers to these basic questions:

- Are users able to use the systems to find the data they need to solve their problems?
- How do the systems add value to the data they deliver in order to facilitate the actionable use of information?

We have the technical prowess to double the number of transistors on a microprocessor chip every eighteen months, and build global networks of computers that can transport millions of messages every hour. We have not, however, matched these skills with an equivalent depth of insight into how people, as sentient human beings, may be helped to make more effective use of information.

Nonetheless, as this book has tried to show, the problem is not intractable. The results of research by social scientists and information scientists, and the innovative practices of a growing number of organizations, have helped us gain a better grip on what has formerly been inscrutable or ignored dimensions of information use.

Information use is a social process of constructing meaning and making collective interpretations, and then acting out plans and intentions. Information grows out of the relationships that people create between themselves and the data, messages, and documents that they encounter. These relationships need to be expressed at three levels. At the *cognitive level*, the information user seeks information to fill a cognitive gap (Dervin 1992)—looking for more information in order to answer a question, solve a problem, understand a situation, and so on. At the *affective level*, the information user experiences emotional states in searching for and encountering information (Kuhlthau 1993). The user may begin information seeking in a state of uncertainty, anxiety, or diffidence. Affective responses change as information is found and assimilated: if the search is successful, the feeling of confidence and satisfaction increases; if unsuccessful or unhelpful, confusion, doubt, and frustration result. A useful theory of information seeking should address these emotional states and identify ways of helping users to cope with these affective symptoms. At the *situational level*, as we have discussed in detail earlier (Chapters 2 and 3), the user is subject to the contextual demands of a problem situation, and applies information traits as criteria that go beyond the subject matter to judge the information's value or usefulness (Taylor 1991).

Any organization attempting to create an information and learning culture that promotes knowledge creation and use will need to start from the recognition that information use is a social, collective sense-making process. It must then develop strategies to manage the cognitive, affective, as well as situational dimensions of information use. Education and training may be required to raise the awareness of the value of information, to increase understanding of what information has potential significance, and to enhance information-searching and information-use skills. Organizational norms and structures may have to be modified to engender the cultural shift: information gathering and sharing could be formally recognized in job descriptions and reward systems; forums and group or team structures may be initiated to facilitate information sharing and cooperative collaboration. Information systems and communication networks may be designed to promote the free and relaxed exchange of formal as well as informal information, to connect users to the best information resources or expertise help that is available, and to provide information that does not truncate the context or history that could assist users in finding meaning. Finally, managers and supervisors may need to show by their example, and demonstrate in their day-to-day practice, the value of systematic information gathering and vigilant information processing as the necessary preconditions of sound decision making.

Coda

Individuals working in organizations, as well as practitioners and researchers, have a great deal more to learn and understand about managing information as a process of discovering meaning, as a collection of resources and skills, and as an intellectual infrastructure for organizational intelligence. Like the seventeenth century physicists who first detected and measured the properties of air, we are only starting to comprehend the character and behavior of an entity that has for so long been transparent, invisible, and taken for granted. Just as no living thing can long survive without air, no social organization can endure without information.

Yet in many organizations, the vital respiratory systems are barely functioning. Like an ill-trained athlete whose respiratory system cannot support the physical demands of running a race, the organization with an underperforming information physiology has neither the energy nor the capacity to withstand the rigors of competitive growth. The goal of information management is to develop processes, structures, and systems that function both as the circulatory system that filters and distributes nourishing information throughout the organization, and as the central nervous system that synthesizes incoming information into representations and interpretations for collective action.

Learning to be intelligent begins by learning how to manage information. The process promises to be a dance of many recursive cycles; in effect, it means learning about how to learn.

References

Achleitner, Herbert K. and Robert Grover. 1988. Managing in an Information-Rich Environment: Applying Information Transfer Theory to Information Systems Management. *Special Libraries* 79, no. 2 (Spring): 92-100.

Achrol, Ravi S. 1988. Measuring Uncertainty in Organizational Analysis. *Social Science Research* 17: 66-91.

Aguilar, Francis J. 1967. *Scanning the Business Environment.* New York, NY: Macmillan Co.

Al-Hamad, Fahaad Murad. 1988. *Scanning Organizational Environments.* D.P.A. thesis, State University Of New York At Albany.

Aldrich, Howard E. 1979. *Organizations and Environments.* Englewood Cliffs, NJ: Prentice-Hall.

Aldrich, Howard E. and Jeffrey Pfeffer. 1976. Environments of Organizations. In *Annual Review of Sociology*, ed. A. Inkeles, 79-105. Palo Alto, CA: Annual Reviews Inc.

Aldrich, Howard E. and Sergio Mindlin. 1978. Uncertainty and Dependence: Two Perspectives on Environment. In *Organization and Environment: Theories, Issues, and Reality*, ed. Lucien Karpik, 149-170. London, U.K.: Sage Publications Inc.

Allen, Bryce L. 1991. Cognitive Research in Information Science: Implications for Design. In *Annual Review of Information Science and Technology*, ed. Martha E. Williams, 3-37. Medford, NJ: Learned Information.

Allen, Thomas John. 1977. *Managing the Flow of Technology: Technology Transfer and the Dissemination of Technological Information within the R & D Organization.* Cambridge, MA: MIT Press.

Anastasi, Anne. 1986. Intelligence As A Quality of Behavior. In *What Is Intelligence? Contemporary Viewpoints on Its Nature and Definition*, ed. Robert J. Sternberg and Douglas K. Detterman. Norwood, NJ: Ablex Publishing Corp.

Anderson, Rebekah E. 1992. Gathering Competitive Intelligence - A Seminar Developed and Offered by 3M's Business Library. In *Professional Papers from the 83rd Annual Conference of the Special Libraries Association held in San Francisco, CA, June 6-11, 1992*, 169-173. Washington, DC: Special Libraries Association.

Argyris, Chris and Donald Schon. 1978. *Organizational Learning: A Theory of Action Perspective.* Reading, MA: Addison-Wesley.

Arrow, Kenneth J. 1964. Control in Large Organizations. *Management Science* 10, no. 3 (April): 397-408.

Arthur, W. Brian. 1988. Self-Reinforcing Mechanisms in Economics. In *The Economy as an Evolving Complex System*, ed. Philip W. Anderson, Kenneth J. Arrow, and David Pines, 9-27. Redwood City, CA: Addison-Wesley.

Arthur, W. Brian. 1990. Positive Feedbacks in the Economy. *Scientific American* (Feb 1990): 92-99.

Ashby, W. Ross. 1956. *An Introduction to Cybernetics*. London, UK: Chapman & Hall.

Auster, Ethel and Chun Wei Choo, ed. 1995. *Managing Information for the Competitive Edge*. New York, NY: Neal Schuman.

Auster, Ethel and Chun Wei Choo. 1992. Environmental Scanning: Preliminary Findings of a Survey of CEO Information Seeking Behavior in Two Canadian Industries. In *Proceedings of the 55th Annual Meeting of the American Society for Information Science held in Pittsburgh, PA, October 26-29, 1992*, edited by Debora Shaw, 48 - 54. Medford, NJ: Learned Information, Inc.

Auster, Ethel and Chun Wei Choo. 1993a. Environmental Scanning by CEOs in Two Canadian Industries. *Journal of the American Society for Information Science* 44, no. 4: 194-203.

Auster, Ethel and Chun Wei Choo. 1993b. Environmental Scanning: Preliminary Findings of Interviews with CEOs in Two Canadian Industries. In *Proceedings of the 56th Annual Meeting of the American Society for Information Science held in Columbus, OH, October 22-28, 1993*, edited by Susan Bonzi, 246-252. Medford, NJ: Learned Information, Inc.

Auster, Ethel and Chun Wei Choo. 1994a. CEOs, Information, and Decision Making: Scanning the Environment for Strategic Advantage. *Library Trends* 43, no. 2 (Fall 1994): 206-225.

Auster, Ethel and Chun Wei Choo. 1994b. How Senior Managers Acquire and Use Information in Environmental Scanning. *Information Processing & Management* 30, no. 5: 607-618.

Basch, Reva. 1996. *Secrets of the Super Net Searchers*. Wilton, CT: Pemberton.

Bates, Mary Ellen and Kimberly Allen. 1994. Lotus Notes In Action: Meeting Corporate Information Needs. *Database* 17, no. 4 (Aug 1994): 27-38.

Bateson, Gregory. 1979. *Mind and Nature: A Necessary Unity*. London, UK: Wildwood House.

Beer, Stafford. 1974. *Designing Freedom*. Ontario, Canada: CBC Publications.

Beer, Stafford. 1981. *Brain of the Firm*. 2nd ed. New York, NY: John Wiley.

Bernhardt, Douglas C. 1993. *Perfectly Legal Competitor Intelligence: How To Get It, Use It, and Profit from It*. London, UK: Financial Times/Pitman Publishing.

Bernhardt, Douglas C. 1994. "I Want It Fast, Factual, Actionable" – Tailoring Competitive Intelligence to Executives' Needs. *Long Range Planning* 27, no. 1 (Feb 1994): 12-24.

Bigelow, Barbara, Liam Fahey, and John F. Mahon. 1993. A Typology of Issue Evolution. *Business & Society* 32, no. 1 (Spring 1993): 18-29.

Birks, Grant. 1995. Value-added Information Services: The Art of Being Synchronous with Your Corporation. *Bulletin of the American Society for Information Science* 21, no. 2 (Dec/Jan 1995): 23-25.

Blandin, James S. and Warren B. Brown. 1977. Uncertainty and Management's Search for Information. *IEEE Transactions on Engineering Management* EM-24, no. 4 (November): 14-19.

Boland, Richard J., Jr., Ramkrishnan V. Tenkasi, and Dov Te'eni. 1994. Designing Information Technology to Support Distributed Cognition. *Organization Science* 5, no. 3 (Aug 1994): 456-475.

Bowonder, B. and T. Miyake. 1992. Creating and Sustaining Competitiveness: Information Management Strategies of Nippon Steel Corporation. *International Journal of Information Management* 12, no. 1 (Mar 1992): 39-56.

Box, Thomas Morgan. 1991. *Performance Predictors For Entrepreneurial Manufacturing Firms: an Empirical Study Of Psychological, Background and Environmental Scanning Attributes (Firm Performance).* Ph.d., Oklahoma State University.

Boyd, Brian Kenneth. 1989. *Perceived Uncertainty and Environmental Scanning: A Structural Model.* Ph.D. dissertation, University of Southern California.

Braman, Sandra. 1994. The Autopoietic State: Communication and Democratic Potential in the Net. *Journal of the American Society for Information Science* 45, no. 6 (Jul 1994): 358-368.

Brand, Stewart. 1988. *The Media Lab: Inventing the Future at MIT.* New York, NY: Penguin Books.

Browne, Mairead. 1993. *Organizational Decision Making and Information.* Norwood, NJ: Ablex Publishing.

Budner, S. 1962. Intolerance of Ambiguity as a Personality Variable. *Journal of Personality* 30: 20-50.

Burns, Tom and G.M. Stalker. 1961. *The Management of Innovation.* London, UK: Tavistock.

Carroll, Jim and Rick Broadhead. 1994. *Canadian Internet Handbook.* Scarborough, ON: Prentice Hall Canada.

Chang, Shan-Ju and Ronald E. Rice. 1993. Browsing: A Multidimensional Framework. In *Annual Review of Information Science and Technology*, ed. Martha E. Williams. Medford, NJ: Learned Information.

Choo, Chun Wei and Ethel Auster. 1993. Scanning the Business Environment: Acquisition and Use of Information by Managers. In *Annual Review of Information Science and Technology*, ed. Martha E. Williams. Medford, NJ: Learned Information, Inc. For the American Society for Information Science.

Choo, Chun Wei. 1991. Towards an Information Model of Organizations. *The Canadian Journal of Information Science* 16, no. 3 (September): 32-62.

Choo, Chun Wei. 1993. *Environmental Scanning: Acquisition and Use of Information by Chief Executive Officers in the Canadian Telecommunications Industry.* PhD, University of Toronto.

Choo, Chun Wei. 1994. Perception and Use of Information Sources in Environmental Scanning. *Library & Information Science Research* 16, no. 1: 23-40.

Choo, Chun Wei. 1995. IT2000: Singapore's Vision of an Intelligent Island. In *Intelligent Environments*, ed. Peter Droege. Amsterdam, Netherlands: Elsevier Science, BV.

Choo, Chun Wei. 1998. *The Knowing Organization: How Organizations Use Information to Construct Meaning, Create Knowledge, and Make Decisions.* New York: Oxford University Press.

Choudhury, Vivek and Jeffrey L. Sampler. 1997. Information Specificity and Environmental Scanning. *MIS Quarterly* 21, no. 1: 25-54.

Chu, Heting, and Marilyn Rosenthal. 1996. Search Engines for the World Wide Web: A Comparative Study and Evaluation Methodology. In *Proceedings of the 59th Annual Meeting of the American Society for Information Science*, held in Baltimore, MD, edited by S. Hardin, 36-142. Medford, NJ: Information Today, Inc.

Churchman, C. W. 1971. *The Design of Inquiring Systems: Basic Concepts of Systems and Organization.* New York, NY: Basic Books.

Crick, Francis. 1994. *The Astonishing Hypothesis.* New York, NY: Simon & Schuster.

Cronin, Blaise, K. Overfelt, K. Fouchereaux, T. Manzanzvike, M. Cha, and E. Sona. 1994. The Internet and Competitive Intelligence: A Survey of Current Practice. *International Journal of Information Management* 14, no. 3 (Jun 94): 204-222.

Cronin, Blaise and Elisabeth Davenport. 1993. Social Intelligence. In *Annual Review of Information Science & Technology*, ed. Martha E. Williams, 3-44. Medford, NJ: Learned Information.

Cronin, Blaise. 1992. What Is Social About Social Intelligence. In *From Information Management to Social Intelligence: The Key to Open Markets*, ed. Blaise Cronin and Neda Tudor-Silovic, 103-110. London, UK: Aslib.

Cronin, Mary J. 1993. *Doing Business On The Internet: How The Electronic Highway Is Transforming American Companies.* New York, NY: Van Nostrand Reinhold.

Culnan, Mary J. 1983. Environmental Scanning: The Effects of Task Complexity and Source Accessibility on Information Gathering Behavior. *Decision Sciences* 14, no. 2 (April): 194-206.

Cyert, Richard Michael and James G. March. 1992. *A Behavioral Theory of the Firm.* 2nd ed. Oxford, UK: Blackwell.

Daft, Richard L. and Karl E. Weick. 1984. Toward a Model of Organizations as Interpretation Systems. *Academy of Management Review* 9, no. 2: 284-295.

Daft, Richard L. and Robert H. Lengel. 1984. Information Richness: A New Approach to Managerial Information Behavior and Organization Design. In *Research in Organizational Behavior*, ed. B.M. Staw and L.L. Cummings, 191-233. Greenwich, CT: JAI Press Inc.

Daft, Richard L. and Robert H. Lengel. 1986. Organizational Information Requirements: Media Richness and Structural Design. *Management Science* 32, no. 5 (May): 554 -571.

Daft, Richard L., Juhani Sormunen, and Don Parks. 1988. Chief Executive Scanning, Environmental Characteristics, and Company Performance: An Empirical Study. *Strategic Management Journal* 9, no. 2 (March/April): 123-139.

Davenport, Thomas H. 1993. *Process Innovation: Reengineering Work Through Information Technology.* Boston, MA: Harvard Business School Press.

Davenport, Thomas H. and Laurence Prusak. 1993. Blow Up The Corporate Library. *International Journal of Information Management* 13, no. 6 (Dec 1993): 405-412.

Davenport, Thomas H., Robert G. Eccles, and Laurence Prusak. 1992. Information Politics. *Sloan Management Review* 34, no. 1 (Fall 1992): 53-63.

de Geus, Arie P. 1988. Planning as Learning. *Harvard Business Review* 66, no. 2 (March/April 1988): 70-74.

Dedijer, Stevan and Nicolas Jéquier, ed. 1987. *Intelligence for Economic Development: An Inquiry into the Role of the Knowledge Industry.* Oxford, UK: Berg.

Dedijer, Stevan. 1991. *Development and Management by Intelligence: Japan 1857-1990.* Institute of Economic Research, School of Economics and Management, Lund University, 1991. Working Paper

Dennett, Daniel C. 1991. *Consciousness Explained.* New York, NY: Little Brown.

Dervin, Brenda. 1992. From the Mind's Eye of the 'User': The Sense-Making Qualitative-Quantitative Methodology. In *Qualitative Research in Information Management*, ed. Jack D. Glazier and Ronald R. Powell. Englewood, CO: Libraries Unlimited.

Desai, Bijel H. and David Bawden. 1993. Competitor Intelligence in the Pharmaceutical Industry. *Journal of Information Science* 19, no. 5: 327-338.

Dill, William R. 1958. Environment as an Influence on Managerial Autonomy. *Administrative Science Quarterly* 11, no. 1 (March): 409-443.

Dill, William R. 1962. The Impact of Environment on Organizational Development. In *Concepts and Issues in Administrative Behavior*, ed. Sidney Mailick and Edward H. Van Ness, 94-109. Englewood Cliffs, NJ: Prentice-Hall Inc.

Dilno, Dennis L. and Denise I. Whitmire. 1992. Lotus Notes and Quality Competitive Intelligence. In *Professional Papers from the 83rd Annual Conference of the Special Libraries Association held in San Francisco, CA, June 6-11, 1992*, 139-147. Washington, DC: Special Libraries Association.

Ding, Wei, and Gary Marchionini. 1996. A Comparative Study of Web Search Service Performance. In *Proceedings of the 59th Annual Meeting of the American Society for Information Science*, held in Baltimore, MD, edited by S. Hardin, 36-142. Medford, NJ: Information Today, Inc.

Dollinger, Marc J. 1984. Environmental Boundary Spanning and Information Processing Effects on Organizational Performance. *Academy of Management Journal* 27, no. 2: 351-368.

Dommer, Jan. 1991. Maintaining the Competitive Edge at Upjohn Company. *Inside Business* (Spring/Summer 1991): 13.

Drucker, Peter F. 1993. *Post-Capitalist Society.* New York, NY: HarperCollins.

Drucker, Peter. 1994 Infoliteracy. *Forbes ASAP*, Aug 29, 1994, 104-109.

Duggan, Patrice and Gale Emenstodt. 1990 The New Face of Japanese Espionage. *Forbes*, Nov 12, 1990, 96.

Dumaine, Brian. 1994. Mr. Learning Organization. *Fortune* 130, no. 8 (Oct 17, 1994): 147-158.

Duncan, Robert B. 1972. Characteristics of Organizational Environments and Perceived Environmental Uncertainty. *Administrative Science Quarterly* 17, no. 3 (September): 313-327.

Eccles, Robert G. and Nitin Nohria. 1992. *Beyond the Hype: Rediscovering the Essence of Management.* Cambridge, MA: Harvard Business School Press.

Edelman, Gerald M. 1992. *Bright Air, Brilliant Fire - On the Matter of the Mind.* New York: Basic Books.

Eisenhardt, Kathleen M. 1989. Making Fast Strategic Decisions in High-Velocity Environments. *Academy of Management Journal* 32, no. 3: 543-576.

Eisenhardt, Kathleen M. 1990. Speed and Strategic Choice: How Managers Accelerate Decision Making. *California Management Review* 32, no. 3 (Spring): 39-54.

Elenkov, Detelin S. 1997. Strategic Uncertainty and Environmental Scanning: The Case for Institutional Influences on Scanning Behavior. *Strategic Management Journal* 18, no. 4: 287-302.

Ellsworth, Jill H. 1994. Business Growth on the Internet. In *The Internet Unleashed*, ed. Kevin Kelly, 723-730. Indianapolis, IN: SAMS Publishing.

Emery, Fred E. and Eric L. Trist. 1965. The Casual Texture of Organizational Environments. *Human Relations* 18: 21-32.

Etzioni, Amitai. 1967. Mixed-Scanning: A "Third" Approach to Decision-Making. *Public Administration Review* 27, no. 5 (December): 385-392.

Etzioni, Amitai. 1986. Mixed Scanning Revisited. *Public Administration Review* 46, no. 1 (January/February): 8-14.

Ewing, R. P. 1990. Moving from Micro to Macro Issues Management. *Public Relations Review* 16, no. 1 (Spring 1990): 19-24.

Fahey, Liam and Vadake K. Narayanan. 1986. *Macroenvironmental Analysis for Strategic Management.* St. Paul, MN: West Publishing.

Fahey, Liam and William R. King. 1977. Environmental Scanning for Corporate Planning. *Business Horizons* 20, no. 4 (August): 61-71.

Feldman, Susan. 1997. "Just the Answers Please": Choosing a Web Search Service. *Searcher* 5, no. 5: available online at http://www.infotoday.com/searcher/may/story3.htm.

Fidel, Raya. 1994. User-Centered Indexing. *Journal of the American Society for Information Science* 45, no. 8 (Sep 1994): 572-576.

Fletcher, Patricia Tobaka. 1991. *An Examination of Situational Dimensions in the Information Behaviors of General Managers.* Ph.D. dissertation, Syracuse University.

Fuld, Leonard M. 1985. *Competitor Intelligence: How To Get It; How To Use It.* New York, NY: John Wiley.

Fuld, Leonard M. 1988. *Monitoring the Competition: Finding Out What's Really Going On Out There.* New York, NY: John Wiley.

Fuld, Leonard. 1991. A Recipe for Business Intelligence Success. *Journal of Business Strategy* 12, no. 1 (Jan/Feb 1991): 12-17.

Fuld, Leonard M. 1996. The Future of Databases: What's Really Needed are Decisionbases. *Information Today*, Feb. 1996, 1, 19.

Gadamer, Hans-Georg. 1975. *Truth and Method.* 2d revised ed. New York, NY: Seabury.

Galbraith, Jay R. 1973. *Designing Complex Organizations.* Reading, MA: Addison-Wesley.

Garvin, David A. 1993. Building A Learning Organization. *Harvard Business Review* 71, no. 4 (Jul-Aug 1993): 78-92.

Gates, Anne Marie. 1990. *Environmental Scanning In Pennsylvania Community Colleges: Does It Exist? Does It Work? (Curriculum Planning).* Ed.d., University Of Pittsburgh.

Gazzaniga, Michael S., ed. 1995. *The Cognitive Neurosciences.* Cambridge, MA: MIT Press.

Gerstberger, Peter G. and Thomas J. Allen. 1968. Criteria used by Research and Development Engineers in the Selection of an Information Source. *Journal of Applied Psychology* 52, no. 4: 272 -279.

Ghoshal, Sumantra and Eleanor Westney. 1991. Organising Competitor Analysis Systems. *Strategic Management Journal* 12, no. 1: 17-31.

Ghoshal, Sumantra and Seok Ki Kim. 1986. Building Effective Intelligence Systems for Competitive Advantage. *Sloan Management Review* 28, no. 1 (Fall): 49-58.

Ghoshal, Sumantra. 1988. Environmental Scanning in Korean Firms: Organizational Isomorphism in Practice. *Journal of International Business Studies* 19, no. 1 (Spring 1988): 69-86.

Gib, Andre and Eileen Walraven. 1992. Teaming Data Management and Competitive Intelligence Professionals: An Approach that Provides a Competitive Advantage. In *Professional Papers from the 83rd Annual Conference of the Special Libraries Association held in San Francisco, CA, June 6-11, 1992*, 128-138. Washington, DC: Special Libraries Association.

Gilad, Benjamin and Tamar Gilad. 1988. *The Business Intelligence System: A New Tool for Competitive Advantage.* New York, NY: Amacom.

Gilad, Benjamin. 1994. *Business Blindspots.* Chicago, IL: Probus Publishing Co.

Glueck, William F. and Lawrence R. Jauch. 1984. *Business Policy and Strategic Management.* 4th ed. New York, NY: McGraw-Hill.

Gordon, Ian. 1989. *Beat the Competition! How To Use Competitive Intelligence to Develop Winning Business Strategies.* Oxford, UK: Basil Blackwell.

Greene, Richard M. 1966. *Business Intelligence and Espionage.* Homewood, IL: Dow-Jones Irwin.

Gregory, Richard L. 1981. *Mind In Science: A History of Explanations in Psychology and Physics.* London, UK: George Weidenfeld and Nicholson.

Gregory, Richard L. 1994. Seeing Intelligence. In *What Is Intelligence?*, ed. Jean Khalfa. Cambridge, UK: Cambridge University Press.

Gulliver, F. 1987. Post-project Appraisals Pay. *Harvard Business Review* 65, no. 2 (Mar-Apr 1987): 128-132.

Haeckel, Stephen H. and Richard L. Nolan. 1993. Managing by Wire. *Harvard Business Review* 71, no. 5 (Sep-Oct 1993): 122-133.

Hales, Colin. 1993. *Managing Through Organization: The Management Process, Forms of Organization, and the Work of Managers.* London, UK: Routledge.

Hambrick, Donald C. 1981. Environment, Strategy, and Power Within Top Management Teams. *Administrative Science Quarterly* 26, no. 1 (Jun 1981): 253-276.

Hambrick, Donald Carrol. 1982. Environmental Scanning and Organizational Strategy. *Strategic Management Journal* 3, no. 2 (Apr/Jun 1982): 159-174.

Hambrick, Donald Carroll. 1979. *Environmental Scanning, Organizational Strategy, and Executive Roles: A Study in Three Industries.* Ph.D. dissertation, Pennsylvania State University.

Hamel, Gary and C. K. Pralahad. 1994. *Competing for the Future.* Boston, MA: Harvard Business School Press.

Hannan, Michael T. and John Freeman. 1977. The Population Ecology of Organizations. *American Journal of Sociology* 82, no. 5 (March): 929-964.

Hart, Paul Jason and Ronald E. Rice. 1991. Using Information from External Databases: Contextual Relationships of Use, Access Method, Task, Database Type, Organizational Differences and Outcomes. *Information Processing and Management* 27, no. 5: 461-479.

Hearst, Marti A. 1997. Interfaces for Searching the Web. *Scientific American* 276, no. 3: 68-72.

Hedberg, Bo. 1981. How Organizations Learn and Unlearn. In *Handbook of Organizational Design: Adapting Organizations to Their Environments*, ed. Paul C. Nystrom and William H. Starbuck, 3-27. New York, NY: Oxford University Press.

Hedin, Hans. 1993. Business Intelligence: Systematised Intelligence Activities in Ten Multinational Companies. *Journal of AGSI* 2, no. 3 (Nov 1993): 126-136.

Herring, Jan P. 1988. Building a Business Intelligence System. *Journal of Business Strategy* 9, no. 3 (May/Jun 1988): 4-9.

Herring, Jan P. 1991. Senior Management Must Champion Business Intelligence Programs. *Journal of Business Strategy* 12, no. 5: 48-52.

Herring, Jan P. 1992. Business Intelligence in Japan and Sweden: Lessons for the US. *Journal of Business Strategy* 13, no. 2 (Mar/Apr 1992): 44-49.

Hickson, D.J., C.R. Hinings, C.A. Lee, R.E. Schneck, and J.M Pennings. 1971. A Strategic Contingencies' Theory of Intraorganizational Power. *Administrative Science Quarterly* 16, no. 2 (June): 216-229.

Hise, Phaedra. 1996. Getting Smart On-line. *Inc.* (*Inc. Technology Supplement*) 18, no. 4: 59-65.

Holland, John H. 1988. The Global Economy as an Adaptive Process. In *The Economy as an Evolving Complex System*, ed. Philip W. Anderson, Kenneth J. Arrow, and David Pines, 117-124. Cambridge, MA: Addison-Wesley.

Holland, John H. 1992. Complex Adaptive Systems. In *A New Era In Computation*, ed. N. Metropolis and Gian-Carlo Rota, 17-30. Cambridge, MA: MIT Press.

Huber, George P. 1991. Organizational Learning: The Contributing Processes and the Literature. *Organization Science* 2, no. 1 (Feb 1991): 88-115.

Jain, Subhash C. 1984. Environmental Scanning in US Corporations. *Long Range Planning* 17, no. 2: 117-128.

Janis, Irving. 1982. *Groupthink: Psychological Studies of Policy Decision.* Boston, MA: Houghton Mifflin.

Jarvenpaa, S., & Ives, B. (1994). Digital Equipment Corporation: The Internet Company. *CIS-FSERV@UBE.UBALT.EDU.*, (Send Cases.DigitalWWW).

Jauch, Lawrence R. and William F. Glueck. 1988. *Business Policy and Strategic Management.* 5th ed. New York, NY: McGraw-Hill Book Co.

Jennings, Daniel F. and James R. Lumpkin. 1992. Insights Between Environmental Scanning Activities and Porter's Generic Strategies: An Empirical Analysis. *Journal of Management* 18, no. 4 (Dec 1992): 791-803.

Johnson, Lynn and Ralph Kuehn. 1987. The Small Business Owner/Manager's Search for External Information. *Journal of Small Business Management* 25, no. 3 (July): 53-60.

Jones, Jack William and Raymond McLeod Jr. 1986. The Structure of Executive Information Systems: An Exploratory Analysis. *Decision Sciences* 17, no. 2 (Spring): 220-249.

Kanter, Rosabeth Moss. 1983. *The Change Masters.* New York, NY: Simon & Schuster.

Kanter, Rosabeth Moss. 1991. Transcending Business Boundaries: 12,000 World Managers View Change. *Harvard Business Review* 69, no. 3 (May/June): 151-164.

Karpinski, Richard, and Rich Santalesa. 1997. Making Push Work for You. *NetGuide*, Issue no. 406, June 1, 1997.

Kassler, Helene S. 1997. Mining the Internet for Competitive Intelligence. *Online*, Sept./ Oct. 1997, 34-45.

Katzer, Jeffrey and Patricia Fletcher. 1992. The Information Environment of Managers. In *Annual Review of Information Science and Technology*, ed. Martha E. Williams, 227-263. Medford, NJ: Learned Information, Inc.

Keegan, Warren J. 1967. *Scanning the International Business Environment: A Study of the Information Acquisition Process.* Ph.D. dissertation, Harvard University.

Keegan, Warren J. 1974. Multinational Scanning: A Study of the Information Sources Utilized by Headquarters Executives in Multinational Companies. *Administrative Science Quarterly* 19, no. 3 (September): 411-421.

Kefalas, Asterios and Peter P. Schoderbek. 1973. Scanning the Business Environment - Some Empirical Results. *Decision Sciences* 4, no. 1: 63-74.

Kickert, Walter J. M. 1993. Autopoiesis and the Science of (Public) Administration: Essence, Sense and Nonsense. *Organization Studies* 14, no. 2: 261-278.

Klein, Harold E. and Robert E. Linneman. 1984. Environmental Assessment: An International Study of Corporate Practice. *Journal of Business Strategy* 5, no. 1 (Summer): 66-75.

Kleiner, Art. 1994. Creating Scenarios. In *The Fifth Discipline Fieldbook*, ed. Peter Senge, Art Kleiner, Charlotte Roberts, Richard Ross, and Bryan Smith, 275-278. New York, NY: Doubleday.

Kobrin, Stephen J., John Basek, Stephen Blank, and Joseph La Palombara. 1980. The Assessment and Evaluation of Noneconomic Environments by American Firms. *Journal of International Business Studies* 11, no. 1 (Spring/Summer): 32-47.

Koch, Christof and Joel L. Davis, ed. 1994. *Large-Scale Neuronal Theories of the Brain*. Cambridge, MA: MIT Press.

Kotter, John P. 1982. *The General Managers*. New York, NY: The Free Press.

Krol, Ed. 1994. *The Whole Internet User's Guide & Catalog*. 2nd ed. Sebastopol, CA: O'Reilly & Associates, Inc.

Kuhlthau, Carol Collier. 1993. *Seeking Meaning: A Process Approach to Library and Information Services*. Norwood, NJ: Ablex Publishing.

Lagerstam, Catharina. 1990. Business Intelligence in Japan. In *The Knowledge Industries: Levers of Economic and Social Development in the 1990's: Proceedings of an International Conference held at the Inter-University Centre for Post-Graduate Studies held in Dubrovnik, Yugoslavia, May 29 - June 3 1990*, edited by Blaise Cronin and Neva Tudor-Silovic, 69-77. London, UK: Aslib.

Langton, Christopher G. 1991. Life at the Edge of Chaos. In *Artificial Life II*, ed. Christopher G. Langton, Charles Taylor, J. Doyne Farmer, and Steen Rasmussen, 41-91. Redwood City, CA: Addison-Wesley.

Larkey, Patrick D. and Lee S. Sproull. 1984. *Advances in Information Processing in Organization*. Vol. 1. Greenwich CT: JAI Press, Inc.

Lawrence, Paul R. and Jay W. Lorsch. 1967. *Organization and Environment: Managing Differentiation and Integration*. Boston, MA: Graduate School of Business Administration, Harvard University.

Leavitt, Harold J. 1975. Beyond the Analytic Manager: I. *California Management Review* 17, no. 3: 5-12.

Lester, Ray and Judith Waters. 1989. *Environmental Scanning and Business Strategy*. London, UK: British Library, Research and Development Department.

Levy, Steven. 1992. *Artificial Life: A Report from the Frontier Where Computers Meet Biology*. New York, NY: Random House.

Liberman, Kristen and Jane L. Rich. 1993. Lotus Notes Databases: The Foundation of a Virtual Library. *Databases* 16, no. 3 (June 1993): 33-46.

Linder, Jane C. 1992. Today A Librarian, Tomorrow A Corporate Intelligence Professional. *Special Libraries* 83, no. 3 (Summer 1992): 142-144.

Locke, Christopher. 1994. Knowledge Exchange. *Internet World* 5, no. 4 (May/Jun 1994): 22-25.

Lottor, Mark K. 1997. *Host Distribution by Top-Level Domain Name.* Network Wizards, 1997. Available at: http://www.nw.com/zone/WWW/dist-bynum.html.

Luthans, Fred, Richard M. Hodgetts, and Stuart A. Rosenkrantz. 1988. *Real Managers.* Cambridge, MA: Ballinger.

Lynch, Clifford. 1997. Searching the Internet. *Scientific American* 276, no. 3: 52-56.

MacMullin, Susan E. and Robert S. Taylor. 1984. Problem Dimensions and Information Traits. *Information Society* 3, no. 1: 91-111.

Maguire, Carmel, Edward J. Kazlauskas, and Anthony D. Weir. 1994. *Information Services for Innovative Organizations.* San Diego, CA: Academic Press.

March, James G. 1991. How Decisions Happen in Organizations. *Human-Computer Interaction* 6, no. 2 (1991): 95-117.

March, James G. 1994. *A Primer on Decision Making: How Decisions Happen.* New York, NY: Free Press.

March, James G. and Herbert A. Simon. 1992. *Organizations.* 2nd ed. Oxford, UK: Blackwell.

March, James G. and Johan P. Olsen. 1979. Organizational Learning and the Ambiguity of the Past. In *Ambiguity and Choice in Organizations*, ed. James G. March and Johan P. Olsen, 54-68. Oslo, Norway: Universitetsforlaget.

Martin, J. S. 1992. Building an Information Resource Center for Competitive Intelligence. *Online Review* 16, no. 6 (Dec 1992): 379-390.

Maturana, Humberto R. and Francisco J. Varela. 1992. *The Tree of Knowledge: The Biological Roots of Human Understanding.* Boston, MA: Shambhala.

Mayberry, Alberta Gale Johnson. 1991. *Effects Of a Selective Dissemination Of Information Service On the Environmental Scanning Process Of an Academic Institution (Information Sources).* Ph.d., North Texas State University.

McGee, James V. and Laurence Prusak. 1993. *Managing Information Strategically.* New York, NY: John Wiley & Sons.

McGill, Michael E. and Jr Slocum, John W. 1994. *The Smarter Organization: How to Build a Business That Learns and Adapts to Marketplace Needs.* New York, NY: John Wiley & Sons.

McIntyre, John Richard. 1992. *A Multi-Case Study Of Environmental Scan As a Component Of the School Planning Process (Strategic Planning).* Ed.d., Rutgers University the State U. Of New Jersey (New Brunswick).

McKinnon, Sharon M. and William J. Bruns Jr. 1992. *The Information Mosaic: How Managers Get the Information They Really Need.* Boston, MA: Harvard Business School Press.

Meyer, Herbert. 1987. *Real-world Intelligence: Organized Information for Executives.* New York, NY: Weidenfeld & Nicolson.

MIDS. 1997. *1997 Users and Hosts of the Internet and the Matrix.* Matrix Information and Directory Services Inc., Feb 1997. Press Release. Available at: http://www.mids. org/press/pr9701.html.

Miles, Raymond E. and Charles C. Snow. 1978. *Organizational Strategy, Structure, and Process.* New York, NY: McGraw-Hill.

Miller, Danny and Peter H. Friesen. 1977. Strategy-Making in Context: Ten Empirical Archetypes. *Journal of Management Studies* 14, no. 3 (October): 253-280.

Miller, Jerry P. 1994. The Relationships Between Organizational Culture and Environmental Scanning: A Case Study. *Library Trends* 43, no. 2 (Fall 1994): 170-205.

Mintzberg, Henry, Duru Raisinghani, and Andre Thêorét. 1976. The Structure of "Unstructured" Decision Processes. *Administrative Science Quarterly* 21, no. 2 (June 1976): 246-275.

Mintzberg, Henry. 1973. *The Nature of Managerial Work.* New York, NY: Harper & Row.

Mintzberg, Henry. 1994. *The Rise and Fall of Strategic Planning: Reconceiving the Roles of Planning, Plans, and Planners.* New York, NY: Free Press.

Montague Institute. 1997. Use of the Internet in Business Intelligence: Survey Report. Available at http://www.montague.com/le/le5962.html. Montague, MA: Montague Institute.

Mooney, Philip F. 1993. The Practice of History in Corporate America: Business Archives in the United States. In *Corporate Archives and History: Making the Past Work*, ed. Arnita A. Jones and Philip L. Cantelon, 9-20. Malabar, FL: Krieger Publishing Co.

Moore, James F. 1993. Predators and Prey: A New Ecology of Competition. *Harvard Business Review* 71, no. 3 (May-Jun 1993): 75-86.

Morgan, Gareth. 1986. *Images of Organization.* Newbury Park, CA: Sage Publications.

Mori, Akio. 1994. The Toshiba Business Information Center Moves Toward the Virtual Library. *Special Libraries* 85, no. 4 (Fall 1994): 277-280.

Murphy, Michael Francis. 1987. *Environmental Scanning: a Case Study In Higher Education.* Ed.d, University Of Georgia.

Nakagawa, Juro. 1992. Intelligence, Trade and Industry. In *The Intelligent Corporation: The Privatisation of Intelligence*, ed. Jon Sigurdson and Yael Tagerud, 39-51. London, UK: Taylor Graham.

NCB (Singapore National Computer Board). 1992. *A Vision of an Intelligent Island: IT2000 Report.* Singapore: SNP Publishers.

Neal, Donn C. 1993. Corporate Archives and History - Introduction. In *Corporate Archives and History: Making the Past Work*, ed. Arnita A. Jones and Philip L. Cantelon, 1-4. Malabar, FL: Krieger Publishing Co.

Netscape Communications Corp. 1997. Netscape Boosts Sales Effectiveness and Productivity at Cadence Design Systems. Available at http://search.netscape.com/comprod/at_work/customer_profiles/cadence.html.

Newgren, Kenneth E., Arthur A. Rasher, and Margaret E. LaRoe. 1984. An Empirical Investigation of the Relationship Between Environmental Assessment and Corporate Performance. In *Proceedings of the 44th Annual Meeting of the Academy of Management held in Boston, MA, August 12-15 1984*, edited by John A. Pearce II and Richard B. Robinson Jr, 352-356. Washington, DC: Academy of Management.

Nishi, Kenyu, Charles Schoderbek, and Peter P. Schoderbek. 1982. Scanning the Organizational Environment: Some Empirical Results. *Human Systems Management* 3, no. 4: 233-245.

Nonaka, Ikujiro. 1988. Toward Middle-Up-Down Management: Accelerating Information Creation. *Sloan Management Review* 29, no. 3 (Spring 1988): 9-18.

Nonaka, Ikujiro. 1990. Redundant, Overlapping Organizations: A Japanese Approach to Managing the Innovation Process. *California Management Review* 32, no. 3: 27-38.

Nonaka, Ikujiro. 1991. The Knowledge-Creating Company. *Harvard Business Review* 69, no. 6 (Nov-Dec 1991): 96-104.

Nonaka, Ikujiro. 1994. A Dynamic Theory of Organizational Knowledge Creation. *Organization Science* 5, no. 1 (Feb 1994): 14-37.

O'Connell, Jeremiah J. and John W. Zimmerman. 1979. Scanning the International Environment. *California Management Review* 22, no. 2 (Winter): 15-23.

O'Reilly, Charles A. lll. 1982. Variation in Decision-Makers' Use of Information Sources: The Impact of Quality and Accessibility of Information. *Academy of Management Journal* 25, no. 4: 756-771.

Olaisen, Johan. 1990. Information Versus Information Technology as a Strategic Resource: Areas of Application of Information and Information Technology in Norwegian Banks and Insurance Companies. *International Journal of Information Management* 10, no. 3 (September): 192-214.

Olsen, Michael D., Bvsan Murthy, and Richard Teare. 1994. CEO Perspectives on Scanning the Global Hotel Business Environment. *International Journal of Contemporary Hospitality Management* 6, no. 4: 3-9.

Onyango, Richard A. O. 1991. Indigenous Technological Capacity: Can Social Intelligence Help? *Social Intelligence* 1, no. 1: 25-42.

Orna, E. 1990. *Practical Information Policies: How to Manage Information Flow in Organizations*. Aldershot, Hampshire, UK: Gower.

Paisley, William. 1980. Information and Work. In *Progress in Communication Sciences*, ed. Brenda Dervin and Melvin J. Voigt, 113-165. Norwood, NJ: Ablex Publishing Corporation.

Pascale, Richard Tanner. 1990. *Managing On The Edge: How The Smartest Companies Use Conflict to Stay Ahead*. New York, NY: Simon and Schuster.

Pask, G. and B. C. E. Scott. 1972. Learning Strategies and Individual Competence. *International Journal of Man-Machine Studies* 4: 217-253.

Pettigrew, Andrew M. 1973. *The Politics of Organizational Decision Making*. London, UK: Tavistock Institute.

Pfeffer, Jeffrey and Gerald R. Salancik. 1978. *The External Control of Organizations: A Resource Dependence Perspective*. New York, NY: Harper & Row.

Pfeffer, Jeffrey. 1992. *Managing with Power: Politics and Influences in Organizations*. Boston, MA: Harvard Business School Press.

Picot, Arnold. 1989. Information Management: The Science of Solving Problems. *International Journal of Information Management* 9, no. 4 (Dec 1989): 237-243.

Polanyi, Michael. 1966. *The Tacit Dimension*. London, UK: Routledge & Kegan Paul.

Polanyi, Michael. 1973. *Personal Knowledge*. London, UK: Routledge and Kegan Paul.

Porter, Michael E. 1980. *Competitive Strategy: Techniques for Analyzing Industries and Competitors*. New York, NY: The Free Press.

Porter, Michael E. 1985. *Competitive Advantage: Creating and Sustaining Superior Performance*. New York, NY: The Free Press.

Porter, Michael E. and Victor E. Millar. 1985. How Information Gives You Competitive Advantage. *Harvard Business Review* 63, no. 4 (Jul-Aug 1985): 149-160.

Preble, John F., Pradeep A. Rau, and Arie Reichel. 1988. The Environmental Scanning Practices of US Multinationals in the Late 1980s. *Management International Review* 28, no. 4: 4-14.

Prescott, John E. and Daniel C. Smith. 1987. A Project-Based Approach to Competitive Analysis. *Strategic Management Journal* 8, no. 5 (Sep/Oct 1987): 411-423.

Prescott, John E., ed. 1989. *Advances in Competitive Intelligence*. Vienna, VA: Society of Competitor Intelligence Professionals.

Prusak, Laurence and James Matarazzo. 1992. *Information Management and Japanese Success*. Washington, DC: Special Libraries Association/Ernst & Young.

Ptaszynski, James Garner. 1989. *Ed Quest As an Organizational Development Activity: Evaluating the Benefits Of Environmental Scanning*. Ph.d., The University Of North Carolina At Chapel Hill.

Quinn, James Brian. 1992. *Intelligent Enterprise: A Knowledge and Service Based Paradigm for Industry*. New York, NY: Macmillan, Inc.

Quinn, Robert E. 1988. *Beyond Rational Management: Mastering the Paradoxes and Competing Demands of High Performance*. San Francisco, CA: Jossey-Bass.

Radosevic, Slavo and Stevan Dedijer. 1990. Knowledge Industries, Information Technologies and Intelligence: The Case of Yugoslavia. In *The Knowledge Industries: Levers of Economic and Social Development in the 1990s*, ed. Blaise Cronin and Neva Tudor-Silovic. London, UK: Aslib.

Radosevic, Slavo. 1991. Techno-Economic Intelligence in the 1990s: A Development Policy Perspective. *Social Intelligence* 1, no. 1: 55-71.

Resnick, Rosalind. 1997. Which "Push" Delivery System is for You. *NetGuide*, May 1, 1997, Issue no. 405.

Rheingold, Howard. 1993. *The Virtual Community: Homesteading on the Electronic Frontier*. Reading, MA: Addison Wesley.

Robek, Mary F., Gerald F. Brown, and Wilmer O. Maedke. 1987. *Information and Records Management*. 3rd ed. Encino, CA: Glencoe Publishing Co.

Roberts, N. and B. Clifford. 1984. *Regional Variations in the Demand and Supply of Business Information: A Study of Manufacturing Firms*. Sheffield, UK: Consultancy and Research Unit, Department of Information Studies, University of Sheffield.

Roberts, Norman and Tom D. Wilson. 1988. The Development of User Studies at Sheffield University, 1963-88. *Journal of Librarianship* 20, no. 4 (October): 270-290.

Roesler, Marina and Donald T. Hawkins. 1994. Intelligent Agents: Software Servants for an Electronic Information World [and More!]. *Online* 18, no. 4 (Jul 1994): 19-32.

Rosenberg, Victor. 1967. Factors Effecting the Preferences of Industrial Personnel for Information Gathering Methods. *Information Storage and Retrieval* 3: 119-127.

Rouse, William B. and Sandra H. Rouse. 1984. Human Information Seeking and Design of Information Systems. *Information Processing and Management* 20, no. 1/2: 129-138.

Sammon, William L., Mark A. Kurland, and Robert Spitalnic, ed. 1984. *Business Competitor Intelligence: Methods for Collecting, Organizing and Using Information*. New York, NY: John Wiley and Sons Ltd.

Schrage, Michael. 1990. *Shared Minds: The New Technologies of Collaboration*. New York, NY: Random House.

Schroder, H. M. 1971. Conceptual Complexity and Personality Organization. In *Personality Theory and Information Processing*, ed. H. M. Schroder and P. Suedfeld, 240-273. New York, NY: Ronald Press Co.

Schwartz, Candy and Peter Hernon. 1993. *Records Management and the Library*. Norwood, NJ: Ablex.

Schwartz, Peter. 1991. *The Art of the Long View*. New York, NY: Doubleday Currency.

Scott, W. Richard. 1987. *Organizations: Rational, Natural, and Open Systems*. 2nd ed. Englewood Cliffs, NJ: Prentice-Hall.

Senge, Peter M. 1990. *The Fifth Discipline: The Art & Practice of the Learning Organization.* New York, NY: Doubleday Currency.

Senge, Peter M., Charlotte Roberts, Richard B. Ross, Bryan J. Smith, and Art Kleiner. 1994. *The Fifth Discipline Fieldbook: Strategies and Tools for a Learning Organization.* New York, NY: Currency Doubleday.

Sharfman, Mark P. and James W. Dean Jr. 1991. Conceptualizing and Measuring the Organizational Environment: A Multidimentional Approach. *Journal of Management* 17, no. 4 (December): 681-700.

Simon, Herbert A. 1976. *Administrative Behavior: A Study of Decision-Making Processes in Administrative Organization.* 3rd ed. New York, NY: The Free Press.

Simon, Herbert. 1977. *The New Science of Management Decision.* Revised ed. Englewood Cliffs, NJ: Prentice-Hall Inc.

Smeltzer, Larry R., Gail L. Fann, and V. Neal Nikolaisen. 1988. Environmental Scanning Practices in Small Businesses. *Journal of Small Business Management* 26, no. 3 (July): 55-62.

Smith, Daniel C. and John E. Prescott. 1987. Demystifying Competitive Analysis. *Planning Review* 15, no. 5 (Sep/Oct 1987): 8-13.

Smith, George David and Laurence E. Steadman. 1981. Present Value of Corporate History. *Harvard Business Review* 59, no. 6 (Nov/Dec 1981): 164-173.

Soergel, Dagobert. 1985. *Organizing Information: Principles of Data Base and Retrieval Systems.* Orlando, FL: Academic Press.

Soergel, Dagobert. 1994. Indexing and Retrieval Performance: The Logical Evidence. *Journal of the American Society for Information Science* 45, no. 8 (Sep 1994): 589-599.

Stabell, Charles. 1978. Integrative Complexity of Information Environment Perception and Information Use: An Empirical Investigation. *Organizational Behavior and Human Performance* 22, no. 1 (August): 116-142.

Stanat, Ruth. 1990. Building a Shared Information Network. In *Online Information 90: 14th International Online Information Meeting Proceedings held in London, UK, December 11-13 1990,* edited by David E. Raitt, 213-225. Oxford, UK: Learned Information.

Stanley, C. D. D. 1985. *Managing External Issues: Theory and Practice.* Greenwich, CT: JAI Press Inc.

Steele, Robert D. 1993. Access: Theory and Practice of Intelligence in the Age of Information. Speech given on Sep 17, 1993.

Stefik, Mark, ed. 1996. Internet Dreams: *Archetypes, Myths, and Metaphors.* Cambridge, MA: MIT Press.

Sternberg, Robert J. and Douglas K. Detterman, ed. 1986. *What Is Intelligence? Contemporary Viewpoints on Its Nature and Definition.* Norwood, NJ: Ablex Publishing Corp.

Sternberg, Robert J., ed. 1982. *The Handbook of Human Intelligence.* Cambridge, UK: Cambridge University Press.

Stewart, Thomas A. 1994 Your Company's Most Valuable Asset: Intellectual Capital. *Fortune*, Oct 3, 1994, 68-74.

Stuart, Anne. 1997. Under the Hood at Ford. *WebMaster*, June, 1997, available at http://www.cio.com/WebMaster/060197_for_content.html.

Subramanian, Ram, Kamalesh Kumar, and Charles Yauger. 1994. The Scanning of Task Environments in Hospitals: An Empirical Study. *Journal of Applied Business Research* 10, no. 4: 104-115.

Subramanian, Ram, Nirmala Fernandes, and Earl Harper. 1993. An Empirical Examination of the Relationship Between Strategy and Scanning. *Mid-Atlantic Journal of Business* 29, no. 3: 315-330.

Subramanian, Ram, Nirmala Fernandes, and Earl Harper. 1993. Environmental Scanning in US Companies: Their Nature and Their Relationship to Performance. *Management International Review* 33, no. 3 (Third Quarter 1993): 271-286.

Sullivan, Jeremiah J. and Ikujiro Nonaka. 1986. The Application of Organizational Learning Theory to Japanese and American Management. *Journal of International Business Studies* 17, no. 3 (Fall 1986): 127-147.

Sutton, Howard E. 1989. Keeping Tabs on the Competition. *Marketing Communications* 14, no. 1 (Jan 1989): 42-45.

Sutton, Howard. 1988. *Competitive Intelligence.* New York: The Conference Board, Inc.

Tank, Andrew. 1993. *Information for Strategic Decisions.* The Conference Board, 1993.

Taylor, Robert S. 1982. Benefits and Costs of Information Use. In *Proceedings of the 45th American Society for Information Science (ASIS) Annual Meeting held in Columbus, Ohio, October 17-21 1982*, edited by A.E. Petracarca, C.I. Taylor, and R.S. Kohn, White Plains, NY: Knowledge Industry Publications, Inc.

Taylor, Robert S. 1982. Value-Added Processes in the Information Life Cycle. *Journal of the American Society for Information Science* 33, no. 5 (September): 341-346.

Taylor, Robert S. 1986. *Value-added Processes in Information Systems.* Norwood, NJ: Ablex Publishing Corp.

Taylor, Robert S. 1991. Information Use Environments. In *Progress in Communication Science*, ed. Brenda Dervin and Melvin J. Voigt, 217-254. Norwood, NJ: Ablex Publishing Corporation.

Teitelbaum, Richard S. 1992 The New Race for Intelligence. *Fortune*, Nov 2, 1992, 104-107.

Tell, Bjorn. 1987. Scientific and Technical Information: Sweden and Malaysia. In *Intelligence for Economic Development: An Inquiry into the Role of the Knowledge Industry*, ed. Stevan Dedijer and Nicolas Jequier, 128-138. Oxford, UK: Berg.

Terreberry, Shirley. 1968. The Evolution of Organizational Environments. *Administrative Science Quarterly* 12, no. 1 (March): 590-613.

Thomas, Philip S. 1980. Environmental Scanning: The State of the Art. *Long Range Planning* 13, no. 1 (February): 20-25.

Thompson, James D. 1967. *Organizations in Action: Social Science Bases of Administrative Theory.* New York: McGraw-Hill.

Thorell, Lisa. 1994. Doing Business On the Internet: Case Studies: DEC, Silicon Graphics, and Sun. *Internet World* 5, no. 5 (Jul/Aug 1994): 52-63.

Tomioka, Akira. 1990. Corporate Intelligence: The Key to the Strategic Success of Japanese Organizations in International Environments. In *Global Corporate Intelligence*, ed. George S. Roukis, Hugh Conway, and Bruce H. Charnov, 211-226. New York, NY: Quorum Books.

Treloar, Andrew. 1994. Architectures for Networked Information: A Comparative Study of Gopher and the World-Wide Web. *Journal of Information Networking* 2, no. 1: 23-46.

Tushman, Michael L. and Thomas J. Scanlan. 1981. Boundary Spanning Individuals: Their Role in Information Transfer and Their Antecedents. *Academy of Management Journal* 28, no. 2: 289-305.

Tyson, Kirk W. M. 1990. *Competitor Intelligence Manual and Guide: Gathering, Analyzing and Using Business Intelligence.* Englewood Cliffs, NJ: Prentice Hall.

Vandenbosch, Betty and Sid L. Huff. 1997. Searching and Scanning: How Executives Obtain Information from Executive Information Systems. *MIS Quarterly* 21, no. 1: 81-108.

Veen, Jeffrey. 1997. Tools: Why Channels Suck. *Wired News*, July 28, 1997.

Ventura, Arnoldo. 1988. Social Intelligence: Prerequisite for the Management of Science and Technology. In *From Research Policy to Social Intelligence: Essays for Stevan Dedijer*, ed. Jan Annerstedt and Andrew Janison, 163-172. Basingstoke, UK: Macmillan.

Vine, David. 1995. Using the Internet as a Strategic Business Tool. *Internet World* 8, no. 1 (Jan 1995): 44-48.

Vogel, Ezra. 1979. *Japan As Number One: Lessons for America.* Cambridge, MA: Harvard University Press.

Wack, Pierre. 1985a. Scenarios: Shooting the Rapids. *Harvard Business Review* 63, no. 6 (Nov-Dec 1985): 139-150.

Wack, Pierre. 1985b. Scenarios: Uncharted Waters Ahead. *Harvard Business Review* 63, no. 5 (Sept/Oct 1985): 72-89.

Waldrop, M. Mitchell. 1992. *Complexity: The Emerging Science at the Edge of Order and Chaos* . New York, NY: Simon & Schuster.

Weick, Karl E. 1979. *The Social Psychology of Organizing*. 2nd ed. Random House: New York.

Weick, Karl E. and Richard L. Daft. 1983. The Effectiveness of Interpretation Systems. In *Organizational Effectiveness: A Comparison of Multiple Models*, ed. Kim S. Cameron and David A. Whetten, 71-93. New York, NY: Academic Press.

West, Joseph John. 1988. *Strategy, Environmental Scanning, and Their Effect Upon Firm Performance: an Exploratory Study Of the Food Service Industry*. Ph.d., Virginia Polytechnic Institute and State University.

Wheatley, Margaret J. 1992. *Leadership and the New Science: Learning About Organization from an Orderly Universe*. San Francisco, CA: Berrett-Koehler.

White, D.A and Tom D. Wilson. 1988. *Information Needs in Industry: A Case Study Approach*. Sheffield, U.K.: Consultancy and Research Unit, Department of Information Studies, University of Sheffield.

White, D.A. 1986. Information Use and Needs in Manufacturing Organizations: Organizational Factors in Information Behaviour. *International Journal of Information Management* 6, no. 3 (September): 157-170.

Wilder, Clinton. 1995. The Internet Pioneers. *Information Week*, Jan 9, 1995, 38-48.

Wilensky, Harold. 1967. *Organisational Intelligence: Knowledge and Policy in Government and Industry*. New York: Basic Books.

Williams, Martha E. 1994. The State of Databases Today: 1994. In K. Y. Maraccio, ed. *Gale Directory of Databases* Detroit, IL: Gale Research, Inc.

Williams, Martha E. 1997. The State of Databases Today: 1997. In *Gale Directory of Databases*, edited by K. Y. Maraccio. Detroit, IL: Gale Research, Inc.

Wilson, Tom D. and I.M. Masser. 1983. Environmental Monitoring and Information Management in County Planning Authorities. In *Representation and Exchange of Knowledge as a Basis of Information Processes: Proceedings of the 5th International Research Forum in Information Science held in Heidelberg, Germany, September 5-7 1983*, edited by H.J. Dietschmann, 271-284. Amsterdam, The Netherlands: Elsevier Science Publishers.

Winograd, Terry and Fernanado Flores. 1987. *Understanding Computers and Cognition: A New Foundation for Design*. Reading, MA: Addison-Wesley Company, Inc.

Witkin, H. 1959. The Perception of the Upright. *Scientific American* 200, no. 2: 50-70.

Wygant, Alice Chambers and O. W. Markley. 1988. *Information and the Future: A Handbook of Sources and Strategies*. Westport, CT: Greenwood Press.

Yasai-Ardekani, Masoud; Nystrom, Paul C. 1996. Designs for Environmental Scanning Systems: Tests of a Contingency Theory. *Management Science* 42, no. 2: 187-204.

Zeki, Semir. 1992. The Visual Image in Mind and Brain. *Scientific American* 267, no. 3 (Sep 1992): 68-77.

Zeki, Semir. 1993. *A Vision of the Brain.* Oxford, U.K.: Basil Blackwell.

Zuboff, Shoshana. 1988. *In The Age of the Smart Machine: The Future of Work and Power.* New York, NY: Basic Books.

Name Index

Includes names of individuals, businesses and institutions. For names of publications and products, see the SUBJECT INDEX.

3M, 206

ABB see Asea Brown Boveri
Abbott Laboratories, 194
Achleitner, Herbert K., 63, 233
Achrol, Ravi S., 87, 233
A.C. Nielsen, 158
Aguilar, Francis J., 72, 75, 82, 83, 84, 85, 90, 92, 94, 96, 233
Aichi Gakun University (Japan), 122
Al-Hamad, Fahaad Murad, 85, 98, 233
Aldrich, Howard E., 3, 5, 233
Allen, Bryce L., 91, 233
Allen, Kimberly, 204, 205, 234
Allen, Thomas John, 42, 43, 143, 233, 239
Allende, Salvador, 209
American Hospital Association, 101
Anastasi, Anne, 11, 233
Anderson, Philip W., 234, 241
Anderson, Rebekah, E., 206, 233
Anheuser-Busch, 194
Annerstedt, Jan, 250
Apple Computer Inc., 9-10, 124, 170
Argyris, Chris, 15, 233
Arrow, Kenneth J., 3, 234, 241
Arthur, Brian, 211, 234
Asea Brown Boveri Inc. (ABB), 117
Ashby, W. Ross, 30, 234
Astra-Draco, 118
AT&T, 36, 110-112, 113, 194, 209
Auster, Ethel, 24, 66, 72, 75, 82, 85, 88 93, 96, 99, 125, 142, 143, 234, 236

Basch, Reva, 165, 173, 195-196, 234
Basek, John, 242
Bates, Mary Ellen, 204, 205, 234
Bateson, Gregory, 23, 44, 234
Bawden, David, 117, 234
B.C. Telephone, 123
Beer, Stafford, 30, 209, 234
Bell & Howell, 10
Bell Atlantic, 124
Bell Canada, 205
Bell Communications Research, 158
Bell, Daniel, 120
Bell-Northern Research, 205
Bernhardt, Douglas C., 74, 189, 197, 234, 235
Bigelow, Barbara, 75, 234
Birks, Grant, 205, 235
Blandin, James S., 59, 61, 235
Blank, Stephen, 242
Boeing, 14
Boland, Richard J., Jr., 45, 235
Bonzi, Susan, 234
Bowonder, B., 215, 235
Box, Thomas Morgan, 91, 92, 235
Boyd, Brian Kenneth, 85, 88, 91, 235
Braman, Sandra, 212, 213, 235
Brand, Stewart, 235
Breklin, Dan, 10
Bristol-Meyers Pharmaceutical, 158
British Library, The, 73
Broadhead, Rick, 168, 235
Brown, Gerald F., 247

Brown, Warren B., 59 60, 235
Browne, Mairead, 65, 66, 235
Bruns, William J., Jr., 64, 244
Budner, S., 91, 235
Bureau of the Census (US), 162
Burns, Tom, 3, 235
Bush Vannevar, 157

Cadence Design Systems, 184
Cameron, Kim S., 251
Canadian Cable TV Association, 126
Canadian Radio, Television and
   Telecommunications Commisson
   (CRTC), 127, 128
Canon, 12, 13, 69, 122, 207
Cantelon, Philip L., 244, 245
Carroll, Jim, 168, 235
Celsius Tech, 118
Central Intelligence Agency (CIA), 78,
   112, 122
Cerf, Vinton, 157
Cha, M., 236
Chang, Shan-Ju, 85, 235
Charnov, Bruce H., 250
Choo, Chun Wei, 6, 17, 24, 66, 72, 75,
   82, 85, 88, 93, 96, 99, 125, 142,
   143, 236
Choudhury, Vivek, 98, 236
Chu, Heting, 171, 236
Churchman, C. W., 45, 236
CIA see Central Intelligence Agency
Citibank, 36, 156
Clifford, B., 62, 247
Conference Board (US), 65
Conway, Hugh, 250
Crick, Francis, 107, 236
Cronin, Blaise, 80, 81, 185, 236, 242,
   247
Cronin, Mary J., 162, 183, 236
CRTC see Canadian Radio, Television
   and Telecommunications
   Commisson

Culnan, Mary J., 95, 143, 236
Cummings, L.L., 236
Cyert, Richard Michael, 3, 6, 7, 84, 237

Daft, Richard L., 6, 7, 8, 61, 82, 85, 87,
   88, 98, 100, 146, 237, 251
Davenport, Elisabeth, 80, 82, 222
Davenport, Thomas H., 25, 67, 68, 150,
   201, 202, 206, 237
Davis, Blaine, 111
Davis, Joel L., 106, 242
de Geus, Arie P., 14, 20, 237
Dean, James W., Jr., 87, 248
Dedijer, Stevan, 75, 80, 118, 120, 189,
   237, 247, 250
Dennett, Daniel C., 109, 237
Dervin, Brenda, 29, 237, 246, 249
Desai, Bijel H., 117, 237
Detterman, Douglas K., 11, 219, 249
Dialog, 191, 194
Dietschmann, H.J., 251
Digital Equipment Corporation, 158,
   177, 183, 206
Dill, William R., 3, 72, 237
Dilno, Dennis L., 204, 237
Ding, Wei, 169-170, 238
Dollinger, Marc J., 100, 237
Dommer, Jan, 205, 238
Droege, Peter, 236
Drucker, Peter, 28, 120, 164, 200, 213,
   214, 238
Duggan, Patrice, 122, 238
Dumaine, Brian, 21, 209, 238
Dun and Bradstreet, 153
Duncan, Robert B., 87, 238

Eastman Kodak, 110, 114, 190 see also
   Kodak
Eccles, Robert G., 53, 54, 55, 237, 238
Edelman, Gerald M., 108, 238
Eisenhardt, Kathleen M., 63, 238

Electrolux, 118, 119
Elenkov, Detelin S., 88, 238
Ellsworth, Jill H., 157, 238
Emenstodt, G., 122, 238
Emery, Fred E., 87, 238
Ericsson, L.M. see L.M. Ericsson
European Council of Information
    Management Executives, 65
European Council on Corporate
    Strategy, 65
Etzioni, Amitai, 73, 238
Ewing, R.P., 75, 238

Faber Castell, 194
Fahey, Liam, 72, 75, 92, 98, 235, 238
Fann, Gail L., 248
Farmer, J. Doyne, 242
Federal Communications Commission,
    178
Federal Express, 209
Feldman, Susan, 171, 239
Fernandes, Nirmala, 249
Fidel, Raya, 37, 238
Fletcher, Patricia Tobaka, 64, 66, 239,
    242
Flores, Fernando, 45, 53, 251
Ford Motor Company, 209, 184
Ford, Larry, 68
Foreign Intelligence Advisory Board
    (US), 112
Forrester, Jay, 209
Fouchereaux, K., 236
Freeman, John, 5, 240
Friesen, Peter H., 99, 100, 244
Fuji Bank, 122
Fuld, Leonard M., 189, 190, 193, 195,
    196, 239

Gadamer, Hans-Georg, 45, 239
Galbraith, Jay R., 3, 239
Galvin, Bob, 112

Gambro, 118
Garvin, David A., 14, 20, 239
Gates, Anne Marie, 95, 239
Gazzaniga Michael S., 106, 239
General Foods Corporation, 154
General Mills, 113-114
General Motors, 110, 114, 158
Gerstberger, Peter G., 143, 239
Ghoshal, Sumantra, 85, 93, 95, 99, 114,
    120, 142, 239
Gib, Andre, 205, 239
Gilad, Benjamin, 74, 75, 79, 110, 113,
    124, 151, 189, 192, 195, 239
Gilad, Tamar, 74, 75, 79, 151, 189, 192,
    239
Glazier, Jack D., 237
Global Business Network, 208
Glueck, William F., 72, 73, 240, 241
Gordon, Ian, 189, 240
Greene, Richard M., 79, 240
Gregory, Richard L., 11, 240
Grover, Robert, 63
Gulliver, F., 14, 240

Haeckel, Stephen H., 10, 240
Hales, Colin, 52, 240
Hambrick, Donald C., 88, 89, 90, 241
Hamel, Gary, 17, 18, 241
Hannan, Michael T., 5, 241
Harper, Earl, 249
Hart, Paul Jason, 194, 241
Hawkins, Donald T., 158, 247
Hearst, Marti A., 168, 241
Hedberg, Bo, 18, 241
Hedin, Hans, 99, 118, 119-120, 241
Hegel, Georg Wilhelm Friedrich, 45
Hernon, Peter, 35, 248
Herring, Jan P., 112, 117, 118, 120,
    189, 190, 191, 241
Hickson, D.J., 67, 241
Hinings, C.R., 240

Hise, Phaedra, 184, 241
Hodgetts, Richard M., 63, 244
Holland, John H., 210, 211, 241
Honda, 13, 69
Huber, George P., 24, 42, 241
Hiff, Sid L., 92, 251
H.W. Wilson Company, 153

IBM, 68
Information Access Company, 153
Inkeles, A., 219
Insurance Group, 118
Itoh, C., 121
Ives, B., 183, 242

Jain, Subhash, C., 89, 92, 98, 99, 114, 115, 242
Janis, Irving, 149, 242
Janison, Andrew, 250
Jarvenpaa, S., 183, 242
Jauch, Lawrence R., 72, 73, 92, 226, 242
Jennings, Daniel F., 88, 242
Jéquier, Nicholas, 75, 80, 189, 236, 237, 250
Johnson, Lynn, 93, 242
Jones, Arnita A., 244, 245
J.P. Morgan, 183

Kanematsu Gosho, 121
Kant, Immanuel, 45
Kanter, Rosabeth Moss, 69, 71, 242
Karpik, Lucien, 233
Karpinski, Richard, 167, 242
Kassler, Helene S., 196, 242
Katzer, Jeffrey, 242
Kay, Alan, 105
Kazlauskas, Edward J., 243
Keegan, Warren J., 94, 96, 97, 242
Kefalas, Asterios, 85, 87, 90, 242
Kelly, Kevin, 238

Kickert, Walter J.M., 212, 242
Kim, Seok Ki, 85, 95, 142, 239
King, William R., 98, 238
Klein, Harold E., 97, 242
Kleiner, Art, 207, 208, 242, 249
Kobrin, Stephen J., 85, 94, 243
Koch, Christof, 106, 243
Kodak, 194 see also Eastman Kodak
Kohn, R.S., 250
Kotter, John P., 60, 149, 243
Kraft, 110, 113
Krol, Ed., 44, 243
Kuehn, Ralph, 93, 241
Kuhlthau, Carol Collier, 216, 243
Kumar, Kamalesh, 241
Kuring-Gai College of Advanced Education (Sydney, Australia), 65
Kurland, Mark A., 250

La Palombara, Joseph, 243
Lagerstam, Catharina, 120, 121, 253
Langston University, 95
Langton, Christopher, 183, 210, 253
Larkey, Patrick D., 6, 253
LaRoe, Margaret E., 246
Lawrence, Paul R., 3, 254
Leavitt, Harold J., 85, 254
Lee, C.A., 227
Leibniz, Gottfriend Wilhelm von, 45
Lengel, Robert H., 61, 146, 237
Lester, Ray, 73, 93, 95, 99, 115, 163, 243
Levy, Steven, 210, 243
LEXIS-NEXIS, 194
Liberman, Kristen, 204, 243
Linder, Jane C., 206, 243
Linnerman, Robert E., 97, 242
L.M. Ericsson, 117
    Ericsson Radio Systems, 118, 119
Locke, Christopher, 166, 243

Locke, John, 45

Lorsch, Jay W., 3, 243

Lotus Development Corporation, 204

Lumpkin, James R., 241

Lund University (Sweden), 80, 118

Luthans, Fred, 63, 244

Lynch, Clifford, 170, 244

MacMullin, Susan E., 26-28, 57, 144, 244

Maedke, Wilmer O., 248

Maguire, Carmel, 41, 244

Mahon, John F., 75, 235

Mailick, Sidney, 237

Manzanzvike, T., 236

March, James G., 3, 6, 7, 8, 9, 12, 84, 141, 236, 244

Marchionini, Gary, 169-170, 238

Markley, O.W., 151, 252

Martin, J.S., 120, 244

Marubeni, 121, 122

Massachusetts Institute of Technology (MIT), 21, 209

Masser, I.M. 97, 252

Matarazzo, James, 202, 247

Matrix Information & Directory Services, 161

Matsushita, 13, 69

Maturana, Humberto, 183, 212, 244

Mayberry, Alberta Gale Johnson, 95, 244

McDonnell Douglas, 205-206

McGee, James V., 25, 244

McGill, Michael E., 16, 244

MCI Communications, 204

McIntyre, John Richard, 98, 244

McKinnon, Sharon M., 64, 244

McLeod, Raymond, Jr., 61, 242

Metropolis, N., 242

Meyer, Herbert E., 78, 79, 120, 122, 137, 138, 189, 244

Miles, Raymond, E., 84, 85, 86, 89, 90, 245

Millar, Victor E., 247

Miller, Danny, 99, 100, 245

Miller, Jerry P., 89, 90, 245

Mindlin, Sergio, 2, 233

Mintzberg, Henry, 46, 47, 57, 59, 61, 65, 73, 84, 149, 245

Mitsubishi, 121, 122

Mitsui, 121, 122

Miyake, T., 215, 235

Monsanto, 158

Montague Institute, 184-5, 245

Moody's, 153

Mooney, Philip F., 36, 37, 245

Moore, James F., 18, 245

Morgan, Gareth, 12, 212, 245

Morgan, J.P. see J.P. Morgan

Mori, Akio, 203, 204, 245

Motorola, 110, 112-113, 158, 190, 196, 207, 209

Murphy, Michael Francis, 101, 245

Murthy, Bvsan, 246

Nakagawa, Juro, 121, 122, 123, 245

Narayanan, Vadake, K., 72, 92, 238

NASA, 162

National Computer Board (NCB) of Singapore, 17-18, 124, 245

National Science Foundation, 157, 177

Neal, Donn C., 36, 245

NEC, 13, 69

Newgren, Kenneth E., 100, 246

Nichimen Corporation, 121, 122

Nielsen, A.C. see A.C. Nielsen

Nikolaisen, V. Neal, 248

Nippon Steel Corporation, 215

Nishi, Kenyi, 85, 87, 90, 92, 246

Nissan, 122

Nissho Iwai, 121

Nohria, Nitin, 53, 54, 55, 238

Nolan, Richard L., 10, 240
Nonaka, Ikujiro, 13, 69, 246, 250
Northern Telecom, 111, 205
Nystrom, Paul C., 90, 226
O'Connell, Jeremiah J., 94, 246
Olaisen, Johan, 193, 246
Olsen, Johan P., 9, 244
Olsen, Michael D., 93, 246
Ontario Securities Commission, 159
Onyango, Richard A., 80, 246
Oracle Corporation, 183
Orna, E., 32, 246
Overfelt, K., 236

Paisley, William, 91, 246
Parks, Don 237
Pascale, Richard Tanner, 13, 14, 69, 247
Pask, G., 91, 247
Pearce, John A., II, 245
Pennings, J.M., 241
Perot, Ross, 172
Perot Systems, 172
Petracarca, A.E., 250
Pettigrew, Andrew M., 67, 247
Pfeffer, Jeffrey, 4, 5, 67, 219, 247
Picot, Arnold, 213, 247
Pines, David, 234, 241
Polanyi, Michael, 12, 247
Porter, Michael E., 74, 76, 77, 78, 81,
   86, 89, 90, 100, 247
Powell, Ronald R., 237
Pralahad, C.K., 17, 18, 241
Preble, John F., 97, 99, 247
Prescott, John E., 113, 115, 189, 194,
   232, 234, 247, 249
Price Waterhouse, 204
Prusak, Laurence, 25, 201, 202, 206,
   223, 230, 232, 237, 244, 247
Ptaszynski, James Garner, 101, 247

Quinn, James Brian, 9, 10, 247

Quinn, Robert E., 89, 247

Radosevic, Slavo, 75, 80, 248
Raisinghani, Duru, 46, 244
Raitt, David, E., 249
Rasher, Arthur A., 245
Rasmussen, Steen, 242
Rau, Pradeep A., 246
Regis McKenna, 10
Reichel, Arie, 246
Resnick, Rosalind, 167, 248
Rheingold, Howard, 162, 248
Rice, Ronald E., 85, 164, 235, 241
Rice University, 172
Rich, Jane L., 204, 243
Robek, Mary F., 34, 248
Roberts, Charlotte, 228, 248
Roberts, Norman, 62, 248
Robinson, Richard B., Jr. 246
Rockwell International, 158
Roesler, Marina, 158, 248
Rosenberg, Victor, 143, 248
Rosenkrantz, Stuart, A., 63, 243
Rosenthal, Marilyn, 171, 236
Ross, Richard, 228, 248
Rota, Gian-Carlo, 241
Roukis, George S., 250
Rouse, Sandra H., 73, 91, 248
Rouse, William B., 73, 91, 248
Royal Dutch Shell, 14, 16, 125, 207
Royal Society of Chemistry (UK), 162

Salancik, Gerald R., 4, 247
San Houston State University, 172
Sammon, William L., 196, 248
Sampler, Jeffrey L., 98, 236
Santalesa, Rich, 167, 242
SAS, 118
SCA Graphic, 118
Scanlan, Thomas J., 43, 141, 250

Schneck, R.E., 241

Schoderbek, Charles, 246

Schoderbek, Peter P., 85, 87, 90, 228, 246

Schon, Donald, 15, 233

Schrage, Michael, 44, 248

Schroder, H.M., 91, 248

Schwartz, Candy, 35, 248

Schwartz, Peter, 208, 248

Scott, B.C.E., 91, 247

Scott, W. Richard, 5, 248

Securities and Exchange Commission, 163

Senge, Peter, 21-22, 209, 228, 249

Shakespeare, William, 137

Sharfman, Mark P., 87, 249

Sharp, 13, 69

Shaw, Debora, 234

Shell see Royal Dutch Shell

Sigurdson, Jon, 245

Simon, Herbert, 6, 33, 54, 84, 141, 243, 249

Singer, Edgar A., 45

Sloan School of Management, MIT, 21, 209

Slocum, John W., Jr., 16, 244

Smeltzer, Larry R., 85, 94, 249

Smith, Bryan, 228, 249

Smith, Daniel C., 113, 115, 194, 232, 249

Smith, George David, 36, 249

Snow, Charles C., 84, 85, 86, 89, 90, 245

Soergel, Dagobert, 37, 249

Sona, E., 236,

Sony, 69

Sormunen, Juhani, 237

Spitalnic, Robert, 250

Sproull, Lee S., 6, 243

Stabell, Charles, 7, 60, 92, 249

Stalker, G.M., 3, 236

Stanat, Ruth, 32, 99, 154, 155, 156, 189, 196, 249

Standard and Poor's, 153, 178

Stanford University, 124, 211

Stanley, C.D.D., 75, 249

Starbuck, William H., 240

Stark, Martin, 110, 111

State Trading Corporation of India, 123

Statistics Canada, 162

Staw, B.M., 237

Steadman, Laurence E., 36, 249

Steele, Robert D., 137, 249

Stefik, Mark, 172, 249

Sternberg, Robert J., 11, 219, 249

Stewart, Thomas A., 21, 250

Stockholm School of Economics, 118

Stuart, Anne, 184, 250

Subramanian, Ram, 85, 89, 97, 99, 100, 101, 114, 250

Suedfeld, P., 248

Sullivan, Jeremiah J., 69, 250

Sumitomo, 121

Sun Microsystems, 158

Sun Tzu, 105

Sutton, Howard, 72, 74, 75, 81, 110, 111, 112, 189, 250

Tagerud, Yael, 245

Tank, Andrew, 65, 250

Taylor, Charles, 242

Taylor, C.I., 250

Taylor, Robert S., 26-28, 39, 57, 144, 145, 216, 244, 250

Teare, Richard, 246

Te'eni, Dov, 235

Teitelbaum, Richard S., 110, 122, 250

Telia, 118, 119

Tell, Bjorn, 80, 250

Tenkasi, Ramkrishnan, V., 235

Terreberry, Shirley, 87, 251

Texas A & M University, 172

Thêorét, Andre, 46, 245
Thomas, Philip S., 97, 99, 251
Thomas Publishing, 153
Thompson, James D., 3, 87, 251
Thorell, Lisa, 183, 251
Tibco Softwqre, 16
Tomioka, Akira, 99, 123, 251
Toshiba, 203, 204
Toyo Menka, 121
Treloar, Andrew, 174, 251
Trist, Eric L., 87, 238
Tudor-Silovic, Neda, 236, 243, 248
Tushman, Michael L., 43, 141, 251
Tyson, Kirk W.M., 189, 251

United Press International, 170
University of California at Berkeley, 124
University of Lund, 118
University of Minnesota, 170
University of Missouri, St. Louis, 172
University of Sheffield (UK), 62
Upjohn, 205
US Council of Information Management Executives, 65
US Council of Planning Executives, 65
US Department of Commerce, 162
US Department of Defense, 167
US Department of Energy, 162
US Department of Transportation, 162

Van Ness, Edward H., 237
Vandenbosch, Betty, 92, 251
Varela, Francisco, 182, 212, 243
Veen, Jeffrey, 168, 251
Ventura, Arnoldo, 75, 251
Vine, David, 178, 251
Vogel, Ezra, 120. 251
Voigt, Melvin J., 246, 250
Volvo, 117, 118, 196

Wack, Pierre, 16, 207, 251
Wal-Mart, 10-11
Waldrop, M. Mitchell, 210, 251
Wallenberg Bank, 118
Walraven, Eileen, 205, 240
Waters, Judith, 73, 93, 95, 99, 115, 163, 243
Weick, Karl E., 3, 6, 7, 8, 45, 72, 82, 84, 98, 236, 252
Weir, Anthony D., 244
Wells Fargo, 36
West, Joseph John, 100, 252
Westney, Eleanor, 114, 239
Wheatley, Margaret J., 212, 252
Whetten, David A., 252
White, D.A., 62, 90, 252
Whitmire, Denise I., 204, 238
Wiener, Norbert, 23
Wilder, Clinton, 183, 252
Wilensky Harold, 9, 252
Williams, Martha E., 186, 235, 236, 242, 252
Wilson, H.W., see H.W. Wilson Company
Wilson, Tom D., 62, 90, 97, 248, 252
Winograd, Terry, 45, 53, 252
Witkin, H., 91, 252
Wong, Seng Hon, 124-125
Wrangler, 10-11
Wygant, Alice Chambers, 151, 252

Xerox Corporation, 158

Yamaha, 13
Yasai-Ardekani, Masoud, 90, 252
Yauger, Charles, 250

Zeki, Semir, 107, 108, 252, 253
Zhuge Liang, 51, 71
Zimmerman, John W., 94, 246
Zuboff, Shoshana, 20, 253

Subject Index

For names of individuals, businesses and institutions, see NAME INDEX. Italicized page numbers indicate information given in a figure or table.

ABI/Inform, 187, *188*

Access to Information Act (Canada), 154

Apple II, 9-10

audits, information, 32

Biobusiness, *189*, 192

browsing, on the Internet, 163-166, 175-176, see also **Internet**

Business Dateline, *188*, 191

business environment *see* **environment**

business intelligence, 74-75, 78-79, 81, 118-120, 122, 123, 137, 163, 183-186, 189, 190, 192-193, 206-207, see also **competitive intelligence, competitor intelligence, environmental scanning**

    Internet sources, 177-182

    online sources, 186-196

    system, *206*, 206-207

        analysis, *206*, 207

        collection, *206*, 207

        dissemination, *206*, 207

        evaluation, *206*, 207

        storage, *206*, 207

Business Week, 132

Business Wire, *188*, 191

Canadian Business and Current Affairs (CBCA), 191

Canadian CEOs

in environmental scanning, case studies of, 125-134

CENDATA, *188*, 191

Chemical Business Newsbase, *189*, 192

communicating, on the Internet, *163*, 172-175, 176, see also **Internet**

Company Intelligence, *189*

competitive intelligence, 74, 76-78, 81, 117, 137, 178, 180, 185-186, 194

competitor intelligence, 74, 81, 205-206, 214

complexity, science of, 223-227

    adaptive nonlinear network, 224-225

    autopoiesis, 226

    complex adaptive systems, 224

    increasing returns, 225

complexity theory, xiii, 60

Computer Database, *189*

computer software see **software**

conditioned viewing,

    as scanning mode, 73, *83*, 84, 158, 159, *160*, 176, *177*, see also under **environmental scanning**, modes of, and **online information gathering**

    Web-based business resources for, *179-181*

cultural knowledge, *11*, 12, 198

databases, see also **online databases**

    collection network within an organization, 31

data warehousing, 34

intelligence databases, 209-210

   at AT&T, 110-111

   at Motorola, 112

online analytical processing, 34

decision making, 6-7, 46-48, *48*, 50, 59, 61-62, 65-66, see also under **managers**, role of

in high-velocity environments, 63-64

protracted, strategic decision processes, 65-66

structure of strategic decision processes, 46-48

Disclosure Database, *190*, 192

discovery, as scanning mode, *83*, 84-85, see also under **environmental scanning**, modes of

Dun's Electronic Business Directory, *190*, 193

Economist, The, 132

EI Compendex Plus, *188*, 191

electronic bulletin boards, 210-211

enacting, as scanning mode, *83*, 84, see also under **environmental scanning**, modes of

end users, 214, 230

and information services, 41-42

as information partners, 212, 219

   as domain experts, 212

as participants in environmental scanning process, 207-209

facilitating use of information by, 39-41

environment

changing nature of, 2, 30, 71-72, 79, 80, 88, 221

   ways to monitor, 32

influence on information behavior, 66-67, 87-88

interpretation of, 8

organization theory and analysis of, 3-5

perceived environmental uncertainty, 87

perceived strategic uncertainty, 87-89

structural characteristics of, 3-4, 72

environmental scanning, 72-103, 137, 158-161, 201-203

and information richness, 146-147

and other types of information gathering, 74-76

   business intelligence, 74-75, 78-79, 81, 118-120, 122, 123, 137, 183-186, 206-207

   competitive intelligence, 74, 76-78, 81, 117, 137, 185-186

   competitor intelligence, 74, 81, 214

   issues management, 75, 152, *160*

   social intelligence, 75, 79-81, 120

and perceived environmental uncertainty, 87, 202

and perceived strategic uncertainty, 87-89

as organizational browsing, 85

as part of organizational learning process, 8

companies or agencies using, 114

   AT&T, 110-112

   British Petroleum, 114

   Eastman Kodak, 114

   General Mills, 113

   General Motors, 114

   in Canada, 125-134

   in Japan, 120-124

   in Sweden, 117-120

   in United Kingdom, 115-117

   Kraft, Inc., 113

   Motorola, 112-113

definition, xi, 72, 73, 82

design recommendations for a scanning system, 189

information behavior

and managerial traits, 86, 90-92, 102

and organizational culture, 89-90, 188, 189

and organizational strategies, 86, 88-90, 102

and situational dimensions, 86, 87-88, 101-102, 184

management of scanning as a strategic activity, 189-191

market-related sectors, importance of, 92-93, 102, 188

methods used for, 96-99, 103, 116-117

formal, structured method recommended, 205-207

in Japan, 120-121

modes of environmental scanning, 72-73, 82-85, 158-161, 175-176, *176*

conditioned viewing, 73, *83*, 84, 158, 159, *160*, 176, *177*

discovery, *83*, 84-85

enacting, *83*, 84

formal search, 73, 158, *160*, 176, *177*

informal search, 73, 158, 159, *160*, 176, *177*

undirected viewing, 72, 83-84, 158, 159, *160*, 176, *177*

scanning interpretation model, 82-85

similarity to human visual system, 105-110

functional specialization, 109

multistage integration, 109-110

parallel vs. hierarchical processing, 109

re-entrant connections, 110

source classification, 93-96

sources used in, 138-156, 157-196

evaluation of, 154,

human, 141, 147-150, 188

information traits as key to user's needs, 145-146

online, 142, 157-196

perceptions influencing source use, 143-144

textual, 141-142, 150-156, 202, 220

stages of development in, 114

styles of, 72-73

use of retrieved information for strategic planning, 99-101, 103

vs. industrial espionage, 137

external sources, 62, *76*, 219

FBR Asian Company Profiles, *190*, 193

Federal Research in Progress, *191*

figures

business intelligence system, *192*

environmental scanning

and information management, *197*

conceptual framework, *86*

interpretation modes, *83*

research, a summary of, *102*

human visual system, perceptual pathways in, *107*

information

behavior of managers, a conceptual framework, *57*

gathering by organizations, external sources, *76*

life-cycle of emerging issues, *152*

management, *xi*

in environmental scanning, *211*

products and services, typology of, *38*

sources, an ecology of, *140*

sources scanned, perception and use of, *144*

Internet information ecology, *163*

knowledge

   experts in the intelligent organization, *212*

   pyramid of the intelligent organization, *213*

learning

   and organizational behavior, *15*

   cycle, *19*

manager as information processing processing system, *59*

managing online information gathering, a framework, *160*

FINDEX, *189*, 192

FINIS, *189*, 192

Forbes, 5, 132

formal search,

   as scanning mode, 73, 158, *160*, 176, *177*, see also under **environmental scanning**, modes of, and **online information gathering**

   Web-based business resources for, *181-182*

Fortune, 21

   Fortune 500, 14, 89, 92, 97, 98, 99, 100, 114, 204

Freedom of Information Act (US), 154

gatekeepers, 41, 43

Globe and Mail, The, 123, 128, 129, 132, 134

Gopher, 165-166

Harvard Business Review, 71

Health Planning and Administration, 192

hermeneutic process, 45-46, 50

Hindustan Times, 123

human information sources, 31-32, 42-43, 44, 49, 60, 62, 63, 64, 96, 134, 139, 147-150, 199, 220

   and informational boundary spanners, 141

and uncertainty absorption, 141

   external, 148-149

   internal 147-148

ICC International Business Research, *190*, 193

indexing, 156, 210

   of online databases, 186-187, 195

   of Web-based resources, 168-171

   subject, 35

   user-centered, 37-38

Industry Trends and Analysis, *189*

informal search,

   as scanning mode, 73, 158, 159, *160*, 176, *177*, see also under **environmental scanning**, modes of, and **online information gathering**

   Web-based business resources for, *181-182*

information access, 42-44, 49, 138

   and external information, 62

   external vs. internal, personal vs. impersonal sources, 93-96, 202

   legislation

      Access to Information Act (Canada), 154

      Freedom of Information Act (U.S.), 154

   models of, 67-68

information acquisition, 24, 29-32, 67, 86, 199

   and uncertainty, 60

   internal vs. external and personal vs. impersonal sources, 93-96, 102, 188-189

   planning of, 138-139

   role of individual, 32

information distribution, 25, 42-44, 68, 185, 200-201

   e-mail and electronic bulletin boards, 173, 210-211, 217

   newsletters, 210

   notice boards and displays, 210

reference binders, 210

information environment
see **environment**

information management, 22, 198-201, 228

and Internet, 161-163

and survival of organization, 2, 14

assessing information gathered by managers, 55-56

audits, 32

collection networks, how to establish, 31

cycle, 23-25, 55

information acquisition, 24, 29-32, 60, 67, 86, 893-96, 102, 199, 201

information distribution, 25, 42-44, 68, 199-201, 210-211

information needs, 24, 26-29, 62, 64, 65, 86, 90, 92-93, 145-146, 199, 207

information organization and storage, 24-25, 33-38, 67, 198, 200

information products and services, 25, 38-42, 198, 200

information use, 25, 45-48, 66, 68, 86, 99-101, 103, 198, 201

functions of, ix

goal of, xi

information gaps, types of, 29

information richness, 146-147

information sharing, 20

strategies for, 209-211

information partnerships, 217

information needs, 24, 26-29, 65, 86, 90, 92-93, 199, 206-207

and operational requirements, 64

information traits as key to user's needs, 144-146, *146*

problem defining, 26-28, 62, 64

information organization and storage, 24-25, 33-38, 67, 198, 200

information products and services, 25, *38*, 38-42, 199, 200

principles for improving, 41-42

value-added, 39-41, *40*

information retrieval systems, 33-38, 49, 68, 186-187, 200-201

efficiency of, 33

intelligent online search programs, 158

unclassified, excluded material in, 34

information richness, 61, 146-147

information sources

human, 141, 147-150, 202, 220

information ecology, 140-141

information traits, 145-146

life-cycle of emerging information issues, 151, *152*

online, 142, 157-197

perceptions influencing source use, 143-144

textual, 141-142, 150-156, 202, 220

internal documents, 151, 155-156

scoring system for evaluation of, 156

published sources, 151-155

evaluation checklist for, 154

information specialists, 220, see also **librarians**

information technology (IT), 17-18, 20, 124, 212, 213, 214-215, 216-217, 219, 220, 228

information traits, 144-146, *146*

information use, 25, 45-48, 66, 68, 86, 99-101, 103, 198, 200-201

information use environment, 26-28

information traits, 144-146, *146*

problem dimensions, 26-28, *27*, 64

value added, 39-41, *40*

INSPEC, *188,*, 191

intelligent organization, 1-22, 67, 197-198, 228, see also **knowledge** or **organizational learning**

and information partnerships, 211-221

  domain experts, *212*, *213*, 214, 217, 220, 221

  users as, 214

    information experts, *212*, *213*, 215-217, 218-219, 220

    information technology experts, *212*, *213*, 214-215, 217, 220, 221

  concepts of, 8-10

  definition, x, 14

  determinants of capacity to learn and adapt, 48-50

  examples of

    Apple Computer Inc., 9-10

    Canon, 12, 13

    Honda, 13

    Matsushita, 13

    NEC, 13

    Sharp, 13

    Wal-Mart, 10-11

    Wrangler, 10-11

  information sources used by, 38-39

  intelligence defined, 11

  "IQ," measures of, 10

  objective of information sharing, 44

internal sources, 220

Internet, 161-176

  and online databases, 195-196

  as information ecology, *163*

  as social information space, 161-162

  browsing on the Internet, 163-166, 175-176

    Web browsing, 163-165

    Gopher, 165-166

    Telnet, 166

  communicating on the Internet, *163*, 172-175, 176

    electronic mail, 173

    mailing list, 174

    newsgroups, 174-175

    Usenet newsgroup categories, 175

  companies using the Internet for environmental scanning, 183-186

    Cadence Design Systems, 184

    Digital Equipment Corporation, 183

    Ford Motor Company, 184

    J.P. Morgan, 183

    Oracle Corporation, 183

  number of people connected by (1997), 161

  origin, 161

  push technology on the Internet, *163*, 166-168, 176

    pushed HTML pages, 167

    channel definition format, 167-168

  searching on the Internet, *163*, 168-172, 176

    Archie, 172

    Jughead, 172

    Veronica, 172

    Web search engines, 168-171

  World Wide Web, 163-165

    business resources, *177-182*

      for conditioned viewing, *179-181*

      for formal and informal search, *181-182*

      for undirected viewing, *178*

Intranet, 183-184

issues management, 75, *152*, 160

Investext, *189*, 192

Japan Economic Newswire Plus, *160*

JAPIO, *188*

knowledge, see also **intelligent organization** or **organizational learning**

  experts, 212-221

domain experts, *212, 213*, 214, 217, 220, 221

users as, 214

information experts, *212, 213*, 215-217, 218-219, 220

information technology experts, *212, 213*, 2124-215, 217, 220, 221

information richness, 61, 146-147

intelligent creation of, 12-14, 68-69

of future, 17-18, 65, 211, 221-227

and environmental scanning, 81, 124-125

complexity, science of, 223-227

scenario planning, 221-222

systems thinking, 222-223

the knowledge society, 227,

types of organizational knowledge, *11*, 11-12, 197-198

cultural, *11*, 12, 198

rule-based, *11*, 12, 197, 198

tacit, *11*, 12, 197, 198

possessed by different employees, 51-52

Kompass databases, 193

librarians, 212, 215, 216, 219, 220

as information experts see under **knowledge**

libraries, 62, 94, 210, 216-217, 220

British Library, The, 73

M&A Filings, *190*

Maclean's, 132

management

American vs. Japanese style, 69

and difficulty of defining problems in, 28

as networks of conversations, 53-54

structure related to environment, 3-4

managerial traits, *86*, 90-92, 102

managers

characteristics of information use by, 54-55

influences on information behavior, 56-66, 86, 87-88, 90-92, 143-144

information gathering style of, 55-56, 89-90

integrative complexity vs. integrative simplicity, 60

cognitive-personality variables, 91

role of

defined, 52-53, 63, 228

in decisions, *59*, 61-62, 65-66

decision-makers or interpreters, 7

fast vs. slow decision makers. 63-64

in environmental scanning, 194

case studies of Canadian CEOs, 125-134

in organizations, *57, 59*, 67

planners linked to company's past, 36

Materials Business File, *192*

Media General Plus, *190*, 193

Moody's Corporate Profiles, *190*, 193

Motorola Intelligence Research Information System (MIRIS), 220

networks, 80, 216, 217, see also Internet

broadband, 18

interpersonal, 42-43, 53-54, 60-61, 110-111, 112, 149, 208

local area (LAN), 208

TradeNet (Singapore), 18

New York Times, The, 129

Newsweek, 132

NTIS, *188*, 191

online databases, 94, 142, 156, 186-196, see also names of individual databases such as ABI/Inform or NTIS and the Internet, 195-196

as decision bases, 195

business sources

  for company-specific analysis, *190*, 192-193

  for demographic analysis, *188*, 191

  for general information and management news, 187, *188*, 191

  for industry analysis, *189*, 192

  for marketing and market research, *189*, 192

  for technology assessment, *188*, 191-192

  companies using online databases for environmental scanning, 193-195

  number available, 186

  studies on use of, 193-195

  value of, 186-187

online information gathering

  conditioned viewing, 159, *160*, 176

  formal search, 160, 176

  framework for managing, 159-160, *161*

  informal search, 159, *160*, 176

  undirected viewing, 159, *160*, 176

online searchers, 187

online sources see **Internet, online databases** or **World Wide Web**

optical character recognition (OCR), 218

optical filing systems, 218

organizational strategies, 86, 88-90, 102

organization theory

  management structure and environment, 2

  organization as system

    decision-making system, 6-7

    information processing system, 5-6

    interpretation system, 7-8, 82-85, 106

open system, 5, 183

organizational intellect, types of, 16

organizational knowledge, types of, 11-12, 197-198

view of environment, 2-5

  as information source, 3-4

  as resource pool, 4

  as ecological system, 5

organizational learning, 69 see also **intelligent organization** or **knowledge**

  and decision making, 46-48, 50

  and Internet, 185-186

  and the hermeneutic process, 45-46, 50

  facilitation of, 39-41

  importance of corporate history, 36-37

  learning loop, 23-26

    single- or double-loop, 15-16, 101, 179

  plan for, 20-22

  process, 8, 14-16, 28-20, 82-85

  vs. organizational change, 16

organizational memory, 35-38

  organizational amnesia, 36

  organizational history, 36

organizations

  and competition, 227-231

  and environment, 2-5, 76, 183, 221, 222

    dependence on, 4

    difficulty of selecting information, 30, 137-138

    example of how scanning coordinated, 112

    information gathering from, 76

    management structure as product of, 3-4

    scanning related to corporate culture, 89-90

  and future, 221-227

complexity, science of 223-227

scenario planning, 221-222

systems thinking, 222-223

and Internet use

Cadence Design Systems, 184

Digital Equipment Corporation, 183

Ford Motor Company, 184

J.P. Morgan, 183

Oracle Corporation, 183

and learning, 8, 14-16, 28-20, 82-85, 198, 230

from online sources, 164

Internet as learning tool, 185-186

vs. organizational change, 16

as systems

decision-making system, 6-7

information processing system, 5-6

interpretation system, 7-8, 82-85, 106

AT&T, 110-112

British Petroleum, 114

Eastman Kodak, 114

General Mills, 113

General Motors, 114

Kraft, Inc., 113

Motorola, 112-113

corporate memory, 34, 36

definition, 30

fortress metaphor, 1-2

information management and survival, 2, 14, 72

organism metaphor, 2, 13, 23, 109-110

Pharmaprojects, *189*, 192

PIRA, 192

PTS MARS, *189*, 192

PTS PROMT, *189*, 192

Push technology on the Internet, *163*, 166-168, 176, see also **Internet**

records management, 34-37, 49, 201

retention policy, 35

records managers, 212, 215

requisite variety, law of, 30-31

rule-based knowledge, *11*, 12, 197-198

searching on the Internet, *163*, 168-172, 176, see also **Internet**

searching online databases, 186-187, see also **online databases**, **online information gathering**, or **online searchers**

scenario planning, 221-222

sense making

Dervin's model of, 29

SEC Online, *190*

situational dimensions, 86, 87-88, 101-102, 144, 199, 230

social intelligence, 75, 79-81, 120

spreadsheets, 196

Standard & Poors (S&P's) Corporate Descriptions Plus News, *190*, 193

systems design

difficulty of identifying information needs, 28-29

systems theory, 222

law of requisite variety, 30-31

system models of organization-environment integration, 197

systems thinking

definition, xiii, 222-223

tables

business intelligence, domain of, *79*

competitor analysis, components of, *78*

environmental scanning

in six large U.K. corporations, *116*

online databases for, *188-190*

human sources

external, *150*

internal, *148*

information

products and services, value added, 40

sources, categories of, *139*

traits, *146*

use in decision phases, *48*

managers as information users, research summary, *58*

online databases for environmental scanning, *188-190*

organizational knowledge, types of, *11*

problem dimensions and information needs, *27*

sources

internal, *155*

published, *153*

Web-based and online sources for viewing and search, *177*

WWW business information resources, *178-183*

tacit knowledge, *11*-12, 149, 197, 205

TIME Magazine, 132

Toronto Star, The, 129

Toronto Sun, The, 129

Trade and Industry Index, *188*

TRW Business Credit Profiles, *190*

undirected viewing,

as scanning mode, 72, 83-84, 158, 159, *160*, 176, *177*, see also under environmental scanning, modes of, and online information gathering

Web-based business resources for, *178*

US Patents Fulltext, *188*

value added

information products and services, 49, 147-148, 200, 219

information traits, 145-146

problem dimensions, 26-28

situational dimensions, 86, 87-88, 101-102, 144, 199, 230

Taylor's model of, 39-41

videotext information system, 220

Visicalc, 10

Wall Street Journal, The, 129, 132

workgroup computing platforms, 218

Lotus Notes, 110, 218

World Wide Web, 163-165, see also Internet

business resources, *177-182*

for conditioned viewing, *179-181*

for formal and informal search, *181-182*

for undirected viewing, *178*